Happy Travels.

Neil Pepper

MARCH 2013.

Not Quite Robinson Crusoe

Neil Pepper, MBE, FRGS

Published by

MELROSE BOOKS

An Imprint of Melrose Press Limited
St Thomas Place, Ely
Cambridgeshire
CB7 4GG, UK
www.melrosebooks.com

FIRST EDITION

Cover designed by Matt Stephens

ISBN 978 1 906561 74 1

Printed and bound in Great Britain by:
CPI Antony Rowe. Chippenham, Wiltshire

FSC
Mixed Sources
Product group from well-managed
forests and other controlled sources
Cert no. SGS-COC-2953
www.fsc.org
© 1996 Forest Stewardship Council

This book is dedicated to all my wonderful friends around the world
including the many members of the Battle of Britain Fighter Association
and their wives who so often encouraged me to go forward with publication.

And also to Debbie for putting up with me for so many years.

Contents

Neil Pepper MBE, FRGS

List of Photographs

Prologue

This book came about from letters containing accounts of my travel experiences that I sent out to friends and family; many of the recipients who were extremely complimentary, my sister Tarina in particular, often pressed me to think of publishing the collection, as it eventually became, and so I hope sincerely that I have repaid their faith in my descriptive abilities.

It is not intended to be a book about me and I hope too that I have managed to keep my obvious presence in it to a minimum. Whilst I am naturally pleased with the end result I must say that I never wanted this to be a glorification of the dubious achievement in prolonged adventurous or downright dangerous travel. So many others in the world have greater stories to tell of personal achievement far beyond anything that I have done.

It is, however, hopefully a truthful and entertaining account of my observations of the various people, places and wildlife that I have been lucky enough to encounter along the way.

I feel that I must explain the obscure title as there is no obvious connection in the text to the exploits of the legendary figure of *Robinson Crusoe*. It is a personal reference to my father and the many wonderful adventure stories that he read to me at bedtime. Along with Defoe's island castaway there were the classics of *Treasure Island*, *Doctor Doolittle* and *James and the Giant Peach*, tales of high adventure in faraway places, fuel for the imagination which took some twenty years to ignite a passion for personal exploration.

All of the places in the collection are available to anyone who has the time and energy to get up and go. I am far from physically fit, I do not come from a wealthy family, I have worked for all of my adult life and have had no great fortune bestowed upon me. In fact when my father died in 1981 he left me with a single pound note and his pocket watch. I am immensely grateful to have been born into a time of relative peace with no great world war to divert my life for six years or more, and conscious that I have been lucky indeed to see and do much of what I have experienced.

I hope now, as I did when the original letters were written, that the following accounts transport you to the various locations and you are able to experience some of the joy and wonder that the world so kindly bestowed upon me.

1. *The Road to Timbuktu*

I had forgotten Africa, or more precisely I had forgotten how much hard work it can be to visit Africa. From the oven-like blast of hot air that envelops you as you leave the aircraft to the insistent assaulting clamour of noise and movement on the streets, the constant begging, the debilitating midday sun and the absolute open-mouthed astonishment directed at an overweight white European covered in tattoos. In a country where body size is directly proportional to wealth the general perception is that anyone looking well-fed and rich is a gift from God, a money cow to be suitably drained of every available penny at every available opportunity. I'd forgotten all of this, but I was certainly remembering it all again very quickly.

The idea had taken root in my mind to visit Timbuktu; the most inaccessible place at the end of the world as the Victorians seemed to believe, a favoured destination for hard-core travellers the world over. I knew it was in Africa, somewhere in the area of the Sahara on the great western bulge of the continent; other than that I was just enchanted with its name and the rare images of sand-blown streets and caravans of camels that are sometimes shown in connection with its mention.

It turned out to be in Mali, a place that I had even less knowledge of than Timbuktu. My education was once again about to be considerably improved! Second or perhaps third largest of all the countries within Africa, it is a huge place, completely landlocked and dependent on the river Niger as its source of irrigation, wealth and commerce. In proportion to the area it covers it has a tiny population of around twelve million and it lays a dubious claim to being one of the least developed countries on the earth, a statement that you read easily with little understanding of the implications until you are faced first-hand with the dire daily struggle for food that motivates so many of its residents!

It is not an easy destination; accurate information is almost non-existent and even the famous Lonely Planet guides are full of error that leaves you totally confused. I struggled hard to obtain a visa, paying a huge sum for the resultant inky endorsement in my passport, only to find that visas were in fact obtainable at the airport upon arrival for a tiny fraction of what I had paid! Not one of the multinational car hire companies provides rental vehicles here, and added to this it is a former French colony, which meant that for me there was the added complication of an almost totally incomprehensible language! My fluent German and the scratchy Swahili and Arabic that I have picked up over the years were to be of no use at all; amidst many drawings and much sign language my only saviour would be a tiny pocket translator with a fifty-thousand-word memory, a time-consuming mode of communication which I eventually found was only a small part of understanding the average Malian. Facial expression, tone of voice and body language become the vital components of comprehension when your verbal skills are suddenly reduced to the level of an average ten-year-old! Happily the people in Mali are a very social bunch; despite their almost crushing poverty they smile and laugh easily and are not at all inhibited about greeting and talking to strangers. Actually I am hard-pushed to think of a place where smiles are so readily bestowed on the visitor, but perhaps they just found my appearance all too amusing?

Bamako, the capital, is a city of contradictions: the whole town appears to be one gigantic marketplace where the clamour of trade and barter is never-ceasing, the overriding impression is one of colour, vibrant, clashing, dazzling colour at every turn; most clothing is loud and bold; the dresses worn by the women are an infinite variation of patterns and primary pigments that shine in the sun and draw the eye until your vision is overloaded. On the streets shiny new four-wheel-drive Jeeps and Mercedes vie with smoking, battered and wrecked minibuses that barely contain their cramped multitude of brightly clad passengers. Internet cafés may be seen on streets where traditional and ornately carved facemasks are offered for sale, and sweating blacksmiths squat at charcoal forges while small boys vigorously pump the bellows. Clean white goats and sheep are held in dusty pens on the roadside where men hawk lottery tickets and phone cards to the passing traffic. You may as easily buy a case for your mobile phone as a fetish ingredient to invoke a curse on your neighbour; in fact the large piles of foetid rotting monkey heads, lion skins, dried lizards, turtle shells, vulture carcases and porcupine quills leave you wondering sadly whether there is any game at all left alive in the country.

I did manage one close encounter with some living wildlife in Bamako when on a Sunday afternoon a large male chimpanzee escaped from its cage in the city zoo and spent some thirty minutes or so terrorising the excited visitors. Observing the fear that normal Africans exhibit when faced with a marauding primate you begin to wonder if we in the west have not lost touch with the primal knowledge of animals; when you are unceremoniously pushed and shoved aside in the fleeing crowd you realise that the cuddly and amusing creature that we are all so familiar with is actually regarded as a very real danger here in its homeland.

Later in the Dogon region when I was trying unsuccessfully to photograph Cayman crocodiles, I was again reminded of the gulf that exists between us. Whilst I only wanted to get closer and closer still to the amazing spectacle, my Bambara guide, eyes bulging, and sweating heavily, only wanted to retreat from the presence of danger!

Whilst Bamako itself is relatively clean, the areas surrounding many villages and smaller towns are littered with the refuse of twentieth-century living. Most noticeable of all are the thousands upon thousands of plastic bags that are used to contain small saleable quantities of chilled drinking water; these clear sausages are sold by hordes of small children who dispense them from yellow-and-black-striped buckets that they balance on their heads. To ingest the water you must nip the plastic between your teeth and squeeze the tube; the bag is then usually discarded without thought; in some areas the ground is littered with vast quantities of these plastic sacks that resemble giant condoms blown into every corner or woodpile. When dusk settles on the city you may view the passage of hundreds of gigantic fruit bats that labour in loose formations across the darkening sky, their huge angular wings silhouetted cleanly against the last quickly fading orange and red twilight as they maintain a direct course out into the surrounding bush. Their numbers are astonishing, as is their apparent single-minded navigation; they are all headed in the same direction for what one expects is a rendezvous with their evening meal!

Some forty miles outside of Bamako to the north is the river-crossing of Koulikoro, which equates to something along the lines of a seaside resort. Here the Niger is wide and slow, and large flat sandbanks are easily accessible; it is a favoured destination of city residents who congregate here in their thousands at the weekend to swim and frolic in the warm flowing water. Great fleets of pinnace boats are arrayed on the shore, and under the shade of a thatched roof skilled shipwrights sit knee-deep in chaff as they chop out new vessels from great baulks of timber, the repeated strokes of the adze like the beat of a tom-tom. Strong, well-muscled boatmen punt lazily back and forth with boats precariously overloaded with escapees from Bamako. The far shore is a huge encampment of straw-thatched beach huts, music blares out loudly enough to reach the opposite bank and the water off of the sandbanks is a heaving mass of bodies reminiscent of a bank holiday at Clacton or Brighton in the thirties. Away from the crowds it is an area of quiet, untroubled lives where the heat washes over you in great stultifying waves, where large black and white kingfishers hover in silent concentration in the clear blue sky before hurtling bullet-like into the water with a clearly audible splash. The river teems with fish, and in the shallows it is a constant moving soup of tiny minnows that dart at any possible food particle that may alight in their vicinity. Families plunder the river and its banks, shovelling loads of dark saturated sand into ancient tip carts that are pulled into the water by reluctant, complaining donkeys. From the nearby villages a constant stream of women and young girls enters the water, sleeping babies strapped to their backs, great jumbled collections of cooking pots and laundry balanced nonchalantly on their heads. All communal activity appears centred on the river, the ritual-like washing of cooking utensils and laundering of clothes seems to take a deceptively long time. The women, stripped to the waist, their wet ebony skin shining in the diamond-hard sunlight, swing the clothes in high arcs over their heads and down onto water-smoothed rocks, with a rhythmic smack that lulls the mind into an almost drugged state where you perceive your surroundings as if from a very great distance, all sounds filtered through the intense wall of heat. The occasional pot or pan escaping into the current bobs past you silently until retrieved by a naked child, and when the work is finally complete, the pots are restacked, the clothes folded in damp piles, the women redress and the babies are hurled carelessly on to the backs of the young girls, pinned in place with large sheets of brightly coloured cloth, the whole procession returning in stately upright posture back to dry land, and the spell is undone.

As I was about to heave myself up from the sand and drive back to the city, a young girl of twelve years or so approached the bank, calf-deep in the water, giggling almost hysterically to her companion as the comatose baby on her back slipped slowly from its perch. She bent progressively further forward at every step in a vain attempt to hold the infant in place, eventually conceding that she must discard the load she carried on her head into the river or lose the baby between her legs. The sleepy child was admonished with two or three well-placed slaps and smartly thrown back into position, where it clung on tightly, wide-eyed and confused!

In the total blackness of pre-dawn my driver and I left Bamako and headed off to Timbuktu along the one thin ribbon of road that traverses the breadth of the country along a roughly similar line as the Niger. Cool and quiet, the morning was in sharp contrast to the bustle of the day, and when the sun rose dramatically on the horizon we were alone on the road in a brown and red baked landscape that offered little relief. The irrigation and the agriculture were soon left behind, replaced by giant baobab trees: devoid of any leaves, they sat, immobile giants as noble and immovable as any English oak, witnesses to generations of life that must surely have passed them by. At regular intervals large termite mounds sprang rigidly up from the flat, blisteringly heated ground, their crenellated battlements providing inspired towers of russet-coloured perpendicular architecture that left one marvelling at the natural intelligence and design of such tiny creatures. Some of the larger colonies had been progressively constructed around a tree so that the green canopy of leaves was all that remained visible, like a huge sweep's brush protruding from the chimney. For the most part our companions on the road were the occasional herd of cows or goats which viewed our passing with indifference as they reared on hind legs to strip the leaves and buds from the higher reaches of the already abused bushes and trees. Ahead of any town or settlement we would begin to overtake the rearguard of a long procession of donkey carts loaded with agricultural produce or gaggles of people clutching market goods; they would veer obligingly off the narrow road at our approach; the sleek panting

4

cattle dogs that trotted lazily beneath the cart in the only shade would alter course instantly to remain protected from the sun, and occasionally a sleeping body could be seen wedged precariously on the axle!

Villages were preceded by numerous rumble strips on the road, protection for the many children who played in the sand, filthily begrimed and apparently content. In every town or village there were numerous roughly made table football games situated beneath shady trees and always the centre of great congregations of young boys or girls. More common still were the children who diligently pushed handcarts full of plastic water containers or firewood, sometimes in company with tiny siblings that rode perched upon the loads. High-tech childhood games do not hold prominence here and the occasional discarded car tyre propelled along with bent sticks generates as much delight as ever any Game Boy managed. My usual practice of providing myself with small gifts and items of trade for such trips was sorely tested here, and my many bags of balloons, cigarette cards and stickers were quickly depleted; the amazing joy that a child can gain from a simple inflated balloon is always a pleasure to behold, a universal language of grinning smiles that breaches any culture or communication gap.

Some of the villages were further protected by lines of empty oil drums in the carriageway: upon stopping they would be pulled aside by rather sullen-looking individuals who represented the most unprofessional-looking non-uniformed police I have ever seen. Remarkably, however, fiscal gifts or bribes were rarely asked for, and when we entered Timbuktu tired, dirty and dishevelled from many hours' driving in the desert sand, the whole complement of the police checkpoint turned out and saluted us prior to examining my papers. We ran through the usual interrogation of country and city of origin and a quick examination of my tattoos, and then left them happily munching on sun-warmed date biscuits from our emergency food reserves.

At Djenne, we diverted away from the road and crossed the river to view the great mosque. Almost all villages have a mosque, constructed in Sahel style from mud and straw, with the tinder-dry ends of the internal wooden beams protruding sharply from the walls, reminiscent of those little towers one builds from matchsticks in moments of quiet boredom. It is an ancient method of construction, which has truly stood the test of time. The great mosque at Djenne is equal to any of the seven ancient wonders; built somewhere around 1905 it is constructed to a design unchanged since the eleventh century. It rears enormously from the centre of the town; its yellow mud walls, smoothly rendered and flat, are punctured at their upper limits by the square ends of ancient beams before the fascia divides into a multitude of exquisitely shaped finials and spires. Before the mosque lies the huge marketplace which storms your senses with its confusion of colours, smells and noises; spices of every conceivable variety lie heaped in colourful perfumed pyramids and the odours are so strong that when you pass close by you are left infused and light-headed. Goods and consumables of every imaginable combination are strewn carelessly on carpets where you must pick your way gingerly on narrow dust-laden pathways between the glittering treasures, ducking beneath the taut ropes of canvas and camel-skin tents that are stretched above the mêlée. Your ears overflow with the ring of hammer on worked steel or bronze and the clatter of thousands of voices engaged in systems of commerce that have changed little in millennia. Tethered goats and sheep bleat their discomfort and motorbikes occasionally nudge between the pedestrians compressed tightly amongst the stalls and displays. Withered old men hunched over tiny work-benches repair ancient watches or spectacles, and women purchase hair beads, ribbons and braiding components in weighed quantities amongst great piles of mangoes and oranges and grotesque dried fish and large chunks of blue-black meat swarming with a thousand flies. Once you leave the clamour of the marketplace you enter a warren of back-streets and narrow alleyways between the yellow mud walls of the houses, where the super-heated air presses in on you even more fiercely. In the middle of each street is an open sewage trench which, crusted with dust and sand, is not the usual foul river that one might expect. People move about slowly here, and the decorated silver-studded doors are left open to encourage the breeze, so that as you pass by you may glimpse momentarily in the cool shadows old men lounging sleepily in string chairs, or naked infants being washed from plastic kettles held above their heads.

So we set off for Timbuktu, turning north, away from the metalled road and into the bush. We progressed along the massive buttress walls of the Gandamia massif which looks for all the world as if it has been transported here from the Indian reservations of south-west America.

As the road gave way to rough, rock-littered scrub and eventually became just a myriad of tyre tracks in the finely grained sand, we met the first of the camel trains heading south, a dozen large camels laden with great slabs of mineral salt that resembled roughly hewn grey and dirty-white paving slabs strapped to either side of their saddles. At the head and tail of the caravan were Tuareg tribesmen clad dramatically in the azure blue robes and turbans that mark them so significantly from other tribes of the desert. It is said that the indigo dye used to colour the cloth is applied without the benefit of water, a scarce and valuable commodity in this landscape; the dye which is therefore not fast in the cloth impregnates the skin of the person wearing it. Thus the early explorers of the Sahara returned home recounting tales of "blue men" who lived in the desert.

The Tuareg are an impossibly romantic bunch to me; they were characters lifted directly from the pages of childhood books that my father read to me whilst I lay in bed imagining the tribulations of castaways and pirates, such as *Robinson Crusoe* and *Man Friday.* The Africans, I was to learn, had a very different view. Tuaregs are Caucasian, they do not resemble the Africans and apparently there is little love between them. Rebel uprisings north of Timbuktu, bandit attacks on caravans of travellers and tourists, and desperately savage retribution by the government have left a history of bitter mistrust and fear. There are tales of mass executions in the dunes of the desert where persons rounded up may or may not have been implicated in the uprisings! My driver often indicated to me that they should not be trusted and when we stood observing the crocodile pools he mused that this was the best place for all of the Tuareg to be deposited. For me they were figures of immense charisma, viewing them astride their camels or Arab-bred horses in full regalia of blue robes, dagger and swords fixed high on the waist by scarlet sashes; they captivate the imagination, and their fiercely independent, noble attitude is strangely akin to those of us born in an island nation.

Later, when we were returning south again, we crested a dune and ran down a narrow trench that was blocked by a Jeep in what I later realised was a classic ambush configuration. There was no way to pass the vehicle which with its hood open and engine parts strewn about was rather obviously in distress. Around the vehicle were six or seven Tuaregs, and as we came to a slow, grudging halt I could sense the anxiety of the driver; he kept the engine running and the car in gear and rocked the vehicle back and forth in its static position so that the wheels would not sink whilst the tribesmen surrounded us and leaned in at the open windows. There were no guns visible and although I cannot speak Bambara I could follow the conversation easily: they wanted a ride to the nearest village; my driver would not agree to take all of them as we already had two hitchhikers on board; he rocked the Jeep gently back and forth and his eyes betrayed his nervous fear. Eventually he agreed to take one of their number on with us and the others cleared a path for us. My driver's fear became contagious when the selected individual returned from the crippled vehicle clutching an intimidating broad-bladed sabre and climbed into the rear seat, perching haughtily on the very edge of the fabric, all but his eyes screened from us by the black cloth of his turban. I viewed him carefully in the rear-view mirror. We dropped our hitchhikers one by one in a remote area of sand that showed no sign of habitation in any direction, and coming to the appropriate village, our Tuareg travelling companion climbed out from the car. He thanked me politely in Arabic and we continued onwards. Later that night when we were safely out of the desert and back in a small town, where we sat eating couscous and mangoes, my driver confessed to me that he had been completely terrified and demonstrated to me that his heart had been pounding uncontrollably at the thought that our Jeep was about to be hijacked. One of the incidents that sparked the original confrontations was the theft of twenty or so Toyota Land Cruisers from a caravan of tourists heading deep into the desert.

The desert defeated the engine of the Jeep, and by the time the sun was directly overhead and the temperature gauge reading well above a hundred degrees, we were stopping every hour or two to refill the radiator from boxes of mineral water that we had crammed into the back seats. I was struck at these moments by the high level of ambient noise in this supposed wasteland: crickets, wasps and other insects called from every bush or stunted tree so that your ears rang with the frequency waves that they generated. Burrow holes of tiny mice, large beetles or snakes could be found in the shade beneath most scrub, or occasionally the tracks of camels clearly defined in the fragile crust of exposed earth. Perhaps most astonishing of all was the large number of wild donkeys that roamed free in this burning and scorched landscape. The sand was incredibly hot and the rubber soles of my deck shoes were noticeably malleable after each sojourn. It soon became clear to me that my driver was not actually following a defined route, but in his defence it must be said that there was no road as one might imagine; there were areas of deeply churned sand where vehicles had obviously been bogged down and dug out, and on the slopes of any large dune there were dozens of tyre tracks from which to choose your preferred passage. At times we would take several runs at the steeper inclines, failing to clear the crest as the flowing grains moved and sucked in the wheels. If we used the tactic of lowering the pressure and increasing the contact footprint we had no pump to reinflate the tyres, and so we hurtled along at high speed so that the sand had insufficient time to part beneath us; bushes flew past, raking the bodywork as we skidded, slipped and slid in a frantic slalom dictated by the most tempting or obvious path of least resistance.

The only other vehicles we encountered were the Land Rovers of several relief agencies, so when the driver began to stop and ask directions from occasional tribesmen plodding resolutely along with camel or donkeys, I began to have serious doubts as to whether he actually knew the way to Timbuktu, but I kept an eye on the compass and the sun and was quietly reassured that we were heading north and must therefore eventually hit the river Niger at some point! Running down a steep slope of shifting sand we careered unexpectedly into the centre of a tiny village of mud and thatch huts protected beneath tall wind-twisted and knurled trees, their bark the colour of coal. All was quiet as we stepped out from the car into the blessed shade, and Osman approached the nearest hut armed with some date biscuits as polite recompense for the required directions. Through the trees I could see some tiny children running towards us, eyes bulging in inquisitive delight; they were soon joined by several others, all completely naked, caked in crumbling grime, faces glazed with crusted mucus. Some had the bulbous distended belly-button that was regarded in times past as a mark of great fertility. In need of a drink I opened the back door and retrieved a bottle of near-boiling water, and was instantly engulfed in a waving field of gesticulating hands. It took a moment for comprehension to dawn on me: it wasn't the water that they wanted but the two dozen or so empty plastic bottles that we had accumulated during the trip. I learnt a deep lesson of humility in that moment; these items that we so readily discard in our indulgent and wasteful society had real value here in this place where people live their lives consuming little and owning less. I stood in shocked contemplation of this fact as adults and children alike grabbed at the bottles and scampered away, testing the thread of the lids and clutching their treasure to their chests with determined protectiveness. We departed the village with two or three chattering piccaninnies riding on the spare tyre and bumper!

And here I was in Timbuktu! Tired, dusty and sunburnt, my shoes half melted and overflowing with abrasive sand, the sun low on the horizon and bathing us in soft shimmering pastel colours that monopolise the eye but are never adequately captured by any camera. It was all that I had expected, not paved with gold or bedecked with treasure but a very run-down, decaying and dilapidated sand-laden town that clings to existence on the fringe of the massive Sahara, for all that it was a place of mystery and wonderment, soaked in a culture that is far beyond the realms of our own green and water-rich land. I reported to the chief of police to register my arrival and stood beneath the barely moving fan in his sweltering, dimly lit office where I could view the miserable inhabitants of the one and only medieval cell, crouched low to the floor, their hands stretched out through the bars in a silent plea for food. The complete array of rubber stamps held on the desk were applied to my passport with such enthusiasm that he managed to tear one of the more ancient imprints in two, and I waited whilst running repairs were completed before I signed the large log book and parted with the required one thousand francs.

In the cool of the evening I ventured out to explore some of the town and found that I was apparently, quite literally, the one and only tourist in the whole of Timbuktu at this time. What at first seemed to be an incidental honour turned quickly into an ordeal of incessant hard and soft-sell tactics for goods and services of every imaginable description. Within moments of leaving the hotel I would find myself accompanied by an ever-increasing band of merchants, Tuareg traders, potential tour guides or schoolchildren just eager to demonstrate their spoken English and invite me to their homes. Two young Tuareg boys who spoke the most perfect English assured me that during the present hot season it was most unusual for tourists to land in Timbuktu, and as such I was certainly the intended target of almost every salesperson in the town for the foreseeable future. It took me a little time to realise that this was not just another cynical fleecing operation, the people here were genuinely in need, near-starving in some instances, and the marked vehicles of the various relief agencies were a permanent reminder that this was a Third World country with all its incumbent destitution. My two young Tuareg walking companions trotted out the mantra of wanting to study to become doctors and return to Mali to help their people, a statement which, in my past experience, most usually precedes a request for some kind of fiscal aid. However, when they refused to partake of a glass of Cola with me, stating that their whole family would be able to eat breakfast for the purchase price of the drinks, it began to dawn on me just how desperate things were for many of the people here. A queue of patient, hopeful traders would be waiting for me to leave the hotel and I was moved by the plight of these friendly and noble people, when the difference between eating and going hungry relies wholly on the willingness of a tourist to part with their money.

For all this, Timbuktu is a fascinating place to visit: in the streets you pass multiple discarded and dismembered vehicles stripped of every usable component, donkeys are driven past you burdened with impossibly huge loads of timber or crops, and women produce piles of unleavened bread cakes from clay ovens that are domed in shape like old-style haystacks. Children scamper in the sandy alleyways with buckets laden with water or laboriously mix great pools of mud and straw before fabricating it into huge bricks. Those that attend school use wooden slates and chalk and sing loud learning songs before the master whilst sitting cross-legged in the street. Flocks of brightly coloured zebra finches swarm down on to carpets of green millet laid out to dry in the sun on window sills or doorsteps. Beaten and near-disabled by the pounding sun, men and women lounge in dilapidated string chairs in open doorways or beneath the wilted and dust-laden trees. The magnificent blue robes of the Tuareg are the most vibrant splash of colour in this sand-blasted vista. At night the few street lights barely shed illumination into the wide main boulevard and in the back streets there is no lighting and one can only venture there with either a torch or local knowledge of where the open sewer trenches are situated. Accepting one of the many offers of hospitality, I was guided to a stone courtyard on a dim street and initiated into the Tuareg tea ceremony. Three glasses of tea produced from the same pot, the first strong like death, the second heavily thick with sugar, sweet like life, the third, depleted and weak, soft like love! Each draft was slurped readily from the same, increasingly dirty, glass by the assembled circle. Here where no light save the glimmering torches can invade your eyes, the night stars are pure crystals of concentrated white, and the constellations are a clear diagram of mythology scribed on the blackness.

There is a library of Islamic literature which holds the world's largest collection of Koranic scriptures: one imagines an ancient fortress-like stone building with high barred windows where light falls in gentle shafts on to great rows of dust-covered tomes bound in exquisitely worked leather and gold; the truth however is somewhat less romantic - a small concrete room where great metal filing cabinets hold crumbling disorganised piles of disintegrating handwritten pages which are being slowly and painstakingly preserved by a team of conservationists and equally slowly downloaded onto the official website. The two ancient mud-built mosques are not on the scale of the great building in Djenne but they are of a geometric shape that is rarely seen in construction and their ancient walls, banked high with blown sand, are weathered by the desert and cracked with deep fissures like the mud of a dried river bed. I had been very much aware that this was a predominantly Muslim country and that with the current political situation I may well encounter some hostility. Until now Bin Laden, his al-Qaeda and September the eleventh had been a non-issue; people faced with the daily grind of providing food do not overburden themselves with international politics, and the most tangible effect of the war in Afghanistan was the drastic drop in foreign visitors and the resultant decline in tourist-generated revenues. However on attempting to enter the main mosque in Timbuktu I heard the guardian refer angrily to 'Americans' and I was sure that I was only permitted access after my guide pleaded my English citizenship. For the next few days I found myself repeatedly denying that I was an American, and whilst feeling rather dismayed that I obviously have the appearance of one I was feeling rather pleased at the reactions demonstrated towards me as a Briton; Tony Blair, it would seem, does not carry as much anti-Muslim news coverage!

Perhaps the most surprising aspect of Timbuktu is the large colonies of hippopotamus resident in the Niger some ten or twelve miles to the east of the town. These fascinating animals appear to maintain a passive disinterest in the many fishing boats and other craft that ply the river back and forth in an almost endless stream. When you enter their territory and cut the engines of the boat the quiet silence is obligingly broken as their massive pink and raw-looking heads surface from the dark waters with the mandatory loud snort and ejected cloud of spray and twitching ears. The family groups that I was able to observe were extremely active and noticeably vocal, the young adolescents gambolling like huge puppies, rolling and flopping joyously in the churning water and bellowing deep vibrating calls, something like a cross between a cow and a lion, as they measured the size of their gigantic gaping mouths in mock confrontations, their massive sabre-like teeth clashing together before they sank below the waters. One or two, leaving the general mêlée, would haul themselves up onto shallow waterlogged sandbanks, their massive glistening girth almost completely visible as they stared dolefully around them. The large bull that obviously controlled the group kept a wary eye on us and at one point surfaced in a churning froth directly adjacent to the bows, warning us that we had approached too closely. I was struck by the unchanged timelessness of the scene, the rock-like heads of the hippos breaking the surface as fishermen perched on the bows of roughly hewn wooden boats, swinging at the hips like Olympic hammer-throwers, cast their nets in great curving arcs that fell onto the water like giant circular spiders' webs. It was almost as if one had stepped into the pages of those beautifully illustrated Sunday school books or a scene from some Hollywood biblical epic.

For me the most enduring memory of Timbuktu will be the Caravanserai on the extreme northern edge of the town where the wind-blown dunes of the desert reach down to the Tuareg camps and threaten to swallow the inhabitants. This is where the great caravans strike out into the Sahara for the salt mines of Taoudenni and the fifty-day trip to Marrakech in Morocco. At times there may be anything up to two thousand camels arrayed here. The camps of the Tuareg are loose and informal with few specific boundaries; cooking utensils, clothing and bundles of possessions are left unattended around the tents and no one seems unduly concerned with their security. Close by is a grand memorial for the dead of the Tuareg uprising which incorporates a multitude of decommissioned weapons before its fountain-like kiosk, and on the sloping field of sand that leads to the dunes a hundred children and young men play energetic games of football. Armed with my camera and pockets full of balloons I spent a wonderful time here in the camp of two young families where indescribably dirty children rambled barefoot in the sand and darkly elegant Tuareg women gigglingly hid their faces from the camera beneath the folds of their robes. The young men of the family, fiercely intent on displaying their football skills, would indiscriminately apply their long camel whips to the storm of squealing children that constantly invaded their unmarked pitch or disrupted a pass in the pursuit of newly inflated and escaped balloons. As the sun set, deeply orange, and the sky became a marbled purple and red pallet of sand-reflected light, small camel trains led by tall men in flowing blue robes passed us by, bound for the endless sand and the desert night. The whip that was so readily deployed amongst the children now hangs proudly in my living room!

Retreating south from the desert we headed out into the elephant reserve of Gourma and eventually arrived at the tiny village of Banzina on the shores of a large and abundant water hole surrounded with lush vegetation. In view of our experiences in the desert I was surprised to see Osman greet the Tuareg chief like an old friend! An extremely tall and noble-looking man who was dressed unusually in full-length green robes, he made us welcome in his tent with dirty pillows and glasses of tea, and whilst Osman observed the polite etiquette leading up to enquiring where the elephant herds might be, I was entranced by my surroundings. The camel skins of the structure were open at either side, allowing a pleasant breeze to pass through; in one corner a young goat, hobbled at the ankles, was being quietly milked by a woman who modestly kept her eyes averted from her guests. From the supporting poles beneath the roof skins hung half a dozen sabres in ornate leather scabbards with bright red sashes and silver embossing. I was surprised to see arrayed against one wall a bank of free-standing shelves constructed from wicker-like canes and strangely reminiscent of those functional pigeonhole shelves you see offered for sale in the more trendy Scandinavian furniture stores. I presented a gift of cola to the chief, a semi-narcotic nut that is chewed like tobacco and used widely by the Tuareg and other tribes. It is usually the preserve of old grey-bearded men but occasionally the younger fellows use it also; it is said to be a stimulant of some effect, great for sustained weight loss but also likely to make you overreact, or as one guide put it, 'explode your head'. Long-term use stains the teeth a dark red like Indian betel nut; it has a musty damp smell like wet leaf mould and tastes absolutely foul to my untrained and unwary palate, a distinct tobacco aftertaste, acrid and astringent. In this region, as with the Dogon, the presentation and thoughtful chewing of cola nuts accompanies all transactions or negotiations. I observed my hosts carefully; all had brilliant white teeth that obviously knew neither fillings nor decay; their bare feet, however, resembled cracked and weathered elephant hide complemented with massive thickly projecting toenails. Their robes of various dark colours appeared clean, and one man sat carefully darning a tear in the skirts of his djellaba whilst the conversation progressed slowly and the chief distributed cola nuts that were split with the thumbnail and shared into economical halves or quarters amongst the group. Eventually it transpired that the elephants had departed the area just three days previously following heavy rainfall that would provide them with fresh grazing on their annual migration to Burkina Faso! I never managed to see any elephants but I was about to see another spectacle that I had neither expected nor planned.

My ignorance of the Falaise de Bandiagara, or Dogon country as it is known, was quite complete. I knew absolutely nothing about it and had read very little before venturing into this extraordinary World Heritage Site. The Bandiagara escarpment rises on dramatically sheer cliffs to a height of some several hundred feet from the flat and sun blasted plains south of Mopti. The Dogon people maintain a remarkable culture and religion that have been little affected by the outside world since the thirteenth century. Their villages are a fairy-tale assembly of weird and wonderful structures that defy adequate description. Before the Dogon occupied this area the Tellem peoples lived in caves and houses carved high in the sheer rock walls of the escarpment; today you stare upwards in consternation at the hundreds of windows and doorways, walls and towers constructed on ledges and beneath overhanging masses of rock where you imagine it is quite impossible to climb. On the more accessible lower ledges you walk amongst the debris of thousands of skeletons, fragile desiccated bones scattered on the dusty ground from decaying and tumbledown burial chambers. The Dogon have settled on the scree-covered lower slopes beneath the giant cliffs and it is here that they continue to live in ancient settlements of mud and timber-built houses that ramble in twisting and convoluted random patterns and angles that would defy architectural balance. The centre of each village is the Tonguna or men's meeting house, a square structure with a multi-layered thatched roof set on stone piles; open on all sides it provides shade and ventilation but can only be entered by sitting down. This simple tenet of construction prevents any violent escalation of discussions, as anyone rising to their feet in anger will sustain a considerable welt on the head; it would be very difficult to maintain a heated argument bent double at the waist!

Dotted between the maze of houses are the multiple grain stores that give the Dogon villages their fascinating signature: squat seven or eight-foot tall circular or square towers like miniature windmills, raised on large stones from the ground to prevent vermin infestation, each is topped with a point and circle of thatch, like multiple garden umbrellas. Around the villages you come across fetish patterns marked in the sand, spiked with twigs and groundnuts, the components of fortune-telling rites or magic spells cast for good or bad results. The groundnuts are used to tempt the foxes onto the sand; their footprints in the boxes of the patterns will indicate the desired result.

fig 1. Dance of the Masks, Dogon Country, Mali

fig 2.   Mask Dancers, Dogon Country, Mali

fig 3. Fortune Tellers, Dogon Country, Mali

fig 4.   Tuareg using antelope bone to smoke tobacco

fig 5. Timbuktu

2. Finding Labrador

Losing your passport is not generally something which leads to good things or significant changes in one's life; most people who have experienced such an event will tell you that the stress and aggravation are best avoided, and so would I if it had not been for the most unforeseen and far-reaching effect it was going to have in my yearly routine of travels.

I had laboured on plans to return to the West African country of Mali; it had made a big impact upon me during my first excursion there and I had been toying with the idea for some time. I'd booked flights and contacted my friends in Bamako and then I'd set about applying for the required visa. This involved sending my passport off to the embassy in Brussels; unfortunately they do not maintain an office in London or how different might things have been. The clock began to tick down to the time when I would expect the return of my passport and nothing appeared, and so I engaged, ever hopefully, in what was to be a fruitless and harrowing battle of wits with the Mali embassy and British consular office in Brussels. In the twenty-five years that I have been travelling it has been my considered misfortune to only ever meet three members of the diplomatic service, and those encounters have left me with a risible contempt and thorough disgust for the corps of superfluous, arrogant and irritating personalities employed therein. I expect there are some decent, affable and agreeable characters amongst this huge and unwieldy organisation; however, nothing that I experienced whilst dealing with the consular staff in Brussels encouraged me to revise this vexing, irksome assessment.

So my passport was lost, buried somewhere amongst the imagined dust-laden files and crowded desks of a dimly lit, shabby establishment somewhere amid the back lanes of the European capital. For a charge amounting to fifty percent of the cost I was able to cancel my airline ticket to Mali, and as all of my carefully laid plans unravelled before my still-disbelieving eyes I began to consider what could be salvaged. Annual leave had been booked with my employing company and I was locked into the dates of travel due to various other trips I had planned and paid for early in the year. I replaced my passport in a single day with the assistance of an extremely helpful manager at the Peterborough passport office and I cast around for somewhere else to go, feeling all the time that it would be a sad second best compared to the high adventure and romantic far-flung mystery of sub-Saharan Africa.

A regular traveller in the less-visited areas of the United States, I plumped for a cheap flight into New York, intending to travel up to Canada through the enticing and as yet unrevealed states of New England. It was my intention to seek out some remote and desolate place to assuage my wanderlust and I scoured the maps to find a suitable location. To the east of the great land mass of Canada there was a large area of terrain that had few marked settlements and what appeared to be a single road terminating abruptly at the town of Goose Bay. I knew some small details about this place named Labrador; it had a huge airbase that had been built during World War Two to enable newly constructed American bombers a suitable staging post on their mammoth flights across the Atlantic. It had also been home to the fascinating English doctor named Wilfred Grenfell whose great exploits travelling the frozen wastes by dog sled whilst delivering medical care and attention to the native peoples had featured heavily in certain books I had read. Beyond that I had no valid knowledge of the land, its peoples and customs, but now, almost four years on from that time, I am proud to say that I have filled that yawning gap in my education.

Many people who live outside of Canada seem never to have heard of Labrador; some are, however, familiar with the name at least of its giant offshore relative, the island of Newfoundland; although if asked I suspect few would be able to place their finger upon it on any world map! When I stopped off briefly with friends in Toronto, the subject of my intended destination arose at dinner one evening and was met with incredulous silent stares until one family member managed to splutter out, 'What do you want to go there for? There's nothing but trees and moose!' In some respects that gentleman was more than correct; there certainly is a great surfeit of both trees and moose in Labrador, but there is also a whole lot more than that if you are prepared to spend your time looking and listening.

To reach Labrador by road from mainland USA you must cross from New England into the gigantic province of Quebec. I had only ever passed through on trains prior to this expedition and so was supremely ignorant of the cultural differences that set this former French colony so firmly apart from the rest of Canada. The contrasts with the other ten provinces are exceptional; there is little of the Americanised feel that exists in the greater portion of the country, its architecture is notably divergent and its people are fiercely proud of their Gallic heritage; so much so that their politicians regularly attempt to promote secession from their bondage to Canada and the British Commonwealth.

I can never quite convince myself that I am actually in Canada whilst I am travelling in Quebec; its feel, its atmosphere and ambience are so alien to the other provinces that you may easily convince yourself you have left the continent of North America completely. It has little of what I think of as the comfortable

21

known quantity so readily available just across its sprawling elongated provincial borders. It has some quite remarkable attractions and historical places of interest, the most notable of these being the fairy tale fortified ramblings of Quebec City. The huge citadel fortress perched atop a great cliff of near-vertical stone shouts the former historical glory of this colonial power base across the frozen Saint Lawrence with unmistakable authority. The narrow lanes and cobbled streets of the old town, designed with defensive strategy in mind, fan out in a rough star shape from the central Place d'Armes, the prodigious stone walls of the buildings, perforated with ornate shuttered windows and arabesque wrought iron grilles, often terminate in medieval turrets or crenellated mock battlements. Tourists bundled up in layers of warm clothing flock amongst the high-class outlets for artworks and luxury goods, and horse-drawn open landau carriages ply their trade amidst the tangle of an oddly effective one-way system.

Close by the walls of the old town, just before the glass and steel sprawl of modern Quebec takes firm hold with its wide boulevards, high-rise international banking houses and multi storey car parks, are the parklands and open green spaces of the Plains of Abraham. This narrow plateau of land runs parallel to the river atop the huge stone ramparts for a distance of perhaps three football pitches; the near precipice bastion was considered an impregnable defence for the emergent French government in the seventeen-hundreds, and Canada might easily have remained a French colony but for the audacious and unconventional attack of General Wolfe. Sending his marines to scale the cliff under cover of night, he took the French troops by surprise and inflicted a crushing defeat upon Montcalm's army which led eventually to the French withdrawal and British command of all of Canada.

Quebec is dominated by the gargantuan Saint Lawrence River; a great churning artery of trade and commerce, it is dotted with affluent port towns and busy ferry settlements thrumming with local maritime history. In the summer it is one of the world's premier spots for observing the great whale migrations, with humpbacks and other baleen cetaceans delighting crowds of international visitors with their energetic sporting antics and complex mating rituals. A large area of the river is set aside as a marine national park and is home to a resident population of the peculiar white Beluga whales and at Tadoussac, where you must transit the mouth of the Saguenay River by ferry, you may see distant family pods of these intriguing creatures bobbing amongst the storm blasted waves and troughs of the fierce grey waters. The Saint Lawrence is choked with great ice floes for much of the winter, and giant jigsaw shaped slabs of metre-thick ice are driven into futuristic architectural piles along the shoreline by the incessant Arctic winds. In the spring it is home to one of the great wildlife spectacles of North America when millions of immaculate white snow geese descend upon the shallow marshes and water meadows of the river's flood plain. Amassing to feed in gigantic flocks, they completely cover the surface of the muddy brown marsh water, making the lakes appear as if covered with an undulating blanket of ploughed snow or a carpet of giant cotton blooms stirred by gentle murmuring breezes. The main east-west highway runs immediately next to the edge of the marshlands and the drivers of the great transcontinental trucks often sound their horns to frighten the geese into massive swirling clouds of agitated wings and honking alarm calls; the rising mantle of birds swarming in chaotic disorder forms momentary complex geometric designs that flit briefly before the eye with tantalising suggestion before the throng descends in unison back onto the water's surface.

Heading eastwards along the great river bank you come upon Baie St Paul, a large town hemmed in by the water on one side and steep hills on the other. It is home to the massive Church of Saint Paul, a popular destination for many thousands of American and Canadian Catholic pilgrims. The huge cathedral-sized chapel is famous for its magnificent stained glass diorama and the steep hillside parks adjacent to the church are decorated with imposing gilded statues representing the harrowing details of the Stations of the Cross. Eventually you come to Baie Comeau, a large uninspiring port nestled tight against the northern shore of the yawning Saint Lawrence estuary, and you turn north onto the snaking gravelled surface of the trans-Labrador highway. This thin winding ribbon is a tiny thread of dull yellow civilisation woven erratically into the colossal green and white tapestry of untamed wilderness that sweeps away for hundreds of miles on either side, its awesome proportions dwarfing even the massive logging trucks that thunder along its slush-laden slippery chicanes.

The road runs in a giant north-eastwards arc, sweeping to its current termination point in the town of North West River, some six hundred miles distant in the very heart of Labrador on the shores of Lake Melville. It rises and falls in a tortuous rollercoaster of deep sun-shaded valleys and steep mountain crests which offer tantalising glimpses of the staggering snow-laden forests tumbling away to the distant horizons with limitless abandon. Exploitation of the gigantic natural resources in these areas has only recently taken a step into the twenty-first century with tremendous strings of hydroelectric power plants. Previously it was the exclusive haunt of the lonely weather-beaten trapper and hunter with sparse service centres controlled by the all-powerful Hudson's Bay Company; now huge dams hold back billions of tons of water, cloaking the savage unworkable lands with serene calm water lakes where eager sports fishermen come to wrestle with giant pike and pickerel. Occasionally as you progress northwards along the road you pass close beside the alien bailiwicks of hydro compounds where large tangles of throbbing conductors and booster cabinets hum loudly with surging waves of copper-borne current. Tiny shrines to man's scientific endeavour deep amongst the inspiring grandeur of nature, these temples of electricity decorated with porcelain finials and steel pinnacles will one day, no doubt,

23

be reclaimed by the solemn, patient forest and perhaps their former significance and purpose will be hotly debated by scholars of ancient history in the millennia to come! Even the stern monumental pylons that stride out across the rugged landscape, laden with their transient cargo of streaming energy, are dominated by the greater power of nature, with the untidy nests of eagles and herons decorating their high geodesic crossbeams.

Shortly before you reach the provincial border between Quebec and Labrador, you will begin to see large clouds of white steam reaching skywards against the wide blue horizon; these static featherlike plumes are a distant smoke signal announcing your arrival at the second great wellspring of resource hidden amongst the unceasing forests and lakes. Separated by a scant eleven miles are the towns of Fermont and Labrador City, the first in Quebec, the second in Labrador itself; low-level nondescript communities, their terraced housing, grid roads and street lighting dropped into the wilderness like Lego brick towns on a pristine child's play mat. It is curious at first to find two almost identical townships immediately adjacent amidst the otherwise vast open spaces, but the dual construction has a very definite fiscal motivation. Stashed beneath the land here are gigantic, perhaps immeasurable, deposits of iron ore; the tremendous wealth of minerals hidden in this distant corner of nature's larder is thankfully ignorant of provincial economics and jealousies and provides astonishing wealth to both sides of the imaginary line amongst the trees. Both of these communities are peculiar in their very existence but are also remarkable present-day reminders of an earlier colonial, almost feudal, system rarely found in present-day society. They are company towns, built, owned and controlled by rival mining companies; they exist for a single purpose only, to service the massive open-cast excavations where the precious ore is torn from the earth by unceasing monstrous diggers, trucks and conveyor belts. The processed ore, pressed and moulded into dull marble-sized pellets, is loaded upon impossibly long freight trains with hundreds of high-sided wagons; each departing train that slithers slowly away to the distant coast on the single rail line, like huge snakes passing along well-worn jungle trails, is said to carry a million dollars in revenue!

You may be forgiven for thinking that life in such isolated company-owned towns could be an ordeal, an unpleasant interlude of barely acceptable incarceration forced by pressing financial need. It is safe to say that in mid-winter, with desperately short hours of daylight and the gigantic snowfalls, minds turn to sunnier locations and less demanding climates. Lab City receives twelve feet of snowfall a year and it has the longest of all snow seasons, with a six-month period when nature finally manages to conquer the stubborn impacted ice and expose the land to summer's splendour. However, wages are good and the town is not short of activities to amuse its many residents; they have their own ski slopes and a huge snowmobile club that maintains many hundreds of miles of carefully groomed trails. Almost every house has one, if not more, snowmobiles, and hunting, fishing and shooting are popular pastimes. There is a small enclave of welcoming dog-mushers that maintain the traditions of Arctic dog teams and sledding, and in past years they have run their own international sled races, covering distances between one hundred and twenty and four hundred miles. For those with less sporting dispositions there are restaurants and fast food cafés including the ubiquitous McDonald's, and there are plenty of churches and bars, although it has to be noted that the latter outweigh the former!

From Lab City you head off eastwards out onto the often unwelcoming highway towards Goose Bay. The road traverses great open plains of lake and stunted boreal forest where flocks of tiny snow buntings and elegantly plumed ptarmigan feed on miniscule seeds and trace minerals exposed amidst the surface slush. Insidious wind-sculpted tongues of snow flicker out like decorative tournament pennants onto the gravel, forming dangerous low-lying bevels; natural minacious sleeping policemen reaching greedily for the wheels of your car with treacherous intentions to spin, flip and wreck the vehicles of unwary travellers.

Approximately halfway between Goose and Labrador City the road pushes in close to the massive Churchill River. Originally the waters plummeted over a gigantic cataract at this point, and during the period of early exploration Churchill Falls were reported to be greater in height and volume than Niagara. This enormous thundering wild turbulence has since been trapped and tamed and dressed as a slave in an immense concrete livery; today it lives in a depressed state serving up never-ceasing meals of energy and power to the incessantly hungry homes of tremendous North American plantations. To maintain the giant's chains and ensure its continuing subdued state, a community of dedicated technicians was established, and just like industrious worker bees servicing their enormous oversized queen, the company town of Churchill Falls was constructed as their protective hive. By comparison with the mining towns this is a sleepy medieval hamlet; there is a single hotel and bar, a library, a school and a gas station, there are no shops and a tenuous slow paced link with consumerism is sustained only by mail order catalogues. There is no cemetery here in this hydroelectric company bastion, for no one is ever buried here; the transient workforce moves back into civilisation long before the depredations of old age and retirement.

The last section of the highway that stretches between Churchill Falls and Happy Valley, Goose Bay, is usually the most engaging should you be at all interested in wildlife, for here you may often make contact with the great caribou herds that roam abroad in this fantastic wilderness. These large gentle and shy creatures with their huge splayed hooves, dense insulating fur and straggling narrow antlers are genuine migratory nomads: passing back and forth across the sub-Arctic tundra of Canada in their unending search for food, they travel ancient ancestral routes mapped only in the collective consciousness of the gargantuan herd. There are two significant groups of these fascinating hardy creatures - the George River herd, which with a staggering seven hundred thousand animals lays claim to being the largest migratory herd in the entire world, and the Red Wine herd. I am told that the Red Wine animals are a distinct smaller forest subspecies and are easily distinguishable from their larger more plentiful open tundra cousins; however I have never managed to discern any notable differences in the various groups I have seen, but this fine point of distinction rages back and forth in unceasing, often heated local debate.

Regardless of the academic and zoological detail, caribou have been a source of sustenance for the aboriginal peoples of Labrador for thousands of years and despite strict regulation dependent upon which tribe you belong to, and closed areas of reserve, this tradition shows no signs of abatement at the current time. The tents of hunting camps are scattered along the road at regular intervals and one sometimes passes large four-wheel-drive vehicles labouring heavily to pull flat trailers stacked high with the frozen carcases of many dozens of these cattle-sized beasts; their eyes glazed from violent high-velocity death, their strong limbs stiff and solid, a sad caricature of their powerful, almost elegant thoroughbred trot.

Eventually you will climb over the high crest of Popes Hill and start a long-drawn-out descent into the town of Happy Valley, Goose Bay. Conceived and constructed during World War Two as a suitable stopover point for the thousands of bomber aircraft that were ferried across the Atlantic to Great Britain, this community is centred on a gigantic airbase with one of the longest runways in the world. Home to the American, Canadian and lately the German air forces, this important strategic base provided employment and relative wealth for the eight thousand or so residents marooned here in the very heart of Labrador. On 11th September 2001 it also served as a temporary safe haven for thousands of airborne travellers diverted away from US airspace after the attacks on the World Trade Center. Those stranded involuntarily on that fateful day were welcomed with the finest Labradorean traditions of hospitality and cared for in private homes and school halls over a period of a week or so until they could resume their onward journeys.

The resident German training squadron departed Goose Bay in 2006, leaving the huge sprawling estate of the airbase a virtual ghost town. However, the gradual economic decline of both base and town has been ongoing for some years now since the Americans redeployed in 1975. The former special glories of this odd isolated locality can be judged in the extraordinary quantity of exceptional recreational and business facilities that struggle on bravely despite the depleted customer base; there are plentiful fast food joints and restaurants, several reasonable sized hotels and large numbers of retail outlets as well as a bowling alley, ice rink and other sporting amenities. Goose

Bay is far from typical of the isolated, traditional and self-sufficient small communities of Labrador; it has a notably eclectic mix of peoples drawn from all the constituent groups of the province and a reasonable proportion of international representation also; it suffers from high rates of crime, usually theft and burglary, and there are significant problems with drug, alcohol and solvent abuse. Despite the underlying social and economic problems the people are welcoming and friendly, they have an easygoing attitude and those travellers that have sought out this quiet, little-known area of Canada are usually swamped with exceptional hospitality; or at least that was the case for me, for during the years I have been visiting Labrador I have had the enormous pleasure of being welcomed into various communities and developing a number of outstanding and remarkable friendships.

Despite its appearances on certain maps, Goose Bay is not actually the end of the road in Labrador; sixteen miles further on to the north-east, perched on a bluff overlooking the shores of elongated Lake Melville, is the town of Sheshatshiu. During my first visit to Labrador I made enquiries about visiting indigenous communities at various tourist offices and was told to avoid this town as I wouldn't be welcome, that I could expect to have rocks thrown at my car and be abused by the local Innu residents! Social conditions, I was told, were as bad as those reported in the early nineteen-hundreds when Arctic and Eskimo cultures were a great source of national fascination, fuelled by the various high-profile expeditions to both poles. At this time I'd never heard of the Innu. I was familiar with the differences between the Canadian Inuit peoples and the Alaskan Inupiat, but had no idea that there was a further cultural division here on the east coast of the continent. Today, I am pleased to say, I have significantly more knowledge about this fascinating indigenous tribe than back in 2004!

The Innu are a semi-nomadic people, skilled trappers, and efficient hunter-gatherers; they have lived in the deep forests of north-eastern Canada for centuries, subsisting completely upon natural resources just as the Inuit of the high Arctic did.

Unlike the coastal communities or those of the well-known treeless and icebound bays along the North-west Passage, they did not rely upon dogs and sleds for transportation but travelled on foot, moving between forest and coastal camps depending upon the season and its associated harvest bounty. They hunted the great herds of caribou and lived in domed tents fashioned from the thick skins before eventually turning to the easier and more adaptable canvas brought in by European fur traders. As recently as the late fifties the township of Sheshatshiu was a summer camp of tents where the bands of Innu came together on the sandy and pebble beaches of Lake Melville to hunt, fish and socialise. Sometime shortly thereafter it was decided, perhaps by faceless well-meaning bureaucrats, that it would be in their best interests if they were forced out of this traditional itinerant lifestyle and made to live in houses with fixed services and amenities and be given access to hospitals, schools and other perceived social benefits.

The price that the Innu have paid for this compelled cultural remodelling is staggering and a mere three generations later the painful results of disenfranchisement and alienation are brutally clear and almost certainly irreversible. Despite the dry status of the town, alcohol is freely available just those few short miles away in Goose Bay, and large cubes of beer cases are stacked on the shop floors and dismantled daily as their clinking building blocks are loaded into taxis bound for Sheshatshiu. Solvent and drug abuse is rampant amongst much of the youth and there is widespread teenage pregnancy; most adults are unemployed, with little or no prospect of work, and many are bitter and resentful over their marginalisation by the greater non-native majority. Houses are often surrounded with great piles of festering garbage and expired vehicles, and there are tales that abound of families destroying the inner fabric of the wooden homes and setting up their traditional tents inside the vandalised structure. The roads are badly surfaced and deeply potholed, almost impassable in some of the streets, and sizeable numbers of stray dogs roam the neighbourhood scavenging food and procreating at an almost unstoppable rate. The large ice hockey stadium sits on the edge of town, squat and threatening with unscalable windowless walls; the toilets and the seating areas are damaged and abused and the two small unwelcoming stores that operate in the town have sophisticated closed-circuit television watching over the dusty tins and cans stacked on their bare plywood shelves.

When I first visited the community in 2004 there was one single RCMP station situated in a metal box similar to a ship's cargo container, which had been daubed with abusive graffiti. At this time the local assembly building, or Band Council House as it is known, was boarded up and derelict, having been completely ransacked during violent rioting just weeks previously. These riots had caused such alarm that the Canadian government had flown in large SWAT teams to quell the disorder that the local police from Goose Bay had been unable to handle. Today, the Band Council House is still boarded up and out of use but the town has a very new and considerably larger police station and attractive additional medical centre. The Innu suffer from extremely poor health, perhaps another symptom of the relatively recent change in their culture, and gross obesity and diabetes are prevalent amongst both sexes; life expectancy is notably shorter than the national average.

There seems to be no shortage of cash showered down upon this community by local government attempting to reverse the damage that has been done to this fragile culture; traditional festivals, workshops and seminars are common and well financed and cash appears to be plentiful for any activity that will guide these people away from the self-destructive abyss and back along their traditional routes. There is a long way to go and I can vividly recall standing in the queue at one of the local post offices when a woman in front of me stooped down to pick up an official-looking document on the floor; it was an electricity bill and when she tried to hand it into the woman working behind the single counter she was told to place it in the bin from which it had fallen; it had been disposed of there only moments before by the recipient, who had no intention of paying it because they were confident the local authority would assume responsibility for the charge prior to any disconnection!

Sheshatshiu, despite its obvious metaphorical status, is also not the end of the road here in Labrador and half a mile further on, where a new steel bridge crosses the narrow channel of water between Lake Melville and Grand Lake, is the termination of Route 520 in the historic town of North West River. Established in 1743 as a fur-trading post for the Hudson's Bay Company it is still a wealthy and well-maintained community, with large prosperous homes and a strong cultural identity. Here the demographic is predominately Inuit and Caucasian, most of whom seem to be in late middle-age. Remarkably the town appears to suffer none of the social deprivation so visible in its close neighbour, litter is rare and graffiti even more so and I have never witnessed anything even approaching antisocial behaviour here in its well-kept streets. The relative affluence and prosperity here are notable and the town boasts a beautiful new visitor centre complete with high-tech auditorium and a fascinating heritage museum housed in the restored trading post.

The differences between these two communities are astonishing and I have never been able to adequately discover why there should be such a marked discrepancy with a mere half-mile separation in the same provincial administration. Previously there was no bridge joining the two towns, and a small cable car was the only link across the intervening channel, with residents of North West River keeping their cars on the far bank to enable access to Goose Bay and the greater, albeit far distant, world. I have been told that the cultural differences between the Inuit and the Innu are extreme and sometimes violent and that members of the two differing tribes enter the neighbouring communities only at risk of physical attack. I have never seen anything that would substantiate this aggressive segregation, and I wonder if this too is outdated knowledge similar to that which I received about the threat of visiting Sheshatshiu? In hindsight I can see that like almost all of society throughout history it suits the power-wielding majority to have a whipping boy, an outcast whom they can demonise and look down upon, and so despite the injustice of the situation it seems merely to reflect the larger worldwide inability of the human race to accept and harmonise.

Every four years the province holds its winter games at Goose Bay, with teams of athletes from every community in Labrador attending to take part in a week-long celebration of Northern Culture. Known locally as the Olympics of the North it recognises and rewards prowess and excellence in sporting events relevant to the needs of the land. There are snowshoe and skiing races, shooting and skating competitions, dog-sledding and curling tournaments ongoing at various locations throughout the town. The track and field events more common in warmer climates are replaced with "seal kicking, blanket tossing and seal crawling" events. The high jump becomes "over the rope", a marathon ordeal of repeatedly hauling one's body over a rope tightly suspended above your head and relevant no doubt to the original seafaring skills of the coastal fishing communities. The triathlon becomes "The Labrathon" where competitors race along a course of obstacles, stopping to chop wood, light fires, boil water and set traps in the shortest possible times. The Winter Games is a massive event with serious pomp and circumstance and is attended by what appears to be a considerable proportion of the entire Labrador population. During this time the cultures of the Innu and the Inuit communities are temporarily accepted and celebrated, and magnificent troops of artists adorned in beautiful traditional outfits are paraded before the TV cameras to charm the crowds with mesmeric performances of ancient drum dancing and throat singing.

Some of the Innu still manage to continue the old traditions of their culture, and each year during the winter months you may find a few tents scattered along the road between Goose and Sheshatshiu. One or two may have large piles of caribou skins stacked beside them awaiting the skilled attentions of the women who will clean, soften and stretch them into workable hides for the remaining vestiges of the once-mighty fur trade. The Labrador tents that they use are both comfortable and roomy and designed especially with travel in mind; they have neither formal poles nor floors, as only the tough fabric shell and stove are ever transported between sites, and the rest of the structure is gathered from the surrounding forest. The heavy white canvas is hung upon an A-frame of lashed fir boughs and the floor is formed by a carpet of woven pine branches that will eventually soften into the comfortable imprint of your body if you sleep on it for any period of time. At one side of the entrance door the galvanised grey box stove is set up on legs made from split logs, and lightweight tubular sections of the chimney pass through a specially strengthened section of canvas in one of the door flaps. The heat that is generated by these stoves in this enclosed space is quite astonishing and one can comfortably sit in just thin summer clothes as long as the fire remains well fed with an endless supply of dry cut timber.

One family of women that I am friends with make this yearly pilgrimage as an affirmation of their own unique identity and family bonds. The mother, an old lady of seventy who speaks no English, was converted to Christianity many years previously; about her neck she wears an enormous heavily carved wooden cross whilst she patiently stitches delicate beaded decorations upon pairs of light cotton slippers that the Innu traditionally wear inside their tents. The three daughters, all either divorced or separated from their husbands, are well educated, computer literate, mature students more familiar with mobile phones and email than the old trapping and hunting skills; however they are impressively relaxed here surrounded by the wilderness and various boisterous generations of children and grandchildren. Comfortably marooned from the worries and woes of the outside world by the bulwark of white canvas walls, they are tangibly close to the ghosts of their ancestors and probably as near to the old ways as they are ever again likely to be!

There is a third group of aboriginal natives here in Labrador which is called the Metis. Widespread throughout most of Canada, this strong indigenous group takes its name from the brown skin of mixed blood lines or Bois Brule; consisting of descendants from marriages between Woodland Cree, Ojibwa, Menominee and French settlers, they are more easily located than the other bands. They are, like the Innu and the Inuit, recognised as their own "nation", with provincial presidents and representation in the wider national assembly. They too struggle to maintain their cultural identity amongst the unending avalanche of American-style television and consumerism, but many are fiercely dedicated to maintaining traditions and a working remembrance of their role in the formidably arduous development of Canada. Similar to many of the native tribes of North America, theirs is a saddening tale of struggle and sometimes brutal repression, particularly in relation to the execution of the emergent spiritual and political leader Louis Riel, who led a small-scale rebellion that managed to particularly scare the British authorities in 1885.

There are still one or two old-style trappers who maintain long miles of trap lines out along the margins of the great silent lakes, taking regulated numbers of pine marten or perhaps the occasional wolf or wolverine once they have attended the mandatory government training courses. A few dedicated people continue the long-standing use of the dog team and flat Komatik sleds, without which the land could never have been opened and explored. Great cords of timber are still cut and stacked as fuel for the welcoming stoves during the long winter darkness when sewing, embroidery and carving are still common pastimes. Doors are rarely locked or knocked upon prior to entering and people continue the social patterns common to my childhood, congregating in animated conversation around kitchen tables loaded with steaming coffee and freshly made bread rather than the inane offerings of the television set.

Despite the tensions and irritations that exist between the diverse groups, this rich and varied mix of differing peoples with proud traditions make Labrador a delight to visit. For all of the modern technology and convenience available, they remain locked in their own unique time capsule, surrounded by almost impenetrable shields of mountain, forest and ice where traditional methods and crafts are maintained not just as a shiny seasonal tourist attraction but as necessary, practical life skills which still fit precisely the demands of living in such a hostile environment. The snowmobile may have supplanted the dog sled and the axe succumbed to the chainsaw, but the rhythms of life here are still just as likely to be dictated by migrating caribou, spawning fish or snow and ice conditions as flight timetables, television schedules and bank interest rates. Long may it last!

fig 6.   Dog sled races in Labrador

fig 7.   Innu family in traditional Labrador tent

fig 8.   Labrador husky close to Rigolet, Labrador

3. *Traffic Jams Amongst the Bison*

The last time I was in Montana, USA, it was April and the snow had melted just enough to make access on some of the Park roads possible. I had been quite alone then, so I was totally unprepared for the five thousand or so snowmobile fanatics that jammed the small town of West Yellowstone.

Only a limited number of roads and trails is open in the Park, and the major circuit that loops past Old Faithful is certainly the most popular route. Unbelievably, here you can be part of an almost urban traffic jam of two thousand sleds!

If you fall in with the accepted culture of "The Sport of Snowmobiling" and rise at six am, to depart for seven am, you religiously return to town by five pm in order to avail yourself of the free fuel that is issued to all persons safely back by curfew. You will spend almost your whole time engulfed in the ear-splitting roar and choking heavy fumes of the numerous sleds. Your progress will be one long overtaking manoeuvre and your forward view will be that of the rear of another sled driver.

The speed limit in the Park is forty-five mph and is rigorously enforced by rangers with radar guns, static speed cameras and ranger speed cops on high-performance sleds. Most of the real hard-core speed freaks therefore shun the Park and head off into the surrounding mountain trails where they hurl themselves at breakneck speed into blind curves with almost suicidal zeal and God help anyone coming the other way!

The group from New York that I tagged along with (fifty-five men only!) were totally bemused by my unwillingness to compete with their activities and obviously felt that riding in the precincts of the National Park was the preserve of children and old ladies. The idea that one might actually want to stop and look at some of the wildlife along the way was obviously an alien concept to them!

I was left more than a little confused as to why it was that no matter how far they travelled, I always seemed to get back to town long after they were safely home, fed and watered! To a man they would all be snug in their bed by nine pm and raging to get back on their sleds at six the following morning.

I have to report that I fulfilled all of their expectation by crashing my sled into a medium-sized fir tree after slipping off the trail in soft powder snow on top of an embankment. Thankfully my low speed saved me injury and contact with the tree saved me from a potentially more injurious descent of the steep bank! Nothing however could save me from the resultant damage to my financial position when I had to pay the insurance deductible!

Having seen the astoundingly ignorant behaviour of some sled drivers around the herds of bison and elk, and the general disruption that is wrought to the winter habitat by these large concentrations of noisy machines, I can totally sympathise with the move afoot by the National Parks Service to ban snowmobiles from all National Parks.

The Park in winter is truly magnificent; the great open expanses of high pasture stretch away from you in an unbroken blanket of pristine snow and the numerous thermal springs and geysers belch massive clouds of sulphur-tainted steam into the crisp winter air. On the high points of the continental divide the trees hang heavily burdened with great overcoats of snow, and should you alight from your sled for any period of time you quickly feel the effects of ten thousand feet of altitude.

The bison are majestic monarchs in this winter kingdom and plough great furrows in the deep snow, pushing the compacted ice before their great humped shoulders in order to reach the grass fermenting below. Unhurried and relaxed, the magnificent bald eagles soar effortlessly in the clearest of blue skies and ravens caw at you from every vantage point. Coyotes share the roads with you and glance nervously, without making full eye contact, as they trot past you seated on your sled. If you are lucky, travel at low enough speed and maintain a painful eye-stinging vigil in the blinding whiteness, you may be rewarded with a glimpse of the famous wolves of Yellowstone. Those reintroduced to the Park are now thriving in several packs that have been reinforced by migrants from across the Canadian border.

I felt it a privilege to be able to spend time here; the value to me is a moving reminder of one's insignificant place in the great scheme of things.

4. *It Rains a Lot in New Zealand*

I t rains a lot in New Zealand. In fact that is somewhat misleading; what I should say is that it rained on me a lot in New Zealand! Like many people I only had a vague knowledge of these small islands that sit directly opposite us on the globe. Of course I knew some of the more recent history, the outstanding war record of the Anzac troops and the ever-present sporting successes. But of anything more than that, well I have to admit my ignorance was quite astonishing really! It was where sheep were produced! And in my mind it was linked by a colonial umbilical cord to Australia.

So when I arrived at Auckland airport at 05.00 hours on a wet and cool Sunday morning many things came as rather a surprise to me! It wasn't hot! It wasn't dry! And it definitely wasn't Australia!! Leaving the terminal building I was fascinated to see the barefooted but rather noble-looking Maori gang member, his jacket blazing with full gang colours, this turned out to be my only contact with the Maori race for well over two weeks; they were almost suspiciously absent from the South Island where I headed that very morning.

A few miles south of Auckland the lovely new three-lane motorway petered out into tortuously winding snakelike roads where the speed limit was all but self-imposed, clean white fog lay on the roads and shielded the first small towns that I encountered, their wonderfully evocative wooden and tin upper storeys seeming to float on the top of a pristine white blanket of fluff. My senses were soon assailed by the smell of wood smoke! The pungent odour now sadly missing from so much of England, it brought vivid memories of childhood spent in my family living room sat with my parents by the crackling coal and log fire, of days spent in the countryside where thick hedgerows had burnt around the edges of drought-scorched fields and of standing crushed up against grubby gypsy families in the queue on the steps of our local town hall awaiting the furious entry to the weekly jumble sale. I could feel myself smiling as my nose triggered all of these long forgotten moments in my mind.

That early morning I was treated to two of the most famous of all New Zealand attractions: firstly kiwis, live ones, awake and very active in the nocturnal birdhouse at Otorohanga. There is something enormously charming about these rather drably coloured chicken sized birds! They are an odd mixture of feathers with strong stout legs and large clawed feet so well adapted for digging. Their bodies balloon over their centre of gravity in a great puff of deep mottled brown feathers, and that impossibly long beak seems far too fragile to be plunged rapier-like into the earth in the quest for food. The nostril, situated somewhat oddly on the very tip of the bill, is cleared of debris after such excavation by great snorting blasts of breath! Later, at another kiwi house on the North Island, I was told by the attendants that even the most hard-baked and antisocial types of New Zealander are often observed to go rather doe-eyed and soft round the jaw at the sight of kiwis in the flesh. To see them wild would take much time, patience and night trekking in the bush; the national population is under threat and introduced predators have all but wiped out many of the indigenous bird species from so many places on the two main islands. However you do see many signs at the sides of the more remote roads and tracks which claim "Kiwi Habitat" and threaten that all dogs will be shot on sight and that cyanide pellets have been dispersed in attempts to control predation.

Second high point that morning was the Glow-Worm Caves at Waitomo. These natural caves, formed by water erosion of the softer rocks over many thousands of years, sit at the bottom of a river valley that is choked with lush rainforest vegetation. Water drips from every surface and the smell of decay permeates the air. The glow-worms are gnats really and even then they only glow in their larval stage when they drop silk-like threads illuminated at the very ends in order to entice prey onto the sticky trap line which can then be reeled in and devoured. Sounds rather obscene but when you take several thousands of such larvae, each emitting its own luminescent glow whilst suspended from the high roof of dark and eerie caves, the sight is one of silent wonder. You pass beneath these uncountable constellations of light in small punt-like boats on the river, and the whole gossamer mass of silken mucus waves gently in the timid breeze that enters the depths of the cave. As your eyes adjust to the deep blackness the number of lights above you appears to multiply into a miniature galaxy where your eyes can no longer adequately measure depth or space.

I crossed to the South Island, arriving on the ferry in the dead of night to find the tiny town of Picton fast asleep and somewhat short on street lighting. The maps that I had, as always, purchased at Stamford's in London were rather unhelpful when it came to small population centres. I soon learned that the dot representing a town could mean that it was either a heaving mini-metropolis or a one-horse fledgling ghost town. Once or twice it caused me a problem in finding accommodation but in general it rather added to the mystery of the trip, never knowing what one would find on entering town limits.

From Picton I took a boat out to the Marlborough Sound, an organised Dolphin Watch trip where I found myself the only fare-paying passenger; the other three people were Department of Conservation personnel bound for Motuara, a tiny island on the very mouth of the Sound across from the favourite anchorage of Captain Cook. I never saw any dolphins, but Motuara was a pleasant surprise; predator-free, it has reintroduction programmes for kiwi and South Island robins; there is also a population of the loveable tiny blue penguin whose diminutive size and inquisitive nature make it appear endearingly comical. The birds on this island have no fear of man, and therefore viewing these creatures is an easy enjoyment; the varied songs and strident loud call of the bellbird fill your ears at every turn on the steep tracks to the summit, and struggling upwards overheated and out of breath I was quite astonished to see little blue penguins peeping from nest boxes at such high elevations.

The South Island became my favourite of the two wild and rugged and genuinely unspoilt. The lack of human contact only adds to its magical status. On the west coast road the sights and attractions form an orderly line to astound and bemuse you. At Westport you can peer down from the cliffs onto fur seal colonies battered by ferocious waves hurled onto the shore by forces that have travelled unimpeded across the Tasman Sea. Erosion of the millennia on the coastal rock faces at Punakaiki has provided the sculptural excellence of the Pancake Rocks rising from the surf in stacked orderliness. Large pods of dolphins cavort in the surf outside the sand bar at Greymouth, scene of devastating earthquakes in years past. At Harihari, the site of Guy Menzies' crash landing after successfully completing the first solo flight over the Tasman, is sadly rather neglected; the sign marking the spot is missing and even the posts have been vandalised.

The fantastic Fox and Franz Joseph Glaciers poke their fast-receding tongues out of the mountains; their befouled leading edges, grimy, fissured and fragmented at the moraine, give way to an external vista of the purest Arctic blue in their upper reaches. The tiny connected specks of climbing teams dot the brilliant surfaces and on either side the ancient ice is hugged tightly by dense water-laden and cloud-covered rainforest. Further south on the Haast coast, I walked through the rainforest on specially prepared tracks constructed from timber and helpfully covered in chicken wire to prevent slipping on the constantly drenched surfaces. I eventually came to the tiny and beautifully secluded Monroe Beach. This was reportedly home to a small colony of the rare yellow-eyed penguin; their tracks and burrows were evident beneath the lower limbs and foliage of the impenetrable bush, but the birds themselves were not. I did however meet another member of New Zealand's indigenous wildlife, and very vicious and persistent they are. I was treated to a first-hand viewing of several hundred sandflies, infuriating insects which, no doubt attracted by my perspiration, promptly bit me on much of my exposed skin and some that I had thought was perfectly well-covered, so that for the following three weeks I had a permanent reminder of my visit to the World Heritage Site.

I passed quickly through the self-styled capital at Queenstown, a small community packed to bursting with extremely young men and women hell-bent on challenging their bodies to the utmost limit in feats of contrived adrenaline pumping horror. Here you may career on foaming rapids in the famous jet boats, roll down steep hills strapped inside huge rigid plastic "Zorb" spheres or bungee jump from giddy heights bound together with friends or solo as the mood takes you. During the time that I was in New Zealand there were several incidents of thrill-seeking tourists suffering broken limbs on one or another of these attractions; it all made me feel rather old!

I headed further south and then west out to the dead-end of Milford Sound, one of the only two fjords accessible by road. The journey is billed by tour agencies as the drive of a lifetime and the scenery is undoubtedly spectacular, changing from high mountain pasture to snow covered mountain peaks that threaten avalanche, and eventually into the awesome towering near vertical stone walls and deep untroubled azure blue of the Sound itself. This area has incredible amounts of rainfall - in excess of ten metres a year - and good days are marked rarely on the calendar, so arriving at the water's edge in brilliant sunshine and clear blue skies I felt privileged in the extreme. The Sound is home to much wildlife and the intrusion of man appears to have had little detrimental effect. Juvenile fur seals bask in the sun on flat dark rocks, observing the tour boats with a disinterested sleepy single eye, or twirl in the deep waters, repeatedly tossing half eaten fish on the end of their whiskered noses. At various points around the cliffs waterfalls disgorge great plumes of spray into the depths, forming their own whirlpools and multiple rainbows. Toddling between the rocks, making impressive but rather clumsy leaps, I was even treated to an appearance of a rare Fiordland crested penguin; his slickly oiled plumage and bright yellow crests gave him an air of grandeur that was rather offset by his shambling, hunched, almost geriatric shuffle. Another of the delights of Milford Sound is that it is home to the mischievous kea, a large green parrot with beautiful markings, widely known for its striking confidence and ability to create mayhem among unguarded parked vehicles in its quest for high-energy junk food. They are accomplished thieves of the highest order and delight in destroying the soft rubber seals of windscreens or doors if permitted to do so. I watched in amusement as several of these villains assaulted the vinyl roof of a Japanese tour bus, resolutely declining to descend and pose for photographs until a suitable offering had been produced and inspected. When the bus departed, my car became the centre of their haughty, almost disdainful interest, and eventually my roof was assailed by a half-dozen or so of these avian bandits who, despite my keen vigilance, still managed to damage my windscreen wiper, and whilst my attention was diverted through the camera lens, assailed my roof. I drove away grinning broadly!

Heading further south still, I entered the lonely coastal region of Catlins. The area is one of rugged wind torn beauty where the gravel roads soon camouflage your car in a slippery glutinous skin of mud, and the trees and bushes grow in deformed compliance with the howling winds that beat the shore after their trip across the southern ocean. Hardy looking sheep stand resolute, battered but unperturbed by the constant gale. It is a haven of bird species where great hawks battle the giant gusts, and flocks of pretty introduced European finches scatter from the hedgerows at your approach. On the rocks of the eroded cliffs and in shallow bays you can see colonies of fur seals and hooker sea lions or even the gigantic wallowing elephant seal visiting from Antarctica. In the more secluded coves you may be lucky enough to sight a pod of rare Hector dolphins or yellow-eyed penguins, and at one site there are the ancient fossilised remains of gigantic podocarp trees visible at low tide. At Slope Point I slipped and slithered my way across deeply waterlogged fields festooned with huge quantities of sheep dung until I reached the southernmost tip of the South Island. Mud spattered and somewhat smelly, with saturated feet, I stood on the cliff edge in the roaring wind and contemplated what it was about such extremities that entice one to expend so much time and energy in their attainment?

Slightly north of the Catlins is the sheltered town and harbour of Dunedin, and to the east of that lies the wonderful Otago Peninsula; this is a wildlife paradise and one of my primary objectives in visiting New Zealand. On this small, rather steep area of land that juts out into the Pacific you are able to watch at very close quarters some of the rarest creatures on earth. The large yellow-eyed penguin colony here is on land privately owned; the farmer, having long ago realised the potential available in ecotourism, has built a fantastic warren of hides connected by trenches reminiscent of those from the First World War. He lovingly maintains the unique habitat that these beautiful endangered birds need to survive - a long low beach for manic wave borne arrivals and departures and sandy dunes of tussock grass dotted with specially constructed marital quarters. This was the closest I got to these penguins at any time; they may waddle past the hides mere inches from your face or camera lens and keeping pace with them through the network of tunnels, bridges, slopes and camouflage netting is like a giant game of Snakes and Ladders. Up this close the height of the birds becomes quickly visible; they are the third largest after the giant King and Emperor birds of the Antarctic. Their calls are astonishingly loud and their behaviour on land appears to be a precisely detailed minuet of greeting and display. Some of the juvenile birds may even be found roosting on the ledges inside the observation tunnels, and here you ease past their watchful eyes in reverent silence; their dense feathers seem to be wrapped around them like a coarsely woven winter overcoat.

Otago is, however, more famous for the other bird colony that is maintained here. At Taiora Head on high seaward cliffs at the tip of the peninsula it is possible to

large piles of Moroccan leather and bottles of linseed oil; the whole quarter might have been purpose built as a set for a period melodrama!

On the way to Christchurch I diverted into the stunning lake and mountain scenery of Mount Cook National Park, where for a reasonable sum I was able to fly over the massive peak and gaze down on the crevasse split, ploughed like upper reaches of the huge Tasman Glacier. At dozens of points the ancient ice overflows into great tumbling rivers that powerfully descend the forested valleys, the tremendous movement recorded in massive sunlit frozen ripples hundreds of feet deep. At Lake Tekapo I stopped to admire the beautiful bronze statue of a collie sheep dog, a tribute to the thousands of willing canine workers who made such enormous efforts in the development of this young country. I was regularly amused along the way to see his contemporary cousins riding happily on the backs of all-terrain quad bikes in the muddy fields, often with front paws draped in bonded companionship over the farmer's shoulders, his head raised above the rain hood of his chauffeur who drove oblivious of the lolling tongue and grinning contentment of his pillion passenger.

So I came to Christchurch where I had various appointments that waylaid me for three days. It is a pretty town full of trees and blustery squares, low-level by European standards, pleasantly rural almost. From the close by harbour town of Lyttleton, Captain Scott set forth on *Discovery*, eventually to meet his tragic death in the ice-fields of Antarctica. In the Christchurch city museum his and the other heroic names of Shackleton, Amundsen, Hillary and Fuchs are evocatively animated in displays of personal items and relics of those early pioneering days and later mechanised efforts to conquer those formidable wastes. In chill winds and the dim late afternoon light of what was still very much winter, having paid my respects to Scott clad in his Burberry parka on his pedestal in the centre of town, I wandered the smaller streets behind the tower blocks where strip clubs and massage parlours kept company with traditional dust-laden and musky-smelling second-hand bookshops where I bought such quantities of treasured volumes that I spent the rest of the trip ruminating on how best to get them all back to England!

Leaving Christchurch I set off in eager anticipation of Kaikoura and its famous resident whales. I am a great lover of all whale species and whenever my travels allow I will take advantage to spend time observing these fantastic creatures. Therefore I had long known of Kaikoura, the only place in the world where you are guaranteed sightings of the mighty sperm whale of *Moby Dick* legend. The seas create rare phenomena at this point on the continental shelf; huge currents converge slightly offshore to create a massive upwelling of nutrient rich deep water. This tumultuous soup of krill and plankton is a tremendous source of food for many marine animals, not least of which are the giant squid, favoured prey of the sperm whale. It is the preserve of young bachelor males, who roam these waters continuously feeding until it is time for them to venture out into the oceans and find a mate. So confident of sightings are the tour operators here that they offer a money back guarantee should you not be treated to at least one giant tail sliding majestically into the deep, something unheard of in most other commercial whale watch operations.

I have seen many whales around the world but nothing had prepared me for the unique sight of sperm whales up close. Their skin appears to have been wrinkled from too much immersion in the salt water, and the upper surfaces and flanks that break the surface are puckered into lumpy ridges like that of a freshly ploughed field. The coloration is deep brown or mottled pink and grey, and collected battle scars and abrasions are vividly white; the older the animal the whiter the skin becomes, hence Melville's legendary pure white Nantucket behemoth. Occasionally curiosity takes hold and the whale will spy hop, gently raising its gigantic blunt head vertically from the water so that its eyes become clear of the waves. The almost square monolithic bulk remains suspended above the water for a moment before slipping gracefully backwards beneath the surface. When hunting, the great flukes of the tail are raised ceremoniously to the sky, shedding crashing sheets of water as the massive creature dives vertically into the black depths seeking equally huge squid, and an hour or more later when he returns to the surface he vents his compressed lungs with a mighty whoosh of expelled air and salt spray, one of nature's truly magnificent sounds that thrills me anew every time I experience it.

From the air you may view these awesome beasts in a way that I had never before imagined; here you can see the complete length and detail of these monsters contrasted against the deeply vibrant blue waters. With fragile looking flippers extended at right angles either side of its body, it coasts unhurriedly on the surface where from six or even seven hundred feet you can clearly see the expelled spray from the blowhole shimmer in the sunlight.

There are other attractions at Kaikoura: on the same trips where I marvelled at the whales I was also entertained by upwards of six hundred dusky dolphins. Entertained is the only correct description to use: once you have entered the pod the water around the boat becomes an animated canvas of uncountable silkily gliding dorsal fins that cut the surface in ever increasing combinations until your eyes fail to cope with the darting permutations. Every few minutes you are held breathless by the most incredible aerobatic manoeuvres of one or more pod members as they leap from the water in fabulous gymnastic combinations of loops and twists that culminate in sharp ear cracking slaps back into the water.

The other wonder of Kaikoura, and the one that I had no previous knowledge of, was the albatrosses. This was an entirely different experience from my earlier encounters at Dunedin; there is no glass here and the birds are mere inches from you, and seeing adults on the wing is the norm rather than the exception. For a few dollars you can hire a local boat complete with captain, and when you have reached a suitable distance offshore the attendance of albatrosses is guaranteed by the smelly shark's liver chum that is thrown overboard in a towed plastic cage. Within minutes the first giants arrive: slowly circling the boat on huge wings they skim the very surface of the waves with easy grace and no discernible effort. When satisfied that a meal is on offer they make an approach to land, and this majestic king of the air, so beautifully elegant in flight, becomes a great tumult of wings, feathers and feet as they make barely controlled crash-landings on the least violently rolling wave. Folding up their articulated wings and regaining their noble composure, they paddle in towards you, maintaining careful watch on the large and no doubt menacing fins of the dolphins that appear briefly in the troughs on all sides. I witnessed one bird being lifted bodily out of the water by a playful dolphin scooting at speed between its legs, the first time I could say with conviction that I have ever seen any bird actually look worried! Soon there is a whole collection of these gigantic birds surrounding the boat, both northern and southern varieties enormous and pristinely white, the huge wandering albatross, the smaller bullers with its careful yellow and grey detail, the darkly marked and exceptionally vocal giant petrel and a gaggle of smaller albatross or mollymawks.

Despite the heaving rush and raucous din a distinct pecking order of feeding is maintained, the largest and most aggressive of the flock spreading its lengthy wings out over the buoyant and bloody flesh in order to maintain its feeding space, delivering weighty stabs with its huge bill to any other heavyweight who dares to invade the area, or a rapid and more dignified complete bodily squeeze to any of the smaller of the gulls that attempt to filch a meal from his table. Occasionally fights break out between the feeding birds and hungry contenders; wings beating furiously, their bills clack together with bone jarring smacks as they rise from the water locked together in a flurry of feathers and frothing water until one or the other is defeated and withdraws to a safe distance to wait bobbing in the roll of the waves for its next chance. I shot off reel after reel, entranced by the intimate proximity of these magnificent creatures. I had seen albatross before, flying in gale conditions, even on the desolate Beagle Channel in Tierra Del Fuego - a stunning sight, a memory I treasure, but for close-up study Kaikoura is certainly unbeatable.

Returning to Picton I had somewhat regretfully completed my circuit of the South Island and now returned to the North Island on an overnight ferry through the noticeably calm roaring forties of the Cook Strait. The North Island, sad to say, has nowhere near the fabulous collection of natural wonders that the South Island boasts, but it does claim a relatively less violent weather history and certainly maintains the larger part of the combined population, a fact that is of immeasurable consequence to most South Island residents! It is quite a shock after weeks on deserted roads in Fjordland and the Catlins to be faced with high-speed lineal duels of manic motorists intent on committing ever-increasing acts of violence in their search for that extra ten feet of road space.

I travelled steadily north through the many townships that stud the roads, stopping off at unlikely places such as Foxton, which boasts its own vintage tram service owned and run by a local entrepreneur, through the fruit orchards of Hastings and Napier and into the high desert, as the Kiwis call it. It is not a true desert, although the road is often closed by snow, but the area is a desolate windswept plain covered in wiry hard tussock grass and arid gravel scrub that stretches away in an undulating prairie like carpet of fawn, russet and brown until it meets the elegant purple and rose pastel tints on the snow-capped volcanic peaks in Tongariro National Park. Rather strangely, this isolated plateau is the site that the army has chosen to locate its exceptionally interesting museum. Here, in a genuine middle-of-nowhere you can revisit the many battlefields where Anzacs carved their brief but astoundingly unique military history. All the names of glory are featured amongst the displays, and a whole wall is draped with Victoria Crosses won in campaigns whose names are those of honour fought only short generations past. You may peer across no-man's land from a trench in Gallipoli or Flanders or walk amongst tanks from Tobruk and El Alamein.

After the huge lake at Taupo you enter the active volcanic area which forms part of the Pacific rim of fire that attracts visitors from all corners of the world, around Rotorua you are able to literally immerse yourself in the power of the earth's molten centre. It is a wonderland of steaming vents and vivid green or black lakes fringed with brightly glowing yellow or orange algae. Great pools of boiling mud pop and splutter with embarrassing sounding mini explosions, their molten chocolate surfaces forming an ever changing kaleidoscope of circular etchings which continually pushes the discarded plastic water bottles and food wrappers out to the edges of the pools. Prompted daily with the addition of a pound or two of soap flakes, the Lady Knox Geyser erupts on cue, jetting a huge spout of steam and surprisingly chilled water over the assembled visitors. On wooden boardwalks you may pass between travertines gently forming from mineral rich waters; fragile crusts of fluorescent green or yellow surround tiny spluttering fumaroles and you are continuously enveloped in great sulphur-laden clouds of dense white steam. Close by at the Waimangu valley you may wander through the youngest ecosystem on the planet, created freshly during the catastrophic eruptions of Mount Tarawera in 1886. This valley of deep vegetation and uncountable volcanic steam vents is a genuine part of Eden in ecological terms. Unfortunately the same eruption also managed to destroy one of the world's most remarkable sites of natural creation, obliterating the magnificent white and pink terraces that were reportedly more beautiful than those of Pamukkale in Turkey.

At Whakarewarewa, known more helpfully as just Whaka, there is a whole industry of tourism and Maori culture centred on the huge Pohutu (big splash) Geyser. The area is a fascinating continuation of the thermal activity, boiling mud pools; steaming vents and algae coloured lakes are sought out amongst the huge stands of Gauss. What I found most interesting was how the site appeared to have been divided into two separate concerns by the Maori owners. On one side there was a huge Maori arts and crafts centre with carving schools, concerts displays, a fabulous futuristic nocturnal kiwi house, manicured lawns and professionally paved walking routes. On the other side was the older establishment that consisted of vintage wooden homes occupied by Maori families, a gaggle of churches with graveyards full of beautiful Victorian monuments; the roads and pathways in disrepair wound through wicket fenced mazes of steam vents and hot pools used for either cooking or washing, and children played in the mud or on the river banks. Between the two camps, no doubt quite unmoved by the obvious dividing feed, sat the white scorched and crenellated mound of the geyser, obligingly erupting hourly in order to maintain the respective entrance revenues.

On to Tauranga and the Bay of Plenty, where it rained plenty, for three days in fact! Despite which the surfers could still be seen in the crashing waves along the very upmarket sea frontage where designer apartments of glass and stainless steel led ceremoniously to the perfect cone of Mount Maunganui, once the core of an ancient volcano, long ago extinct but still dominating the pleasant town. Now I detoured out onto the Coromandel Peninsula, a rather eerie place of gravel roads and small towns hemmed in by the all-pervading dense and dripping rain sodden forest. This is a place of quiet enchantment where large dung coloured hawks feed on possum carcases and kingfishers plunge into broiling streams fed from the cloud covered heights. On the Hot Water Beach, thermal currents escape the earth and filter out to sea beneath the sand and at the appropriate moment in the tidal cycle you may dig your own one-man hot tub and parboil yourself if the fancy takes you. On a high mountain back road I found my first kauri tree, a giant almost perfectly square trunk rising above the pungent mouldering canopy of the surrounding bush like a massive temple column that supported the pressing grey clouds, threatening to fall in, crushing triumph on everything within view. Much further north, after I had stayed the night in the dreary town of Thames and passed quickly through Auckland, I came to Waipoua Kauri Forest. These huge trees are every bit as impressive as the Californian redwoods, they manage an unbelievable girth. The largest, Te Matua Ngahere or Father of the Forest, is a staggering fifteen feet in diameter, the bark is light coloured almost like that of the silver birch and it holds a near perfect repetitive geometric pattern reminiscent of the hatching on the wooden handle of a Webley revolver. They rise in beautifully straight elegance with no lower branches and eventually spread their enormous moss and debris laden branches into tangled canopies that maintain communities of smaller plants, which lodge in the crooks of the many sturdy branches. Like all such wonders of nature they were almost wiped from the face of the earth by over logging, and the few areas that were saved are now protected, but will be millennia in their regeneration. The only jarring note in this ancient wilderness was the volunteers guarding the forest car parks in order to prevent break-ins and theft.

At Hokianga Harbour, finally out of time, I reluctantly turned south and headed away from the lonely remoteness of the northern peninsula via the pretty and manicured resort of Kerikeri and the maritime history of Dargaville, which had exported the millions of felled kauri trees. I returned sadly to Auckland to browse in the Sunday junk markets before flying back to the United Kingdom.

I had arrived in New Zealand shamefully lacking any real knowledge about the land and its people; I was leaving suitably re-educated and enormously impressed. Here was England thirty years past! A place where doors could still be left unlocked and the streets were blissfully clean and free from litter or dumped refuse. It was a place where people smiled easily at strangers on the street, where shop assistants and post office clerks were genuinely pleased to serve you and pump attendants cheerfully filled the tank and washed your windscreen whilst they held forth about the rugby or the weather. It was a place where you quickly adjusted to the twenty minutes or so of conversation that accompanied any request for directions and where it was still acceptable to linger with a book after a meal or coffee and watch the world go by. Perhaps it was the company I kept along the way? I have neglected to say that the other major reason for travelling to New Zealand was to visit the eighteen surviving veterans of the Battle of Britain scattered around both islands. These brave men had volunteered for either the Royal New Zealand Air Force or the RAF and had come to our aid that summer of 1940, fighting the Luftwaffe, and eventually beating the awesome odds they had returned home and are now all in their eighties, and many well over ninety. Most of the places that I stopped at were dictated by this consideration. They and their partners gave me the utmost hospitality, opening both their homes and their memories for me and the fifty cassette tapes filled with the events of "our finest hour" are an amazing treasured archive. Perhaps it was the remarkable courtesy and politeness with which these couples treated me, or maybe it was the well cared for stock in the lush green fields; it may have been the cars driving on the left hand side of the road, or the newspapers that were filled daily with as much news from Great Britain as from New Zealand. Whatever the reason, with England twelve thousand miles distant I felt very much AT HOME!

5. *Adrift in Patagonia*

There is a mystery and aura about the vast expanses of Patagonia that exerts a pull upon one's imagination similar to the effect that you feel in the high Arctic. Its endless vistas of low rolling plains coated in stunted prickly scrub stretch away from you towards the distant unbroken horizon in surging waves of churning green and yellow like the tumbling swell of a massive immobile and silent ocean. Adrift on this huge landscape you are drawn inexorably forward as each new crest entices you with the promise of high adventure and fresh discovery. At first you may be forgiven for feeling that the massive open spaces of the land are just one great emptiness of rain starved, desiccated vegetation and scruffy straggling sheep; however the briefest excursion amongst the wind-driven bushes and winding sandy trails reveals a multitude of extraordinary wildlife. The magnificent ragged coastline where billions of fossils are disgorged into the seas from crumbling wind-eroded cliffs is a remarkable habitat too; it teems with thousands of marine mammals and provides unique opportunities to view some of nature's most incredible spectacles.

There are few cities in Patagonia, and those that exist are separated by many hundreds of miles of immense empty space, devoid of trees and high mountains. The arid desert landscape parched in the rain shadow of the Andes far to the west is sometimes regarded as the Siberia of Argentina, a place of desolate exclusion, devoid of amenities, limited in development potential, offering few of the luxuries of civilised society. Yet it is this very monotony and desolation which lays siege to your consciousness and captures the imagination. Of the many exotic locations which Charles Darwin visited during his five years' exploration on the *Beagle* this, by his own admission, was the place that invaded his memory most vividly and most repeatedly.

Still it seems odd that in the mid nineteenth century this was the destination that a group of Welsh nationalists chose as their sanctuary from the domineering repression of the English! Like many who have fled Great Britain, they sought political autonomy and religious freedom, a place where they could speak their own language and retain their cultural heritage. They made an application to the Argentine government and eventually received a land grant in the province of Chubut in 1863. Although only a few had been farmers their intention was to develop the settlement on an agricultural base, and skills learnt in the lush and verdant countryside of Wales were tested to the absolute extreme here in the forsaken wastes of the Patagonian desert. During the early years the colony was almost starved out of existence. Eventually they developed clever irrigation systems, increased their harvests, and the colony spread, founding the towns of Rawson, Trelew, and Gaimen. Today the imported culture is still evident in some of the towns where Welsh surnames are still common, although Spanish is the predominant language. There are obvious examples of stone-built architecture and wonderful homely teashops serving dark rich fruitcakes and other home cooked delights.

As late as 1879 the Argentine government were engaged in an active campaign of genocide amongst the Tehuelche Indians. General Julio Argentino Roca led a war of ruthless extermination known euphemistically as "the Conquest of the Desert". To their credit the Welsh did not participate in this slaughter but their settlement in the region did provide a foothold for the Argentine state in an area previously beyond its authority. With the indigenous population removed, half a million sheep and cattle were imported to graze the former Indian lands of northern Patagonia, and the Argentine government made enormous land grants which became the massive sheep estancias of the present day.

These huge farms represent the concentration of vast areas of land into the hands of relatively few people, creating a regional elite who still maintain a socio-economic power base; even today the estancia remains a prominent economic institution employing a dependent and resident workforce. These agricultural labourers are the remnants of the famed and almost mythical gauchos, Argentine cowboys with an image and culture so widely celebrated amongst the remote urban populations that the reality has been distorted to a degree equivalent to their counterparts in the Wild West of North America.

The primary sites for viewing the incredible wildlife of this southern ecosystem are mostly situated on the Península Valdés, a large protuberance of land bulging out into the Atlantic Ocean, roughly similar in shape to the continent of Australia stood on end or perhaps a blunt Eskimo uhlu knife with its handle as the long thin isthmus connecting it to the mainland. The landscape is flat and unremarkable: divided into several large sheep estancias and crisscrossed with dusty sand and gravel roads, it divulges no hint of the abundant and impressive fauna hidden therein. At its very centre it claims one of the lowest continental depressions in the world, with the blistering white salt flats of Salina Grande and Salina Chica shimmering mystically amongst the heat distorted air forty-two metres below sea level.

There, half a dozen formally recognised wildlife sites are dotted around the coast, manned by rangers and provided with various tourist amenities; you are strictly segregated from the animals by fences and boardwalks but the interior bristles with multiple species which burst upon you with unexpected delight at each new thicket or dune. There are the magnificent and haughty guanaco, huge llama type animals which are actually New World camels; adorned in a beautiful red and white coat equal in richness and tone, if not texture, to a thoroughbred race horse, they stalk elegantly amongst the endless yellow gorse and waist-high grasses, their twitching ears and enormous doe eyes alert to every possible threat. Silhouetted against the low dissipating rays of evening sunlight, they create an image of spectral beauty, their shining evanescent wisps of tussled guard hair shimmering around the body like an ephemeral iridescent aura. Sometimes you may be lucky enough to view the young males jousting for position amongst the herd, rearing up violently upon their back legs like trained circus horses and boxing their opponent with murderous pummelling hoofs. Upon approaching a grazing herd you are met with a forest of inquisitive raised heads, the flicking ears and tense snorted breaths a mistrustful prelude to the sharply barked stuttering alarm call that sets the group bounding away in a graceful loping gait, the young keeping pace on their impossibly long legs as the adults effortlessly leap the wire sheep fences.

Elsewhere you may encounter groups of rhea, the large flightless ostrich-type bird specific to South America, skittish and extremely nervous; they may be viewed easily at a distance calmly placing their enormous three-toed feet amongst the prickly tangled brush, their curved elongated necks darting forward repeatedly to secure food amid the tight restrictive undergrowth. The upper plumage is a dull brown and grey which provides an effective camouflage when the bird is seated amongst the surrounding vegetation, but once on its feet its underside is a pure flashing white. When the birds are alarmed these apparently smooth and compact feathers disgorge into a giant flustering mass of wildly waving plumes, quills and tufts which accelerate rapidly away from you like a large quivering duster perched on giant bony legs, exploding puffs of dust and sand into the air as each tremendous foot hammers into contact with the ground.

Occasionally you may chance upon a mara; sometimes known as the Patagonian or South American hare, these are large rodents the size of a Labrador or retriever dog. They have rabbit-like faces with long tipped ears and their fur is light brown and trimmed with an unbroken line of white which runs around the lower half of the compact round body so that the animal looks as if it were wearing a tailored dog coat or a snug fitting mini-skirt. They are extremely fast and if you happen to surprise one feeding on the verges of the road with no immediate access to the brush trails, it may sprint ahead of your vehicle at an easy thirty miles an hour until it spies a suitable exit from its impromptu race track.

Everywhere the low-level foliage teems with bird life; brightly coloured twittering finches dart amongst the needle-like thorns and buttercup lemon blossoms of the eternal gorse bushes, and high above in the clear blue sky exquisite kestrels and peregrine falcons patrol in swooping watchful arcs and swirls of awe-inspiring aerobatics. At ground level there are families of elegant crested tinamous feeding amidst the debris scattered over the ridges and plains of low sand banks, their erect crests bobbing above their tiny heads like a maharaja's headdress as they progress in line-astern formation, the column declining in what appears to be a strict order of proportional magnitude. Should you decide to sit quietly anywhere in this desert like landscape your ever present water bottle will quickly be visited by bold finches who will attempt to secure a stake in this scarce and valuable resource, drumming like woodpeckers on the unyielding clear plastic.

At Punta Norte, the northernmost tip of the peninsula, there is a large mixed colony of sea lions and sea elephants. Here the crashing waters of the Atlantic thunder onto an endless beach of dull red shingle beneath crumbling cliffs of yellow clay and wind-driven sand dunes. Amidst their harems of snoozing females, massive bull sea lions sit stolidly sunning themselves, their necks craning back, the large whiskered muzzles pointed skywards, their enormous heads and resplendent dense manes badges of regal insignia proclaiming their bellicose sovereignty. Along the surf line swept by the tumbling incessant foam of breaking rollers are the young pretenders to the throne, juvenile males insufficiently bulky and lacking the necessary accoutrements of sexual maturity. They wait in the tumult of spray, ever watchful for the opportunity to usurp an unwary or injudicious monarch. Occasionally one of these adolescents attempts a foray onto the beach to be met with ear-splitting clamorous uproar, each resident bull bellowing raucous and profound indignation. Much of the time these are just probing engagements, feints to test the status quo and the vigilance of the master amongst his concubines. Periodically these reconnaissance missions develop into full-blown savage combat, each gigantic head snapping repeatedly back and forth with the lightning speed of a striking cobra. Fearsome canine teeth slash and tear amongst the thickly packed fur of their opponent's neck, each brutal hacking attack delivered with shattering ferocity and accompanied with tremendous deafening roars. Sustained combats are rare but even so, when the contenders disengage, the patches of slick matted fur, slimy and darkly shining with blood, are clear signs of considerable wounding. When no attempts are being made upon breeding rights, the beach provides periods of pleasant sleepy calm, the sunlit beauty of the sea accompanied only by the sound of the billowing wind and the agreeable twittering of unseen finches.

Intermittently the bulls will relax and lower their mighty heads to a prone position amongst their females and offspring, snoring and slurping loudly for ten minutes of contented slumber before heaving themselves back into a sentry position to give vent to bouts of loud sonorous trumpeting and half-hearted lunging upon their nearest neighbour, each newly woken participant adding its powerful booming song until the beach is alive in one huge resounding chorus.

In the brilliant sunshine of Christmas Day, swept by fierce bursts of wind, I sat in the dunes above the beach and watched in fascination as several sea lion cows gave birth in shallow scrapes excavated amongst the sparkling sunlit pebbles, each new arrival heralded into its harsh environment by a screeching commotion of clamouring gulls descending upon the bloody afterbirth. Occasionally the tiny infants, sleek and glistening wet from the amniotic fluid, could be seen teetering on small wobbly flippers between nipples along the massive recumbent bodies of their mothers. I watched in dismay as one miniscule newborn, separated from its mother, tottered amongst the various groups of adults in desperate search of its parent's comforting nourishment and protection, its agonising high-pitched mewing clearly audible above the wind and waves. Hauling itself with intense effort amongst the various surrounding adults, its pitiful insistent cry was met with complete dispassionate disinterest, each potential saviour a study in accomplished maternal indifference. Surviving the clumsy crushing manoeuvrings of one large bull positioning amongst his females, it eventually settled into the protective chasm between the powerful front flippers of what appeared to be its father, a brief lowering of the massive regal head from its extended position of vigilance the only indication of its tiny fragile presence.

Life on these nursery beaches is fraught with predatory danger; the seas surrounding the peninsula are the domain of the itinerant killer whale, and it is here on these sloping beaches, with large quantities of deeply layered shingle, that these gigantic hunters have developed the tactic of beaching themselves in order to take young sea lion or sea elephant pups. Surging in through the churning green waters at high tide, the whale can often reach youngsters or even adults settled close by the extremities of the breaking surf. Its colossal weight, propelled at immense speed, is powered almost completely clear of the water in this calculated pursuit of necessary protein. Seizing the terrified prey in its incredible monster jaws, the water is regained by tremendous agitated thrashing of the body and tail in violent spiral motions that displace the fluid gravel beneath its polished bulk and raise great clouds of boiling splattering spray as it fiercely slithers sideways back into the enveloping oceanic depths.

Another group of smaller but no less impressive residents of Punta Norte is the large colony of armadillos that inhabits the dunes and gullies of the surrounding countryside. These amazing animals are somewhat repellent when you first meet them; their large armoured shells, fringed with long guard hairs beneath which tiny scuttling legs can be glimpsed, are all too reminiscent of giant cockroaches or massive beetles. Their dark burrows honeycomb the earthen banks with numerous foreboding entrances excavated amongst the entwined roots of the large bushes, adding to the distasteful scabrous image, but actually these small mammals are neither repugnant nor offensive. Usually nocturnal in their habits, this particular group ventures abroad during daylight to scavenge the detritus of human visitors. In the car park of the reserve you may encounter large numbers of them trundling about amongst the vehicles, squinting short-sightedly against the strong sunlight and standing upright on hind legs against the wheels, stretching their inquisitive narrow snouts towards the enticing larder of foodstuffs contained within. If you are patient and sit quietly on a suitable bank they will assemble at your feet like a pack of loyal hounds, their twitching noses and bobbing heads responsive to each movement or sound that you generate. If you should provide them some foodstuffs they will attempt to climb the fabric of your trousers and even scramble up the bank to clamber over your lap and reach up against your arms and chest like friendly puppies, with tiny tongues that carefully lap salt residue from your bare arms or hands. Occasionally one may tumble backwards on the dislodged scree of its own excavation, rolling clumsily onto its curved plates and flipping upright again with a rapid heave of it muscular body before it attacks the offending bank with madly scrabbling claws to construct a more effective pathway.

In such close proximity they are fascinating beyond description, the magnificent symmetry of their segmented plates of armour stretching along their backs onto their foreheads like the helmets of medieval war horses, and when sitting on their haunches, balanced against their extended tail like a begging dog, they expose a reddened under-belly ridged and patterned like chain mail and overhung at the shoulders with a serrated cuirass. The enormous opalescent claws, adapted for maximum efficiency when digging, are sometimes wielded as weapons during brief and voluble squabbling; these high-speed scuttling disagreements are a frenzy of chattering squeals and rapid scrab-bling which resemble fingernails scratching heavy porcelain or thick shiny plastic.

The endless shingle beaches which stretch unbroken along the entire length of the peninsula are a deserted wildlife paradise. The great undulating expanse of shimmering polished stones is marked along its entire length with an constant ribbon of gleaming white sun scorched bones, the tiny skeletal remains of thousands of penguins and other pelagic birds discarded amongst the brittle tangles of festering seaweed and smoothly bleached driftwood, a sad litter of mortality deposited carelessly by the retreating waters at high tide like a wavy trail of sugar granules trickled from a punctured bag. The tiny resident population of humans has little impact on these massive areas of habitat, and small groups of basking female elephant seals can be found on the windward slopes of the tumbled stone ramparts and soft furrows ploughed amongst the pebbles by the incessant sea. These monstrously large beasts spend much of their time in languorous somnolence, baking in the sun like giant overstuffed grey sausages in a butcher's display, their thunderous snoring and equally raucous farting the only indication of life amid the torpid apathetic assembly. If you are quiet and careful you may approach within a few feet of these gigantic slumberous bedfellows before any individual will rouse from its apparent coma and reluctantly focus its large baleful watering eyes upon you. If you are injudicious enough to advance too close you will be warned against further progres-sion by a widely stretched jaw with persuasively numerous and viciously sharp teeth set around the gaping pink maw; this display of impressive weaponry is usually accompa-nied by a rumbling contralto exclamation that vibrates across your senses in foul smelling fishy blasts. Some of the animals have great suppurating wounds in their backs or flanks; the sickly discoloured flesh, torn in deep lacerated crevices filled with shiny yellowing pus, is testament to the staggering damage those teeth can inflict.

The largest colony of sea elephants can be observed at the Caleta Valdes, where the Atlantic surge has constructed a massive gravel spit that encloses a sheltered elongated lagoon. Here below the disintegrating cliffs you may view hundreds of these recumbent female pinnipeds. If you wish to see these great sea mammals engaged in any form of activity it is necessary to visit in the early morning, when they can be seen rolling lazily amongst the surf and coasting in onto the beach, curling their heads and tails into the shape of a taut bow to prevent drag on the stones and maximise the distance the waves might carry their bulk. Clear of the sea they become giant slug-like shapes, propelling themselves with great heaving lunges that ripple along the huge body mass like a colossal tubular jelly rolling forward on a carelessly tilted plate. Often at this time, as they haul themselves to their preferred spot amongst the gravel, they may engage in cursory bouts of hierarchical skirmishing. Swaying back and forth over their centre of gravity like a gigantic rocking horse they build momentum; eventually curling themselves into ginormous bananas they face off with mouths gaping and whiskered noses pointed heavenwards. In the more serious contests they rear up, arching their heads backwards to form a momentary crescent moon before falling forwards against their opponent with a monumental slap of quivering wet flesh, the teeth brought to bear against the opponent's flabby neck in a slashing roll of the head as the bodies smack heavily together. Large juvenile pups shuffle amongst the loose stones calling loudly like Jersey calves at milking time as they search for mothers amidst the dozens of cylindrical bulks, and out in the waves numerous sleek heads bob and dive between the sparkling crests and darkened troughs of the sunbathed swells, seemingly oblivious to the danger of possible Orca attacks.

Elsewhere on the coast, where the shingle gives way to large stones and dry broken patches of clay, rugged bushes of viciously spiked gorse have taken a stubborn hold upon the very edges of the beaches, their wind-distorted canopies a welcome shelter to enormous well-fed hares and sleekly elegant foxes. At one location where I picked my way carefully along narrow beaten animal tracks amongst the fiendish three-inch needles and penetrating spines of flowering prickly pears, I stumbled upon a family of foxes that displayed no fear at a human intrusion. The mother kept a watchful eye upon me and once she moved a dead rabbit to another selected cache, but for the most part she and her partner were quite content for me to be in close proximity to her young and immensely playful cubs. The silver-grey and fawn fur merged perfectly with their surroundings and the four rumbustious cubs played romping games of chase, disappearing amongst the myriad tunnels and cavities of the undergrowth, their wondrous camouflage concealing them completely until they reappeared magically at some other portal of their personal adventure playground. Every now and then one of the more confident would approach to within a few feet of where I was sitting and examine me with curious wide eyes and questioning turns of the head until it was again distracted by its siblings into impish wrestling and frolicsome mischief. Sometimes they would play amongst the cactus plants beneath the magnificent yellow and orange petals of the lotus style flowers or venture out uncertainly onto the flat expanse of the beach pebbles before the mother's sharp warning bark recalled them to her side. I spent several hours with the fox family, mesmerised by the remote paradisiacal atmosphere of sun, wind and sea, captivated by the connection of a cross species communication, a moment of absolute pleasure, a gift of trust and acceptance that touches one's heart and lifts your soul for the joy of life and pleasure of the world we so often pass by in our ever-increasing self-centred clamour.

There are penguins too on the Península Valdés, several large colonies of the Jackass or Magellanic variety; in fact one estancia on the north-western shore boasts the northernmost penguin colony in the Atlantic. However, if it is penguins you desire then the absolute Mecca is Punta Tombo. Situated one hundred and ten kilometres south of Trelew, this provincial reserve is a breeding home to an estimated one-half to three-quarters of a million Magellanic birds, the largest nesting ground anywhere in continental South America. This large area of uncultivated land is a picturesque alliance of tortuous hills and valleys covered in scrub and bright yellow gorse which straggle down to shallow stony beaches at the water's edge. The interior is frequented by large herds of nervous guanaco; numerous bleached skeletons adorned with the cardboard-stiff remains of the beautiful red fur can be glimpsed beneath the thick prickly bushes, and the soil is riven with hundreds of tiny holes excavated by mole rats, lizards and snakes. As you approach the coastal area a mile or even more inland you begin to encounter penguins, waddling through rock-strewn trails or sitting on the crests of grassy banks staring off into the distance with carefree oblivion through squinted dreamy eyes. The massive size of the colony only becomes evident once you have reached the beaches; here the constant stream of shuffling pedestrian birds toddling back and forth from the sea like clockwork minstrels is reminiscent of the miniaturised and slow motion traffic flow of a large city or motorway system. On some of the busiest, most heavily used routes wooden bridges have been constructed above the thoroughfare in order that the equally large numbers of visiting tourists may walk amongst the bustling minuscule commuters without causing significant disturbance. On every side you are faced with birds, tubby fat chicks petitioning quarrelsomely around parents, noisily demanding food and violently thrusting their entire heads into the open bills of mothers and fathers as they regurgitate slimy strings and lumps of foul smelling predigested squid. The baby birds are a patchwork mix of fluffy black down and areas of slick grey juvenile plumage; the wispy clumps of fuzzy fine hair tremble in the blasts of fierce unrelenting wind that thunders in from the crashing ocean, and often twins or even triplets will be found huddled low to the ground against the minimal protective shelter of a single parent. Some have excavated full-blown burrows where only the hard shiny beak of the adult or the fluffy posterior of the chicks can be glimpsed in the twilight earthen dungeon; others have chosen relatively sheltered nest sites tucked in tightly amongst the lowest tangles of wind-beaten branches and debris of the tough prickly bushes; they lie horizontal in the shallow beaten nest scrapes, eyes tightly closed against the endless whirls of stinging windborne dust. At your approach they will heave themselves into a low humpbacked crouch, the head still held parallel to the ground, and display an archetypal warning behaviour; regarding you with wary water-filled eyes they sway their heads back and forth in careful combinations of twists and turns that resemble crude figure of eight manoeuvres, the neck twisting to an impossible angle at the extremity of each sweep to turn the head almost upside down. Should you fail to heed this warning you will be treated to the atrociously loud donkey like braying that provides the bird with its colloquial name of jackass penguin. The colony is home to many other species as well as the penguins: there are king and rock cormorants, kelp gulls and oyster catchers and the murderously efficient giant petrels that patrol the nursery on massive wings, swooping low over your head in swishing passes as they search for unguarded chicks. The ground is littered with tiny dry and withered corpses and plundered eggshells, and yet for all this predation it is in fact starvation that accounts for the majority of infant mortalities.

Their flesh and eggs eaten by early settlers and aboriginal tribes alike, these small characters suffered persecution until relatively recent times: during the years when the whaling fleets were active they were boiled down into residue fat which was used to cap casks of precious whale or seal oil. These days, aside from the plundering of skuas and other large gulls, attacks by leopard seals, killer whales and sea lions, they have also to contend with loathsome polluting oil spills. Forlorn and bedraggled birds coated in suffocating jackets of offensive and malodorous crude oil are a common sight. Their beautiful water-resistant plumage defiled and corrupted by this noxious foul residue, they are unable to hunt and will starve to death, aided in their agony by the poisonous effects of the oil they ingest during their heart wrenching attempts at preening.

Around the sheltered edge of Golfo San Jose, along the northern shore of the narrow isthmus that connects the peninsula to the mainland, there are beautiful deserted beaches. Mile upon mile of flat white sand shelves gently down to the water where huge tidal drops reveal a wonderland of teeming rock pools, ominous sea caves and extravagant marine sculptures. A billion mussels and limpets crowd together in massive glistening cities, coating every surface exposed by the ebbing sea with serrated blue-grey armour plating that swaddles each curve and crevasse with adhesive intimacy.

In the captivity of their pools beneath the perfectly clear water, dozens of hungry sea anemones the size of teacups hold out their delicate flesh-coloured tentacles, beckoning unwary creatures into their fatal stinging embrace. Glutinous blobs of vivid green algae and tiny plants with yellow filigree branches nestle beside the alien-like pods of those that have secured prey, their prehensile filaments wrapped securely in a cage like arrangement over its unfortunate half digested victim. The beach here is littered, not with bones as on the Atlantic coast, but with tangled masses of slippery ghost white seaweed and decaying jellyfish, the viscous fronds slumped on the sand like thick trails of slimy gastropod mucus.

Although the shellfish here is infected with the deadly red tide bacteria, local fishermen are still able to subsist on their offshore catch. They live on the beach in ramshackle shanties constructed from hulks of decaying timber and oxidised sheets of corrugated iron staggering against a central unit consisting usually of an antiquated bus, every rusting surface decorated with skeins of organised net, colourful faded floats and inexplicable tackle. Fat scruffy chickens scratch and kick among the dirt and debris and grubby children amuse themselves chasing footballs or scrabbling in the sand. The perimeter and approach to one large camp was lined with magnificent chalk white whale bones, the huge vertebrae segments alternating with the curved spears of the ribs and giant mandible skeleton of the jaws driven into the sand like the ramparts of some frightful medieval fortress or the grotesque picket fence of some fearsome man-eating ogre in a gruesome children's fairytale. Although we spoke no common language the owner of this camp, a portly man with a scarred bald head and walrus moustache, dressed only in shorts and sandals, invited me into his workshop where a large steel table used for filleting and preparing the fish dominated the entire dimly lit space. Hung on the walls was an array of genuine artefacts and treasures scavenged from the beach or wrested from the sea, an ancient gaucho bolas, a pair of sprung steel sheep shears and even a pair of dried and withered knee-length leather sea boots. He was most proud however of the large frame of perhaps sixty or more Stone Age arrowheads that he indicated he had collected himself from the surrounding Elysian landscape.

The catch from these fishermen undoubtedly makes its way to the nearest large population centre in Puerto Madryn. Originally settled by the Welsh and taking its name from Sir Love Jones-Parry, the Baron of Madryn, this town is now dominated by huge aluminium and fish processing plants, and with its massive beach and surfing culture there is little except the street names to remind you of its past colonial ancestry. The Avenue Roca that parallels the long pristine beach that sweeps around the western edge of Golfo Nuevo is populated by promenading crowds of dark haired barefoot young men; adorned in mirror sunglasses and baggy shorts, they display their bronzed and muscled torsos amongst the groups of equally tanned, elegantly half-dressed teenage females. The numerous street cafés and bars are filled with noisy families and chattering groups of friends sipping fresh aromatic coffee or extravagant jazzy cocktails; the expensive clothes and lavish fashion accessories might convince you easily that this was Florida or Los Angeles rather than a remote backwater of Patagonia.

The one small town of Puerto Piramide actually situated on the peninsula is also now a fashionable resort. Originally constructed to enable salt exports it relies now entirely on tourism; its few dusty streets, crammed with various accommodation units, restaurants, bars and occasional souvenir shops, are immensely popular with Argentineans who flock onto the glorious white beaches here for much of the summer. Close by are camper parks where converted buses and luxury recreation vehicles adorned with sun awnings cluster together surrounded by power boats, quad bikes and four-wheel-drive Jeeps. Mile upon mile in each direction beneath the countless brittle promontories and fragile bluffs, the amazing wealth of fossil deposits exposed by the persistently collapsing cliffs offers the eternal promise of significant historical discovery. Complete fossilised dinosaur skeletons have been recovered from these former areas of primeval seabed and the museum at Trelew displays an incredible collection of assembled genuine remains from these awesome giant creatures.

One of the delights of visiting Piramides, however, is that you may view present-day leviathans at close quarters: the two huge bays of Golfo Nuevo and San Jose are temporary springtime homes and calving grounds for the glorious southern right whale. These massive thirty-ton filter feeders were hunted to the very brink of extinction during the staggering periods of commercial slaughter in the eighteenth century and are only now slowly beginning to recover. Travelling here from their winter feeding grounds in Antarctica they are tolerant and curious towards boats; the very fact that made them so easy to kill and provided their familiar name as "the right whale to hunt", now provides tourists with wonderfully close encounters for the minimal price of an excursion ticket. Even when escorting calves the trusting mothers will approach to the very sides of a vessel, their great backs crusted and mantled with literally tons of clinging white barnacles rising gently out of the water to be caressed by dozens of eager human fingers, the beautiful exhalations of spray-laden breath a pleasant audible heartbeat of shared mammalian obligation. These sheltered havens are also the site where the whales choose to mate, their joyous ritual of courting often observed as impossible breaching jumps, repeated slapping of gigantic tails and flippers and slow leisurely swimming pressed together in close intimate formation. There is a further more curious display that the whales in this location exhibit, known as sailing: this entails repeatedly progressing in straight lines between apparently fixed points in the bay with the tail fully extended clear of the water, the flukes open wide for the duration of each trip, propulsion achieved with the flippers only. Although it is suspected that this too forms part of the complex mating process, it is still not fully understood by observing marine biologists, but whether we comprehend the meaning or not, this fascinating process provides a truly exceptional spectacle, enough just in itself to make the trip worthwhile if perhaps you were still wondering what there was to see in Patagonia!

fig 9. Armadillo, Península Valdés

fig10.   Magellanic Penguin, Península Valdés

6. *Driving to the Arctic Ocean*

T he Dalton Highway that stretches between Fairbanks and the Prudhoe Bay oilfields on the shores of the Arctic Ocean is sometimes also known as the Haul Road. Built in 1978 to enable the construction of the famous Alaska pipeline, it is a thin ribbon of gravel that winds its way through some of the most wild and untamed land on earth.

Originally the oil companies banned private vehicles from the road completely and a checkpoint was established where the road sweeps down out of the unending forests to cross the huge high span of the Yukon river bridge. Eventually, after much to-ing and fro-ing in the courts, where it was finally established that taxpayers' money be used to maintain the highway, the oil companies opened the road over its entire length.

The road has changed considerably in the five years since I first drove it! All but ninety miles are now chip-sealed and there is no sign of the treacherous mire of half frozen mud that sucked at the car wheels for a hundred miles or more once you descended from the awesomely giddy heights of Atigan Pass.

Recalling that first venture on the road, I had loaded my rental Jeep with all the necessary survival equipment, my stomach tight at the thought of the tortuous journey ahead, my memory swirling with vivid recollections of sheet ice and avalanche warnings, of bone-jarring ruts of frozen mud that violently wrench the steering wheel from your unwary grasp when you are fighting heavy sleep laden eyelids. Vivid flashes of chopping accumulated ice from the wheel arches flashed back through my mind as I packed the hatchet, shovel, distress flares and tyre repair kit.

I am rather sad to admit that, unlike five years previously, I had absolutely no cause to use any of this carefully accumulated equipment on this occasion. The road feels tame now, not at all the daunting challenge I remembered. In 1998 I had marvelled in awestruck silence at the incredible wildlife along this barely discernible narrow smudge of road lost in the incredible snow draped scenery. There had been herds of huge prehistoric musk oxen, their great shaggy coats of qiviut hair hanging in tangled mats of yellow, brown and grey, soiled with mud and ice at its lowest points where it swept across the tundra. Their huge heads ensconced in the armoured framework of elegant curving horns lowered to the muskeg as they grazed unhurriedly.

There were herds of caribou, red and Arctic foxes, soaring bald eagles and most thrilling of all, a huge timber wolf who stepped out of the treeline only twenty feet from the car and loped across the road on long rangy legs and huge padding feet, his nose held down amongst the scent he was tracking, he barely condescended to give me even a cursory glance before he disappeared back into the labyrinth of densely packed trees.

The first hundred miles of the road pass through unending forest of spruce, cedar and pine where the dark forbidding loneliness heaves down on your tiny presence with repetitive monotony. Eventually the treeline retreats as the road climbs and you enter windswept tundra of stunted willows, spongy moss and lichen-coated bedrock. Here your view may sweep across countless thousands of acres of open brown and grey land where the silver bands of twisting rivers reflect the weak sunlight and the foreboding ramparts of the Brooks Range can be seen piercing the darkened bases of the low massed clouds.

There are heaving formations of wind-torn and scoured rock that were used as vantage points by early stone age hunters tracking the migrating herds of caribou which their lives so closely depended on, and the navigation aid known as Finger Rock, a curiously shaped crooked finger of stone which rises from the flat ground and points directly at Fairbanks as if a fossilised giant were breaking loose from his tomb beneath the frozen earth!

Where the road crosses the Arctic Circle there is a picnic area and display of information boards set atop a small ridge facing out over the endless open vista that finally disappears into the northern horizon. The brightly coloured map which demonstrates the extent of that imaginary circumpolar line had been defaced with graffiti, and despite having been repainted, the words scored deeply into the wooden surface were clearly legible, the angry demand "keep out of ANWR" carried all the echoes of the vehement protests lodged by native Alaskans over the proposed oil drilling development of the great pristine beauty of the Arctic National Wildlife Refuge.

Eventually, at about the halfway point, the road leads you to "Cold Foot". This extended lay-by holds the record as the world's most northerly truck stop. An enterprising chap called Dick Mackey set up a burger bar in an old school bus as a service station for the truck drivers hauling loads to Prudhoe Bay. Twenty-two years later this swamp of churned mud that swarms around the tiny island of petrol pumps is rumoured to have changed hands for an estimated one million dollars! The barrack blocks which housed the original road construction gangs have been converted into a hotel and the school bus has graduated into a huge wooden cabin where equally huge meals are served twenty-four hours a day and the walls are decorated with dramatic photographs depicting battered, crashed and crumpled cars, vans and camper homes along with various jack knifed or overturned articulated trucks. The highway is an unforgiving place for the unwary or unprepared!

The truck stop at Cold Foot provides the only petrol between the Yukon River and the Arctic Ocean; there is a miniscule post office, a tyre repair and mechanics shop and a tiny gravel airstrip, and yet it is visited by considerable numbers of tourists each year, a large proportion of whom are Japanese! Cold Foot is one of the optimum places in the northern hemisphere to view the aurora borealis or northern lights. During winter months of unforgiving darkness, the sky at Cold Foot and above the Atigan Pass burns with fierce sheets of undulating colour; great shimmering curtains of ethereal green, white and red pulsate across the stratosphere like shrouds of celestial ectoplasm. The Japanese believe that children conceived beneath this spiritual display of solar energy will be blessed with lifelong good fortune, and they flock to this remote site in droves so that they may procreate at the most opportune moment!

Some ten miles further north of Cold Foot the unique town of Wiseman nestles precariously along the bank of the Koyukuk River. Like almost every point of interest along the Dalton, Wiseman claims its own "most northerly" status as the northernmost Gold Rush town in the world. This evocative collection of twenty remaining log cabins was home to a riotous mining camp during 1910; the whorehouses and the saloon are no longer active but the structures are all listed and protected and almost all of the cabins are inhabited. This is a community dominated by subsistence hunters, where cabin gables are decorated with moose or caribou antlers and tanned wolf skins; wolverine and snow hare pelts hang in the entry porches. I stayed with one trapper who owned "Igloo No 8", originally the saloon and meeting house for the fraternal brotherhood of the Arctic. A lopsided ramshackle old cabin roofed in tin with the original sign-painted glass panes of the saloon still forming the windows of the front porch. The trapper and his family originated from Germany and they eked out a living here, eating the food which they trapped or shot.

The cabin was a place of anomalies where the original saloon piano stood in the kitchen along with a huge pot-bellied stove and the wires of a fire alarm system and laptop computer terminals snaked around the caulked wooden walls. The back rooms were an Aladdin's cave of Gold Rush memorabilia and trapping paraphernalia, where wolf pelts hung with tin baths, dog harness, leather horse tack and snares whilst broken freight sleds were piled with gin traps and the skin of a huge grizzly bear loitered next to a wooden barrel washing machine, an ancient gramophone and exquisitely stitched moose skin mukluks.

On the frost-twisted front porch a child's talking "Tigger" character sat incongruously amongst piled bags of dog food and various stored provisions and salvaged tools, horseshoes and assorted ironware cascaded from the eaves, and from every post and beam. The team of huskies chained to their half buried wooden kennel boxes along the snow riven bank of the nearby creek strained eagerly against their lines as large ebony sleek crows pecked raucously at huge chunks of caribou meat which, almost unbelievably, they had managed to move sufficiently far away from the reach of the agitated dogs. Around the yard, tucked into the crooks of tree branches or suspended from wires, were the half exposed skulls and body parts of various trapped animals, the white bone being slowly exposed as the frozen flesh was devoured by the many visiting finches and buntings.

From Wiseman you may venture along the short road to the dead-end of Nolan mining camp and from here you may walk into the gates of the Arctic National Park. This is a huge tract of completely untouched wilderness extending over more than thirteen thousand square miles and straddling the Arctic divide, so that all the rivers either flow northwards to the Arctic Ocean or south to the Yukon River. It is a protected home to numerous wolf packs, solitary grizzly bears, huge shouldered Dall mountain sheep, caribou and moose. When you venture into its white blanketed valleys the silence is so intense that your breathing thunders in your ears with deafening regularity, the packed snow crunches beneath your feet with squeaking protest, setting the teeth on edge, and the blinding sunlight is reflected from thousands of tiny particles as if uncountable flawless diamonds had been strewn across the landscape. In the midst of daylight you may convince yourself that this is a place devoid of animal life but the signs of the many residents are around you on all sides, held by the frozen snow, the fuzzy imprint of feathered ptarmigan feet or the sharply pressed claws of wolverine. With great excitement I recognised the trail of a wolf; the large dog-like imprint of a steadily loping animal which moved forward with unswerving directness was joined at one point by what appeared to be a pup zigzagging back and forth across the larger tracks, and soon my suspicions were proven by the frozen scat which had been deposited in the centre of the trail; the heavy content of undigested animal hair confirmed a carnivorous predator, and whilst I never saw the wolf I suspect the wolf saw me!

Progressing north from Wiseman you leave the very last of the stunted trees and begin the climb over the Brooks mountain range, winding your way carefully up through the icy Atigan Pass where great sheets of snow hang on the steep mountainside preparing to descend in ferocious avalanche; numerous signs warn you of the dangers of stopping in the pass, but the unnatural quiet and the visible slides of snow are more than enough to keep you on the move. The road descends from the pass on an equally steep gradient and pushes on northwards to Galbraith where it climbs again onto the coastal shelf. Here the horizon is unbroken in any way and the great unending whiteness stretches on as far as the eye can see, pierced only by the twin strings of the road and the pipeline. All perspective is soon lost and the white snowbound land joins the white cloud of the sky with a barely discernible change, and when the grey sea fog rolls in from the coast some hundred miles or so distant, the flat plain becomes a twilight zone of complete disorientation where up and down, left and right cease to exist, where only forward or backwards between the reflective road markers has any meaning and your eyes ache for some small point of reference to focus on. You pass the very edge of the Arctic National Wildlife Refuge, a truly massive area of Arctic wilderness which boasts fewer visitors than the surface of the Moon and ever present is the writhing serpent-like pipeline; blind and mute it slithers ever onwards across the ice bound plain, the head searching out Prudhoe Bay and its unceasing ingestion of thick crude oil. Caribou roam here feeding on the meagre lichens they uncover beneath the crusted snow; they eye you cautiously as you pass by, and should you venture too close to the herd the lead male will quickly shepherd his harem and offspring out of your reach, his heavy bull neck stretching forwards and swinging beneath his muzzle as his breath is expelled with audible grunts into the frozen air in small condensed white clouds.

Close to the termination point of the road at Deadhorse I stopped the car and watched in amazement as a beautiful red fox in a magnificent full winter coat chased a huge black crow across the ice, leaping and twisting into the air in vain attempts to capture the crow, which fluttered and flapped in leaps and hops of half flight just out of his reach. With hindsight I have realised that either the crow was injured in some way or perhaps was carrying some large item of food which impeded his aerodynamics; whatever the reason, it was a curiously surreal scene to witness at the end of an equally curious four hundred miles.

Whilst the road actually leads to the oilfields on the Arctic Ocean, no private vehicles are allowed past the town of Deadhorse. This strange town sits a mile or so inland from the sea ice and acts as airport and focal point for the oilfields. It is a sprawling collection of hangars, huts, sheds and steel containers, massive yellow painted earth moving machines sit like immobile monsters half buried beneath great banks of driven snow, and large sea-going tug boats slouch sullenly on steel frames like forlorn beached whales. Everywhere is the technology of oil: pipes and rigs; flare stacks and emergency fire vehicles.

Quite amazingly the population of Deadhorse varies from between three to eight thousand persons; there are three hotels which provide twenty-four-hour meals for the shift workers on the fields, and the centre of the complex is the Prudhoe Bay general store and post office. Here you may purchase anything from fresh fruit to inflatable dolls; row upon row of huge Arctic weather snowsuits fill most of the racks and you may even purchase small vials of genuine Prudhoe Bay crude oil! The wooden walls of the tiny post office are covered with FBI wanted posters containing mug shots and fingerprints of felons, kidnappers and rapists, and alongside these are numerous photographs of more law-abiding travellers: those who have either started or finished at Prudhoe on the marathon trip between Tierra del Fuego and the Arctic Ocean.

Amongst them were those that crammed themselves into beaten old Volkswagen Beetles or other improbable motorised transport, and a half-dozen or so who had cycled! And even one or two complete maniacs who had walked!!!

The oil at Prudhoe is almost expired; the seven hundred and eighty-nine miles of pipeline down to Valdez completed in 1977 have passed their projected lifespan of twenty years and there is talk of constructing a second line to enable drilling of the reserves which lie beneath the ANWR. Drilling in the Arctic National Wildlife Refuge has been on the cards for some time now. George Bush Senior backed a bill for exploitation of the area as far back as 1989, but the terrible ecological disaster brought about by the oil spill from the Exxon Valdez waylaid it. Despite President Clinton's attempts to preserve the refuge it looks almost certain that drilling will go ahead now. There is no personal income tax in Alaska and on top of that the revenue generated for the state by the oil companies is held in a "permanent fund" which pays out a substantial yearly dividend to every resident man, woman and child. Alaskans are so inured to the oil wealth that retail companies selling luxury vehicles or snowmobiles will advance you credit on the strength of your permanent fund cheque arriving each February. Visiting congressional investigators fly over the vast expanse of land and are reported to have commented on not understanding "what all the fuss is about"; even the governor is on record as saying "there's absolutely nothing up there". Combine this with the current anti-Middle Eastern climate and the still far-reaching effects of the previous incumbent in the White House and the fate of the North Slope seems sealed. I wonder how different it will be if I venture back again in another five years?

So I travelled back along the haul road to Fairbanks, wondering, as I invariably do on long trips, why it is that it always feels quicker on the return leg! I expect it is some psychological quirk that kicks in once you know you have passed the furthest point and are headed back to safety and civilisation. With all but the last five hundred yards of loose gravel behind me I was relieved to have made it back with the car intact. Two of the essential items to carry on the haul road are a large sheet of clear plastic and a roll of duct tape so that you may fabricate a temporary windscreen if yours should be smashed. In days gone by it was more than usual for cars to lose both the screen and side windows from projectile stones hurled up by passing trucks. Without doubt I now know that one should never count the chickens before they are safely in the bag; with the hard top in view a huge double trailer truck, a fast closing speed and a large lump of stone managed to crack my windscreen from top to bottom in one loud clattering bang!

Back in Fairbanks I boarded a flight to Barrow, the northernmost point on the American continent and an ancient Inupiat whaling community, approximately one hundred miles west of Prudhoe Bay. The day was dazzlingly bright and clear and from the windows of the aircraft I could clearly trace the thin strand of the road and the pipeline snaking its way over the awesome landscape. From the air the tiny insignificance and temporary nature of those two structures is completely evident. They are mere hairline cracks in the varnish of this immense age-worn and timeless painted landscape, miniscule threads which can be expunged in a moment by the heavy stroke of the careless artist.

Of the many places that I have been privileged to visit, Barrow, Alaska remains one of the most uniquely fascinating, a complete oddity that defies convention and challenges all your preconceptions of Eskimo culture. Unlike the Dalton Highway, Barrow hadn't changed much since I was there last! It had acquired a fancy new post office, a huge shiny supermarket and an even bigger three-storey Inupiat heritage centre where a full size model of a sixty-ton Bowhead Whale hung suspended from the roof, the tastefully decorated galleries were lined with beautiful photographic studies of local people and there were displays of natural history and a few original Eskimo artefacts.

Other than that it was all as I had remembered, haphazard, low-level and dirty, almost every single-storey wooden house was still surrounded with piles of detritus and discarded materials, deceased windowless cars, ancient paint-scarred pickup trucks and broken snowmobiles sat entombed in dirty grey banks of snow that were strewn with engine parts, retired washing machines, dilapidated household furniture and children's redundant toys! The porch railings and side walls of almost every second house were adorned with numerous stiff frozen skins, and many dozens of racks of antlers, often still attached to the desiccated and ice-mummified heads of the caribou, were jumbled in jigsaw confusion on sagging flat roofs.

Complete distended carcases of ring seals protruded upright from wind-driven snow banks like fur coated traffic bollards, full polar bear skins were strung tightly on wooden stretching racks constructed on the roofs of half a dozen homes and everywhere were the remains of the hunted bowhead whale. The great twelve-foot long plates of baleen leant against the walls of what seemed to be every house, some of it still embedded in the fatty yellow gum tissue. Huge vertebrae segments and long curved ribs were piled on roofs or stacked in heaps and now and then large hunks of sickly yellow mottled and gangrenous-looking whale blubber were piled in a driveway or garden. Enter the porch of any Inupiat house and you will find more hunks of this mouldering whale flesh carelessly dumped on the dirty floor surrounded by mud caked shoes and boots. Along the beach where the crushing tangled ice of the Arctic Ocean heaves up against the black sand there are lines of impossibly huge whale skulls, their jawbones lashed into place against the upper mandibles and supported upright on wooden blocks; they possess an odd, alien, sculpture-like quality. The huge tangled pile of thousands of decaying whalebones discarded at the end of the road some ten miles or so from town was regularly visited by polar bears, who would gnaw some sustaining nourishment from them, and they have this winter been bulldozed out on to the sea ice in order that they descend to the bottom of the ocean when the summer sun finally breaks the ice.

In Barrow incongruity is quite normal. Women with beautiful jet-black hair tied in long thick braids hurtle past you on four-wheel all-terrain motorbikes with chubby moon-faced babies clamped tightly into the hoods of their traditional brightly col-oured fur-lined parkas. Young teenagers cruise the limited road system in huge four-wheel-drive Jeeps, their heads bobbing in time to the thumping base of blaring hip-hop music whilst weathered sunburnt hunters hooded in white camouflage fatigues and heavy fur mittens pass by on roaring snowmobiles, large powerful rifles strapped across their backs. Huge aggressive huskies and ferocious mastiffs are chained before most houses and small children play unattended in the mud-choked streets late into the early hours of the brightly sunlit night. It is quite common to find an expensive new car, motorbike or pushchair parked next to a traditional umiak whaling boat manufactured with ancient skills, the precision sawn timber tautly clad with tough white-bearded seal skins.

Some of the more artistic residents have constructed interesting garden sculp-tures from whale vertebrae and in this landscape completely devoid of trees the two half-scale palms are a master stroke, their trunks made from bleached driftwood and the classically drooping fronds ingeniously fabricated from the polished black plates of hair-fringed baleen.

Aside from the scenery and the odd nature of the town the people who live and work in Barrow are fascinating. The native Inupiat are generally slow talking and thoughtful; easy to smile, they all appear to suffer from hereditary eye weakness which forces most to wear glasses, the heavy practical frames solidly black on their leath-ered brown faces. They are difficult people to approach and make acquaintance of but friendly if you take the time to cultivate the relationship. Most of the businesses in Bar-row are owned, managed or staffed by non-native peoples; there are the usual industri-ous Koreans, Chinese and Filipinos and, rather strangely for such a cold and ice-laden environment, a large contingent of Hawaiians, well-fed and sleekly fat; some sport the traditional topknot in their oiled black hair and their flattened facial features are not greatly removed from those of the Eskimo! Like many Inuit communities there are high levels of suicide and, despite the fact that Barrow is officially "dry" and it is not possible to "legally" purchase beer or spirit, there are ongoing problems with alcoholism. It is a strange sight to see young teenagers wearing colourfully printed sweatshirts proclaim-ing their pride in the fact that their parents have "both quit"! Drug abuse appears rife among the younger generation; some teenagers that I spoke with told me that cannabis is regularly purchased by mail order on the Internet.

I have a good friend living in Barrow who keeps a team of huskies, and as we prepared for a trip out on the ice the weather blessed us with the added burden of a mild storm; by the time we left town in the late evening the wind was reasonably fierce and the loose snow driving almost vertically across the land enveloped the dogs in its mantle as they lunged forwards in their harnesses. We were headed for a natural ice cave which had formed in a driven bank of snow some twenty miles to the east of Barrow, and as we worked our way along the ice-laden beach the dogs, used to much shorter trips laden only with one or two tourists and not the added burden of two hundred pounds of equipment and food, looked back over their shoulders, clearly asking why it was we had not turned for home yet?

Fourteen miles or so out, with the wind howling and visibility deteriorating, we stopped to view the memorial for Willy Post and Will Rogers, two pioneering American aviators who had been killed in a crash during the twenties. The original obelisk memorial has been so badly damaged by the severe Arctic weather that it has been replaced with an updated version, but it is genuinely hard to tell which is which; there are no engraved memorial plaques and the cracked concrete pillars formed around steel frames which protrude from the crumbling apex sit lonely and unremarked in the harsh landscape. As a trained pilot I had shivers at the thought of crashing in such an unforgiving and deadly environment.

We didn't know it at the time but our ice cave had been closed by driven snow and we circled the sled in the area searching for any indication of the entrance; the dogs were tired and an immediate return trip to the safety of Barrow would have been long and arduous. My friend John, the owner of the dogs, is a committed member of the Church of Jesus Christ of Latter-Day Saints, more commonly known as Mormons; he is a devout believer and completely dedicated to converting me to his church, and as the weather worsened and the night temperature dropped he suggested that a prayer was in order to enable us to find the cave! I am a long-standing non-believer, I have no faith in the power of prayer, but I have to say that it rather seemed to do the trick; within minutes of John completing his utterly sincere request for help we stumbled onto the remains of the last camp pitched at the cave entrance.

An hour later, after much shovelling of snow and blocks of ice, we had excavated the cave to its original dimensions and set up camp in the protected lee of the twenty-foot snow bank driven hard up against the jumbled sea ice. Unlike many husky teams, John's dogs can be allowed to run free off the tug lines without disappearing over the horizon never to be seen again, and whilst we prepared the camp the team charged around with great exuberance, tumbling and tangling in the loose snow we had dug out of our accommodation. In our protected position the wind was not evident and the utter and sometimes eerie silence of the Arctic quickly settled around us.

Inside the cave we set up our home comforts and prepared food, the fuel tablets for the stove releasing such copious amounts of fumes that eventually, red-eyed and breathless, we had to retreat outside for oxygen. In the early hours of the morning, after much talk of God and Christian values, with the light barely dimming in the grey-streaked sky, we crawled into the cave with three of the dogs and sealed the entrance with a large slab of ice. In hindsight, taking the dogs into the igloo was a bit of a mistake; whilst they generate huge amounts of heat which was sorely needed, they are not the best bedfellows: hogging as much of the limited sleeping space as they could snuggle, stretch and expand into, they spent the rest of the night variously farting, drooling and belching in complete oblivion whilst I, cramped and fatigued, dozed fitfully between bouts of sleep-induced shivering.

An hour before dawn, cold and stiff, we rose and broke camp; slowly loading the equipment back onto the sled and harnessing the dogs, we moved and talked in the subdued tones of the sleep deprived; however as we set off eastwards back to Barrow the sun rose with such stunning, indescribable beauty that all else was forgotten.

Tender pastel hues of red, orange and pink suffused the entire sky in wide bands of fire-laden promise that were dissolved slowly as the massive terracotta orb of the sun heaved itself sedately off the horizon into the perfect shimmering clarity of unpolluted air. The dogs ran onwards into swirling skeins of ground-blown snow, covering their backs and caking their faces with icy rime as they pushed happily for home, unmoved by the intense magnificence of the new day. People often ask me what the attraction is in the snow and ice of the Arctic, and words are generally inadequate to explain, but the awe-inspiring wonder of such incredible moments is worth any amount of cold or discomfort; the exquisite inspiring nature of this land is beyond description; it storms your senses, invades your soul, and captures your heart; what more can be said?

The following evening we took the dogs out onto the sea ice again; this time we were not burdened with supplies or equipment and the lightweight toboggan sled was whipped along easily on the hard wind-polished ice. We followed a trail laid out with tiny fluorescent orange flags placed by the whaling crew who had constructed the roughly hewn passage in the heaving pressure ridges and gigantic jumbled blocks of tumbling ice. These corridors are laboriously hacked out with chainsaws and axes to enable the traditional hunting boats to be hauled out to the open water at the edge of the ice. Here the whalers set up camp and wait for the migrating bowheads to pass by in the leads (or channels) of dark, open water between the strip of coastal ice and the massive sheets of the free-floating pack.

Whaling captains have been known to be more than a little irascible over people using their trails; uninvited visitors to whaling camps have sometimes been accused of scaring away the whales and bringing bad luck to the hunt, and the hard labour and cost of gasoline for the snowmobiles used in the construction is undoubtedly another contributing factor. So when we crested one more concrete hard ridge and saw the tents and boats of the whalers set up on a flattened expanse of ice we were careful to approach quietly and ask permission to stop.

As it turned out, our worries were completely unfounded and the captain of the crew, dressed in dirty blue overalls, his face weathered teak-brown and heavily scarred, was a very amiable chap who was pleased to allow us into his camp. I was amazed to find that apart from the necessary members of his crew, the oarsmen and the harpooner, there were also several young children happily rambling about amongst the piles of equipment and parked snowmobiles!

The international whaling commission allows the continued harvesting of the protected bowhead whale by native subsistence hunters only. The taking of whales is strictly regulated and between the seven coastal communities on the North Slope the whaling crews are allowed a quota of twenty-two whales per year. During the last hunting season the crews in Barrow were allocated eight whales and I was amazed to hear that a "struck" whale that escapes is deducted from that quota. Within the Inupiat hierarchy whaling captains are held in high regard; they feed the native community and in Barrow, which has some of the highest food and gasoline prices in north America, this kudos extends into discounts in the gas station, supermarkets and other services, hence the fact that although there are only eight whales to be taken there are more than twenty whaling captains!

The traditional umiak boats, which must be used to hunt the whales, are superbly crafted, each one manufactured from five bearded sealskins stretched and secured with rope over sturdy oak frames. The captain patiently showed me his equipment and explained to me how the eight-man crew would sit in the boat, allowing the maximum manoeuvring room for the harpooner perched in the bow. The whale must be struck with a traditional harpoon and float in the first instance and then to ensure a quick death it is shot with an explosive grenade. It is easy to underestimate the skill and intelligence required to hunt such massive marine mammals, but pursuing a sixty-five foot leviathan in a tiny rowing boat where a careless stroke of an oar against the side of the craft will send the whale plunging irretrievably into the ocean depths or a thrashing tail may upend the boat and dump its occupants into waters so cold that death is almost inevitable, takes courage, stamina and patience. Whole shelves of coastal ice, complete with snowmobiles, whaling camps and their various residents, have been known to break away when bumped by the massive weight of the unanchored pack and drift out to sea where the men can only be removed to safety by helicopter!

When a whale is successfully struck, the captain raises his flag; these beautiful emblems, hand stitched by wives or daughters, are items of great significance, each design specific to the history of the family and origins of the crew. A raised flag alerts and summons others crews in the vicinity who hasten to help in the recovery of the carcase. Bowhead whales generally weigh in at one ton per foot, and hauling sixty-five tons of inert mass free of the water and up onto the ice is no easy task. The assembled crews, assisted by family members and other residents, erect large wooden A-frames which slot into holes drilled in the ice with chainsaws; block and tackle rigs are attached to the flukes and the whale is slowly inched up onto the ice by dozens of men, woman and children hauling on the ropes!

The blubber and flesh is flensed from the carcase on the ice; a strict protocol of distribution for all participants is observed, dependent on the order in which the assisting crews arrived and the level of help provided; this extends even as far as the one hundred and forty plates of baleen suspended in the giant mouth. The huge blocks of flensed meat are ferried back to the town on sledges and excited women and young girls butcher it into manageable sections on the beds of trailers or large sheets of plywood set up on trestles in front of their homes, their hands dripping with blood while they carve the meat with cleavers or the traditional Eskimo ulu knives.

For me, there has always been repugnance about killing whales; the brutal near-extinction of these huge awesome creatures that demonstrate an intelligence we have yet to fully understand weighed heavily on my conscience. And yet when faced with the genuine reality of a community sustained in part by the death of the whale, a people who observe the ancient rituals of the hunt and give thanks in ceremonies and festivals for the good fortune and bounty provided them, your knowledge expands, your perception is altered and you falter in that previous condemnation.

fig 11. Wolf on Dalton Highway

fig 12.   The Arctic Ocean, Barrow, Alaska

fig 13.   Inupiat whale hunters

7. *In the Dragon's Lair*

I had thought that my travels during the last nineteen years had equipped me with a reasonable knowledge of geography and the world in general; 2002 left me in no doubt as to my ignorance of vast areas of the globe, places I had often glanced at on maps with a smug knowing smile, believing that I knew what was there, what was on offer! This time I was on the fast track to an education in Indonesia! I had always thought that I would like to see the famous Dragons of Komodo, yet again an easy statement to make, an easy thought to conceive, but as the years rolled past I never seemed to get any closer to making the trip. There always seemed to be something else more urgent to be done, some more attractive place to visit. However the BBC and David Attenborough kept my interest on the boil; their regular television programmes centred on these massive reptiles tugged at my conscience and eventually I knew it was time to be on my way.

This is the point in all trips when my ignorance begins to challenge my intention. I made reservations for flights to Bangkok, believing that this was the nearest port of entry to the tiny islands that I wanted to arrive at. I was in the process of booking flights for several other trips at the same time and so I didn't give it too much thought at the time. However something nagged in my mind and I eventually scanned the pages of the atlas that covered Southeast Asia only to find that Komodo was nowhere near Bangkok and that in fact I would have to fly to Bali in Indonesia in order to be as close as possible to the dragons upon arrival.

Bali, the holy island, I had heard a little about - popular with Australians as a holiday destination. Indonesia, well, I knew it comprised a large straggling connection of islands that we used to call the Dutch East Indies and that was about the sum of it; and oh yes, I knew that orang-utans lived in Borneo! I was about to undergo yet another course of intensive, and expensive, education in matters geographical. The Independent Travellers Club that I belong to did a wonderful job in misinforming me about the tribulations of reaching the isle of Komodo, and I spent many weeks fretting about what I had been led to believe would be an arduous journey fraught with danger on violent rip tides across narrows where ferries ran to erratic timetables if at all! A further complication was that my planned departure date clashed with the Queen's Golden Jubilee celebrations, and there were many moments along the way when I almost cancelled the trip in favour of staying home to participate in the massive festivities. As it was, I did my part to arrange our local Jubilee street party before I left for Singapore, and Debbie made a roaring success of the event in my absence. For me, missing the Jubilee was a huge trade-off but in the end it paid a dividend I am unlikely ever to forget, for on the Jubilee Monday my rented boat docked at Rinca Island where my first komodo dragon sat basking in the sweltering sun in the very centre of the jetty!

It was a close-run thing, however; I had arrived in Denpesar to find that neither of the two small internal airlines flew to Flores on Sundays and it rather looked as if I would miss making it to the dragon island for my own very private celebration of our Queen's Jubilee. I was the only passenger that left the aircraft in Labuanbajo. The trip from Bali had taken us out over a stunning panorama of countless tiny islands that sat like piped green and yellow decorations on an iced cake of the deepest imaginable royal blue; freshwater rivers could be seen spilling their discoloured contents far out into the deep ocean in great churning turmoils that took on the appearance of wide roads on the water's surface. On the larger islands the patchwork quilt of cultivated fields and rice terraces crowded in; on the steeper ridges a twisted tangle of dense green jungle blanketed every contour; occasionally the massive thrusting cone of a volcano broke through the upper surface of the clouds and appeared as if floating, suspended on the billowing white fluff. The pilot declined to reduce, even slightly, the revs on his engines as I clambered down the steps, and by the time I had walked across the scorching tarmac to the terminal building he had already begun his take-off run, heading off further east to Maumere.

I took my bag from a sleepy official with a bandaged cheek and eye which made him look like Errol Flynn, and turned towards the exit where I was stopped dead in my tracks by the huge clamouring crowd of people that were pushed up tightly against the glass doors; all were shouting and waving their arms frantically, some held pieces of paper with hotel or tour agency names flat against the windows; there was, I realised, NO escape! I took a deep breath and a tighter grip on my bag and walked through the automatic door into the storm. When I surfaced on the far side, dishevelled, hot and irritated, I had managed to retain my bag, but had also accumulated two resolute fellows who held tightly to the straps and smiled engagingly at me as they politely enquired whether I would like to go to the Pelita Air offices and make my return reservation? This was a master stroke of genius on their part; the dire advice of the sales agent in Bali on week-long delays to return reservations still rang in my ears and I allowed myself to be ushered into their Jeep and chauffeured off to their planned schedule of soft-sell tactics designed to part me from substantial amounts of my cash. Actually that is a little unfair, as they turned out to be very genuine chaps who arranged everything that I needed to get to and from the Dragon Islands. However, at this time I was still under the misguided impression that government ferry boats ran to and from Komodo and their insistence that this service was now defunct rather led me to think that I had been snared by some villainous characters about to lead me astray! In an open-air restaurant perched high on the cliffs overlooking the harbour of Labuanbajo we drank milk shakes and viewed the distant heat distorted coastline of Komodo whilst we fenced elegantly through the bargaining process, arriving eventually at a reasonable price for the hire of a boat and crew and a very flexible itinerary to visit both Komodo and Rinca Islands.

My boat and crew arrived at the harbour within an hour of the deal being struck; it had a small wheelhouse at the stern, a sun canopy stretched over the bleached deck from the foremast and its pale green paint was peeling and flaked, but I was suitably impressed with its solid traditional wooden construction and strong sounding engines. The crew looked rather young, three brothers not more than twenty-five years old at most; it took me some time to be able to discern who was who, but the captain presented an air of quiet confidence that reassured me and as the boat belonged to their father I felt it was a safe bet that they would like to keep it afloat and in reasonably good repair. We loaded the provisions that I had purchased for the coming week: crates of bottled water, bags of bananas and ripened oranges, packets of biscuits and a plastic bottle sealed with cling film and a rubber band containing half a litre of Arac, the local palm wine that is fermented to incredible alcoholic potency somewhere around seventy percent proof! As it turned out I had rather underestimated the stores required: I had agreed a deal that did not include feeding the crew; however when I saw what they actually had to eat I felt compelled to provide more adequate and decent food for them, and whenever we chanced upon a fishing boat I purchased large grotesque looking sun-dried fish which they stored on the wheelhouse roof and seemed to be quite partial to, although I never did see how they cooked it!

The dragons actually inhabit three islands - Komodo, Rinca and a very small area on the north coast of Flores, which is almost impossible to reach and has no national park status like the others. Of all the information I had gathered, the most accurate item turned out to be that which suggested Rinca was the better of the islands to visit for dragon viewing. Within two hours of arriving on Flores all my weeks of fears and worries of how I would manage to successfully complete the necessary hiring of a boat and navigating to the islands were put firmly to rest. Like so many other places I have visited around the world the logistical reality is far more simple and accommodating than the perceived obstacles one imagines before arrival. We set sail for Rinca that afternoon. It was Monday 3rd June and I would make it to the Island of Dragons on the Queen's Golden Jubilee Bank Holiday!

The sun was broilingly hot, but once we were out to sea the breeze beneath the canopy was an exquisite caress on the skin and the captain produced a deeply padded clean-smelling mattress from the hold and I lay on the deck bathed in shimmering reflected light, the deep chugging thrum of the engines reverberating through the deck like a friendly heartbeat. The captain took the wheel, showering me with broad happy smiles whenever I glanced at him; his brothers settled down to sleep on the bows and we surged along through the brilliant blue-green waters capped with small foaming rollers from which flying fish occasionally erupted to skim above the waves, their skittering tails and fins smacking loudly on the water as if it were a hard, compacted surface. By the time we rounded the cove at Rinca where the National Park maintains its dock I was nodding into sleep and it was only the change in engine note that awakened me to our imminent arrival.

I took in the face of the island before me; steep hills covered in deep golden sunburnt savannah grass and topped along the ridges with tall spindly palm trees reared up from shallow beaches that were fringed with deeply tangled foreboding salt water mangroves. The engine was cut, the anchor heaved overboard with a great splash and we coasted to a gentle stop against the weathered timbers of the jetty. My powers of observation failed me sadly; lulled by the sleepy voyage I was quite divorced from what was happening around me and when the captain advanced along the jetty holding a large boat pole used for punting the craft away from the shore, I followed his track with my eyes and was electrified to see the huge dragon lying squarely in the centre of the gable roofed gateway that covered the jetty entrance. It was quite still, its legs stretched out at its sides, its head slightly raised; the skin was brown but dappled with yellow or light green patches that I was later to learn were the new areas of skin generated after shedding which takes place in rotation rather than all at once. Its black eyes were impenetrable and I was only just in time to stop the captain from assailing the beast with his boat pole. I hastily grabbed for my camera and advanced to the side of the captain where I shot off dozens of photographs. I could hardly believe it; I had travelled so many thousands of miles after years of anticipation and here I was finally face to face with the largest lizard in the world, living dinosaur, an awesome creature of fable and legend. The film in my camera quickly expended, I indicated to Amir that we could proceed and he again advanced on the dragon, pole outstretched before him. As the tip of the ten-foot shaft came into gentle contact with the flank of the animal I was completely astounded at the lightning transformation that occurred; in a split second it exploded from its immobile, mannequin-like rest to direct a vicious bite at the proffered pole, its neck whipping sideways like a sprung trap, heaving its massive body from the floor in the same instant, its strong legs taking up the four-square stance that a bull terrier adopts when confronted by an enemy, its huge tail swinging hard to counterbalance the head thrust in its attack on the wooden stave. I was awestruck; despite having seen them on television hundreds of times I was completely unprepared for the savage strength and power of the animal at close quarters!

It comes as quite a shock to realise that this giant reptile is entirely capable of killing and devouring you!

The second prod with the pole had the desired effect and the dragon turned in a moderately fast retreat; its walk is truly primeval, a lumbering swagger of opposite fore and back legs accompanied by the swinging of both head and tail in opposite directions like the mechanism of a crude clockwork toy; its head is held aloft, the huge veins and muscles form great ridges on the leathered scaled surface of its massive neck and its split yellow tongue snakes out from the mouth in regular time to taste the air before recoiling back into the maw. We followed him at a cautious distance and watched him position himself with a great thump on a sunlit rocky ledge close to the water's edge, where I imagined he hoped he would be free from further intrusion. There were four more dragons lining the stony pathway to the park headquarters but none was as large and forbidding as the guardian of the jetty; at our approach they raised themselves from the ground where they had been roasting in the sun and slipped into the shadowy mangroves, with the exception of one medium-sized fellow who trundled along in front of us for some time, his huge tail sweeping back and forth in the dust before he startled me by clambering up a steep rain-washed, crumbling bank and magically disappearing into the long tinder-dry yellow grass. The short walk to the ranger camp was through a blasted and baked landscape; insects and mosquitoes swarmed in buzzing clouds just above the surface of tiny pools and streams of water that were beating retreat from the blistering sun in the very bottom of the parched and cracked river beds, and troops of monkeys picked carelessly through the debris of storm-tossed branches and crackling parchment-like leaves.

The Park Headquarters and rangers camp is a small collection of rustic bungalows raised high off the ground on stout wooden piles where electricity is provided only between seven and ten pm nightly and water is a diminishing resource that has to be carefully managed. The rangers live here for a month at a time in near prison-like confinement, and during the four days that I stayed on the island I was the only tourist who slept in the rented guest bungalows. Without exception the many groups of tourists that visited the island each day were gone again within two hours of arrival, leaving me to enjoy the amazing peace and coolness of the evenings, the frantic noise-filled nights and the sunlit mornings when the dragons were most active. I could hardly believe my luck; it seemed impossible to me that I would be granted the privilege of having the whole place to myself, and the following days and nights provided me with endless moments of fascination and wonder that would certainly have been denied me had I opted to limit the visit to the ranger-escorted tour only. There were for instance four dragons that lived within the confines of the camp, all fully grown, between thirty and forty years old and magnificently huge at almost ten feet long. They were fully deserving of their indigenous name of Land Crocodile. The Rangers on Rinca have no guns and rely only on their intimate knowledge of the dragon behaviour and a rack of stout, forked wooden sticks as protection from these mighty beasts.

When I first walked into the camp area to be confronted by these four grand specimens I began to take pictures of them as quickly as possible, but this is not the one-sided event that you may imagine, and within moments one of the animals had taken a very keen interest in myself and the captain and began to advance on us. Amir, who had been obligingly carrying my bag, quickly climbed a rickety wooden ladder leant against a large tree, and a ranger came rapidly to my defence with forked stick held firmly before him. I must admit that I was quite fearful of its awesome power and predatory alien intent. They have a very successful mode of killing prey that is more than adequate to deal with humans: their saliva is packed full of impossibly nasty bacteria which will mortally infect any bite which they are able to inflict; they do not chase their prey, but lie in ambush on forest and grassland tracks where they can seize unwary deer and pigs or even water buffalo, and once they have bitten the animal it is merely a matter of tracking the beast until it dies of blood loss or infection. I was, therefore, more than respectful of these giant predators, and on occasion when I could hear their distinctive heavy footfalls beneath my bedroom I would descend the steps from the bungalow only after careful examination of the area from the veranda.

The toilet facilities were naturally basic, separated from the main buildings and at ground level with no raised flooring, so that washing myself from the tile-lined tank in the foul-smelling darkness of the tiny room one morning I was dismayed to recognise the scraping signature of a dragon walking very close to the door! A door that was held shut only with a flimsy wooden latch! I felt distinctly trapped and more than a little insecure as I held my breath and waited for him to pass. I later realised that the dragons were attracted to the toilets because of the ready supply of water that was held in the waist-high tanks. There are no showers here and washing is accomplished using a saucepan with which you scoop water onto yourself, the excess running off into the pit or septic tank beneath the toilet itself. I watched in utter astonishment from the door of my cabin one afternoon as a fair-sized dragon advanced out of the forest and disappeared into the open door of the toilet! I grabbed my camera and cautiously approached the door of the outhouse; the dragon had his head thrust into the pan of the toilet and was gulping noisily at the contents. I stood very still and waited; the dragon raised his angular reptilian head and flicked his tongue out towards the water tank and then with careful slow deliberation he stretched his front feet up to the ledge of the tank, and gripping the edge of the tiles with his massive claws he heaved himself into the tank, splashing water onto the floor. For a few minutes his rigid foil-like tail remained sticking up out of the tank, and I smilingly wondered how an unwary visitor would have reacted to chancing upon this monster in their bathwater when attending to their ablutions? Adjusting his position in the water, his tail also disappeared into the tank and the only indication of his presence was the great gurgling slurps that sounded for the entire world like a thirsty dog at its water bowl. Eventually, having drunk his fill, his head reappeared from the tank, and hooking his black shiny claws over the lip of the tank, he heaved himself upwards and outwards, falling sideways in an ungraceful tangle onto the concrete floor with a resounding whump! that made me think of beef carcases being loaded in refrigerators. He quickly regained his feet, and when he stepped out from the door his distended stomach, full of water, swung heavily beneath him and scraped a neat furrow in the dust as he returned to the forest. It didn't dawn on me for some time, in fact not until I had left the island and returned to Flores, but despite the dragon and his toxic saliva having been in the tank, myself and the rangers continued to use the same water to wash in daily.

In the evenings, when the sweltering heat of the day began to disperse and the rangers prepared their evening meal in the communal mess room, these camp dragons would assemble beneath the steps of the kitchen in order to pounce upon the fish-bones that the chef discarded through the open window. These gatherings occasionally degenerated into bouts of fighting when their incredible speed and strength was displayed to full effect. The enormous thudding of their bodies thrown against each other shook the ground and raised great sprays of billowing dust that clouded the air. I was able to watch from just a few feet as one large dragon pinned another beneath its huge heaving body and bit into the back of its neck with massive heaves of its jaw before the victim could shake free and scuttle to a safe distance, leaving the victor with noticeably blood-spattered lips.

The nights were a continuous symphony of animal calls; wild pig families grunted in constantly differing pitch, nosing through piles of rocks and leaves while the heavy-set deer, with suitably small antlers that enable safe passage in the forest, barked loud conversations back and forth from all sides that woke me in the night with startling heart-thudding alarm. When I swept a torch out from the steps of my bungalow a whole host of reflecting eyes shone back at me. Rinca teems with wildlife, including many feral dogs that have been left here by poachers that raid the herds of buffalo and deer. The excess of game is the primary reason that the dragons have been so successful, for although the dragon can swim to other surrounding islands there is no surfeit of available food like that on Rinca.

In the early mornings I would trek out from the camp in the company of one of the rangers and head off into the forest before the hammering sun made things too uncomfortable. It is not allowed to walk in the park without an escort and I was more than happy to be in the company of the rangers. I was very conscious that this was not a place in which to take unnecessary risks; one needs a great deal of bushcraft to spot a dragon in ambush, and as they are able to tackle the massive ton weight of the water buffalo, usually ripping into the soft under belly or testicles, I had no desire to push my luck! An unfed, hungry dragon can be extremely aggressive and on the occasion that we met two such beasts I was astonished at their malevolent interest and their unexpected loud hissing that sounded like the steam venting from an old whistling kettle. Beneath the forest canopy the dappled soft light shot in beams and fell in pools onto the deep carpet of fallen vegetation where great decaying palm fronds lay in abstract tangles; their mandible shape and spiked serrated edges appeared to me like the beaks of giant swordfish. The massive lizards are superbly at home in this environment; moving easily through the tangles of roots and lianas, they will round the tremendous girth of an ancient fig tree, becoming completely immobile in an instant, head held ridged high above their backs, the only indication of life their flickering tongue tasting the scent on the air before they proceed. They present an incredible image of prehistory that leaves you invigorated at the encounter. Imagine the impact they must have had on those early explorers and travellers that came here in the early nineteen-hundreds in response to foreboding reports of giant dragons that lived on the Lesser Sunda Islands!

One morning, on the edge of the forest where the hills climb steeply covered in a deep saffron cloak of parched savannah grasses, we found a dragon wallowing in a muddy water hole in the bed of a deep creek. He was gigantic, well over nine feet long; my guide estimated his weight at eighty-five kilos and his age to be around forty-five years. He had fed that morning and his lower jaw was coated with blood, his neck and mouth bulged with flesh from the kill which he tried to force down his gullet with great convulsive heaves of his straining neck muscles; when his mouth opened at each gagging convulsion you could clearly see the great slab of hair-covered meat that he was trying to force into his stomach. Occasionally he rested from his efforts and squashed himself down into the treacle-like water, squirming his tail and legs into the mud whilst his body squelched from side to side. The fur is indigestible and if you examine the sun-dried faeces that litter the trails you can clearly see the knitted hair content and chalky white texture from the bone calcium of the prey. Sometimes we would chance upon two or three dragons in the same small area where, depending on their state of hunger, they would stalk around one another in a slow motion ballet of shooting tongues, ridged legs and stiff tails. The lack of water forces the massive buffalo into the same habitat as the dragons and it was not uncommon to find a dragon sleeping on a large flat rock in a pool of bright sunshine just feet away from a giant water buffalo wallowing in the heated mud of a stagnant water hole, the crusted earth and clay forming a distinct high-water mark along its huge flanks, its head and tail waving side to side in an attempt to dispel the mass of swarming flies.

A short boat trip from the ranger station brings you to Rinca village, a tiny community of Muslims that grind out a living by fishing the fertile seas around the island.

The village is very ramshackle and dilapidated; the rows of wooden and tin houses stretch back away from the shore, each sitting high above the sand on large wooden stilts; the steep gabled roofs are deeply thatched with sun-bleached palm leaves and long grasses, canoes are drawn up on the beach and the sun burns down on great piles of rancid smelling sea cucumbers or tarpaulins covered in legions of tiny silver sardines. Family groups sit in the deep shade beneath the houses where they play cards or backgammon in the funnelled breeze, and women wrapped in colourful sarongs patiently groom the tangled matted hair of grubby children. Well-fed cats with torn ears and battle-scarred faces stalk between the houses, unaffected by the stifling heat, and high above in the clear blue sky giant fish eagles soar on massive wings in huge lazy orbits whilst they search for prey. Amidst this timeless scene of desert island tranquillity, familiar yet jarring twentieth-century technology intrudes at regular intervals; like giant mushrooming sunshades, the dishes of half a dozen television satellite receivers rise on sturdy metal pylons before the wealthier homes; these ominous black and silver discs seem to rear above the children and animals like giant predatory beasts or silent hostile warders in a futuristic prison. There have been no recent dragon-related deaths; one small child was taken some time ago and the village schoolmaster who was attacked has managed to retain his leg, albeit without sensitivity below the knee and fifty-odd stitches to remind him of his good fortune!

In the company of two rangers I left the village and we set out to visit a cave on the nearby mountainside which houses a colony of fruit bats, or flying foxes as they are often called. We picked our way along the inner edges of the mangroves where the detritus of the ocean had been trapped in the tangled roots and twisted boughs: mineral water bottles and plastic bags, aluminium cans and nylon fishing net deposited here amongst the thousands of sand crab holes on high tides that one day may release the decaying litter back into the surging sea. I was not at all comforted by the fact that my guides managed to lose the track on a number of occasions, and eventually we progressed in single file as the lead ranger cut a path with his panga and I kept close watch for lurking dragons and snakes. Shortly we came to the foot of the hillside and began to climb upwards. The straw-like grass was waist-high, the earth beneath it a treacherous scree of loose volcanic rock and broken tree branches, and what had appeared to be an easy climb soon left me light-headed, breathless and weak from heat exhaustion. Sitting down, before I fell down, I doused a handkerchief from my water bottle and tied it on my head, much to the amusement of my ranger guides, who were obviously not acquainted with British seaside fashions!

Staggering onto the ridge, the entrance of the cave was approached through a steep descent of shattered rock and a deeply layered mulch of leaves. Ducking beneath a natural lintel in the face of the rock you are suddenly presented with a wide expanse of sheltered cave that was surprisingly airy, dry and well-lit by sunlight which poured in through a huge rent in the stone roof. The floor was a soft cushion of fine dark brown bat guano and the stench of ammonia in the dull heavy air was stingingly acrid in my nostrils. I could hear the bats but apart from a few of the smaller variety that flew tight laps high against the curving roof I could not see the larger foxes.

One of the rangers indicated a deep and ominously black crevice taller than a man in the far rock face, which was overhung by a natural hollowed dome in the pitted and scarred lava. As I approached the jagged rent in the wall I could hear the high-pitched shrill calling and loud leathery flapping of what was obviously a huge number of bats, but I was still totally unprepared for the sight that met me when I switched on my torch and swung the beam into the blackness. The walls and roof were an obscene moving carpet of tightly packed heaving velvet bodies that writhed in constant turmoil as if the very rock of the cave was alive and pulsing with blood beneath its veined furry skin. An inestimable profusion of tiny yellow eyes reflected back at me like a miniature milky way suspended in the gloom, and as I swept the light across the multitude of bodies I slowly became aware that the inner concave surface of the rock dome beneath which I was standing was home to a further massive colony of throbbing bats which were suspended less than a foot above my head. I am not usually repelled by any form of animal or insect but this huge community of uncountable individuals, each wrapped inside the translucent shroud of their folded wings and suspended above me in an incessant palpitating mass, had an occult quality that sent my spine into a deep shuddering spasm, the after-effect tingling in my teeth and scalp in a most unpleasant way that people often refer to as someone walking on their grave. The light could not reach the very depths of the cleft and when I raised my camera and fired off some shots, thousands more burning eyes were momentarily visible in the harsh flash; the pitch of the squealing increased immediately and the walls erupted from their previous almost rhythmic throb into a blurred confusion of thrashing limbs and long bodies; bats began to stream past my face, beating loudly at the heated air with their almost parchment-like wings; I had a momentary glimpse of narrow snouts, tiny sharp teeth and pointed ears in each flash as I shot off the roll of film. Before I was finished two of the agitated bats had crashed directly into me, one glancing briefly against my left cheek to leave me shocked at its deep warmth and downy velvet-like touch. The second thumped squarely onto my chest, momentarily clutching at my shirt and clambering upwards with a loose ineffective shuffle before it took to the air again. Those that left the roost swung above me in the bright sunlight at the very top of the cave, flocking together on the roof to form small tightly packed groups; others left the cave completely and we later saw them hanging in the upper branches of thorn trees as we descended the hill. It is an experience both visual and tactile that I am never likely to forget.

Back on board the boat we waited for the tide to float us off the beach, and I passed the time by inflating several packs of balloons, letting them fly into the onshore wind to the delighted cries of the village children, who dived fully clothed into the shallow surf in excited clamouring groups to retrieve them. Others, completely naked and presumably the better swimmers, hauled themselves out of the water onto the bows of the boat, and having received a handful of uninflated balloons, dived back into the foam with near-suicidal leaps, much to the bemusement of the crew who obviously felt that children should not be clambering over their boat. Johannis, my ranger guide, added to the general uproar; being unable to inflate even one balloon despite puffing arduously at it for some minutes, and contemptuously flinging the offending article over the side he stalked off behind the wheel house, scowling and muttering loudly. The children waved us off far out into the sea and we set sail for Komodo itself.

I had been amazed at the wildlife that seemed flocked on Rinca and therefore I suppose it was inevitable that Komodo itself would be a disappointment. It is considerably more tourist-oriented; with a large village of upmarket guest bungalows, museum, restaurant and tiny gift market, they cater to the larger cruise ships and boats that are able to anchor amongst the coral reefs in the wide bay that provides the only landing point. There were one or two dragons that lived in the camp area but they were not as animated as those on Rinca, occasionally one would startle a wild pig when they roused themselves in order to drink from the cooking water being discharged into the concrete drains, but on the whole they were a quiet bunch. Despite trekking some miles I managed to see only one other dragon on Komodo: sound asleep in a contrived drinking pool, he appeared well-fed and content and barely condescended to open a sleepy eye when I positioned myself for close-up shots of his incredible japanned claws. Some years ago the rangers would stage regular feedings of the dragons to coincide with the visits of larger tourist groups. A goat would be killed, and the carcase suspended from a rope in a dried river bed below a huge viewing gallery where the gruesome feast could be observed in all its grisly glory. This practice has now been abandoned following three years of detailed surveys of visitors and the apparent notable disruption that was caused by a thousand visitors crowded into the arena for such events. What did impress me on Komodo, which I was unable to see on Rinca, were the eerie burrows that the dragons use for sleeping. These holes, excavated horizontally into high earthen banks, as large as the open mouth of a dustbin, had a most chilling primeval quality, half shrouded by tangled roots and creepers, all but the first foot or so quite impenetrable; even in the midday sun their unseen depths and imagined lair had a dark malevolent character that made me clench my teeth and raised the hair on the nape of my neck.

The other very notable item on Komodo was the massive profusion of shattered coral that was scattered on the wide beach; great tangled dumps of brittle stag's antlers, broken spines and large brain shaped globes were tossed into the lee of surf washed rocks or fallen trees. I picked a careful path through these bone yards of bleached fragments and sun-dried starfish, examining the more unusual pieces, each step the jangling audible equivalent of walking on broken fine china. The rangers, somewhat oddly, offered to entice a dragon out onto the beach for me to photograph but I was happy to paddle in the warm soup-like water and lie on the heated sand whilst I watched several large sail boats disgorge their loads of tourists and lie offshore to await their return a mere hour or so later.

I had spent a week with the dragons and it was time to head back to Flores, and I could not help but feel a little sad to be leaving this place of enchantment. However, I had seen my dragons, up close, first-hand, in the boilingly hot sun and the parched landscape of their awesome home. Now I was in for a further introduction to the astonishing ways of Indonesia by way of the road to Kelimutu. I had already learnt two valuable lessons along the way: one was to never open your bag in the presence of any people as they would certainly take it as an invitation to come and squat at your side and curiously but ever so politely examine everything that you owned, carefully fingering any item that you did not keep hold of. The second was that no matter where you were it was almost impossible to actually use a personal stereo! Whenever I popped the earphones on my head and inserted a music tape I would become aware almost immediately of the inquisitive hopeful eyes that were following me. Once such eye contact had been established it was a matter of mere moments before I would be parted from my music only to be reunited with the machine once the batteries had been completely expended!

Back on the island of Flores I eventually located my hire Jeep and driver which I had arranged before leaving for Komodo. The vehicle looked rugged enough but the young driver, a mere twenty years old, didn't fill me with a great deal of confidence. This was a feeling that was very quickly reinforced when we set off on a four-day trip to the famous three coloured lakes of Kelimutu. The grandly named Trans-Flores Highway turned out to be an ordeal of constantly twisting, turning, swooping snake-like convolutions and hairpin bends that left me feeling decidedly seasick through repeated ten-hour periods of driving that scared the hell out of me! All drivers in Indonesia appear to feel that they have precedence over every other vehicle on the road, and we would hurtle at a breakneck speed into blind curves where we would invariably be met with an oncoming truck, bus or motorcycle barrelling along at an equally suicidal speed in the very centre of the narrow tarmac. The horn was applied with great gusto at every available opportunity as we swerved to miss each new danger. The general feeling of queasy sweat-inducing fear was added to by the congestion of the road with children, cows, pigs, goats, dogs, cats and chickens in every imaginable combination and it was a complete mystery to me how we managed to traverse the length of Flores, some three hundred miles, and back without killing a single pedestrian or animal! Sometimes the road deteriorated into great craters and potholes that had to be negotiated an inch at a time whilst one prayed fervently that no giant trucks would dash around the hairpin bend while you were unable to escape their murderous intentions.

The scenery, however, was quite incredible; the roads were fringed with dense, lush vegetation; huge stands of bamboo towered into the sky, each segmented trunk as thick as a telephone pole, and giant palm and banana trees formed high vaulted roofs above the road so that sunlight dribbled through the canopy in shimmering dappled shafts like spilled metallic paint. When we climbed the steep exposed switchbacks up out of the valley floors we could see the massive cones of volcanoes rising above the surrounding jungle, their upper reaches a delicate pastel red and pink of crumbling rock with sulphur-stained vents that spouted plumes of drifting white steam. On the higher passes of the mountains we left the stifling heat behind and entered the rain and fog of the cloud base and here, where rivulets of water ran from every surface and leaf, the people were wrapped in blankets and coats against the damp grey drizzle.

Flores was named by the Dutch for its abundance of flowers, and the deep green and dark shadow of the forest was decorated with many thousand blooms of fragile yellow and white orchids or tangled sprays of scarlet and purple creepers. On the tops of the mountains, where the trees thinned and the valley sides could be seen, the intricate manmade beauty of the terraced rice fields swept in on the eye, where the blue sky and cotton-wool clouds were reflected in the perfectly still mirrors formed by hundreds of crescent-shaped paddies that tumbled down each hillside as if a giant net curtain had been draped over the undulating contours. Ankle-deep in the water of the rice fields, workers wearing the sampan straw hat were bent double, planting new shoots whilst tiny children played on the raised dykes of earth that separated each pool. In an attempt to fend off the fierce sun, many of the women had daubed their faces and arms with the light grey sludge from the fields, and wearing these mud packs their wide-eyed, camouflaged appearance made me think about stories of belligerent cannibal tribes deep in the Amazon, or commandos preparing for combat.

The people of Flores are incredibly friendly; as each vehicle approaches along the road they will turn to examine the occupants, smiling broadly and waving with happy enthusiasm as you zoom by. As we passed through the small villages I noted women sat working at ancient wooden looms before the front door of their houses and men lounged playing ukuleles that had been cut from flat pieces of rough timber which had no sound box beneath the strings. Occasionally you would see an old woman of almost troglodyte appearance, withered and wrinkled with incredibly matted grey hair and the bloodlike stains of betel nut on her lips, so that she appeared to be in the throes of a particularly bad haemorrhage. They were almost always crouched in a simian posture over a small child whilst they carefully removed parasites from the infant's head. Both men and women washed themselves, remaining fully clothed whilst they showered beneath small waterfalls at the roadside, and in many places ingenious constructions of bamboo had been rigged together with string and wire to divert the water running down from the hills into water chutes where women did their washing or filled containers for use in the home. Completed damp laundry was draped over bushes and small trees around almost every house, and I was struck over and over by the clean, washed and pressed appearance of almost everyone I saw. Once we rounded a bend in the road on a high remote hillside and came across a bunch of young schoolchildren in beautifully laundered uniforms of crisp white shirts and dark red shorts and skirts that were so totally out of place in the deep jungle that surrounded us I could hardly believe my eyes!

The contradiction of large satellite dishes standing before houses constructed of rattan matting, bamboo and thatch was remarkable; dyed skeins of thread hung on thorn bushes to dry in the sun and old women stood guard with long canes against hungry poultry whilst rice was spread on large tarpaulins to be dried and bagged. Almost every man carried a parang or machete on his belt, often in an elaborately carved bamboo scabbard, the polished handle of the knife usually terminating in the head of a duck or some such bird. Women and children gathered in groups at the roadside to offer oranges and bananas for sale, and should you stop to buy some such fruit you would immediately have a half-dozen or more chipped and battered enamel bowls piled high with ripening oranges thrust into your face through the open window. In one town where a market was obviously in progress we passed a line of men casually walking along the grass verge, each with a large black and rust-brown hog on the end of a length of twine; these fat, round pigs walked along eagerly in front of their owners like trained dogs on leads, their big floppy ears bouncing over their eyes with each bob of the head. Sometimes a crowded bus would pass us with overflowing passengers clinging dangerously to the sides of the vehicle, and perched amongst the packages and bags lashed to the roof, the presence of a bound and indignant swine would be announced clearly by the constant loud squealing from somewhere amongst the piled boxes and travellers high above us. I wondered idly how ten hours in the company of such a vocal travelling companion would be?

Arriving in the village of Moni I found that the sixteen-hundred-metre summit of the extinct volcano, which contains the three coloured lakes, was inconveniently covered with several hundred feet of cloud. Undeterred, my driver told me that the best time to visit Kelimutu was at sunrise when the views would be most spectacular and the clouds completely dispersed. Nursing our first flat tyre of the trip we cruised to a convenient halt outside a local guesthouse, and still feeling more than a little seasick I settled in and tried to sort my bag into some semblance of order from the tumbled tangled puzzle that the bumpy road had transformed it into. Moni is a small village that stretches itself out along the road for a mile or so; there was nothing of any note to be seen except for the massive dominating bulk of Kelimutu that disappeared sharply into the thunderous boiling clouds long before any of the cone shape could be discerned. The cook in the local café was a slightly built young man with very feminine looks and an engaging smile. Min, as he was called, sat listening to my Walkman and improvising his own versions of Abba songs in a delightful falsetto voice whilst I ate. It turned out that Min was a member of a local dance group which performed traditional folk songs and storytelling dances to tourist groups in order to boost their small incomes. He politely enquired if I would like to see his group perform and I was more than happy to pay the small price for a personal performance. Solo travelling can be arduous and frustrating, scary and dangerous, but it is also rewarding in the extreme when fate drops a pleasant unexpected experience just for you. We picked our way gingerly through the alleyways of the houses with only my tiny torch for illumination and came to a small earthen square surrounded on all sides by low thatched bungalows, then seated beneath fierce floodlighting I watched as the group paraded into the square. They were mostly women, ranging from pretty young teenage girls with beautiful skin and round dark faces to ancient grandmothers, tiny and withered with the blood-like staining of betel nut running from their thin lips. The musicians were all young boys and the whole group was dressed in costumes of vibrant pink blouses and wrapped in the famous intricately woven sarongs of dark brown, indigo and saffron which are produced only in the nearby town of Nggela.

In no way could I have expected the beautiful music and song that was to come. When the gong was struck, the drums took up the beat and the women began to sing; I could hardly believe that the exquisitely melodious and soft gentle sounds were being produced by the people in front of me; the perfect tones emanating from what appeared to be the oldest of the women carried the group along as each beautifully clear voice was added to the lulling mesmeric combination. Each song was accompaniment to a dance which related to some item of Indonesian or Flores history; two small boys rode around the dance floor with carved shields and swords on wooden hobby-horses that represented the introduction of the animal to this area, and I was able to follow each story easily if not the words of the songs. Another dance illustrated the sewing, harvesting and winnowing of the rice whilst the song paid homage to the spirits of Kelimutu Mountain; the women took positions at the end of thick bamboo poles which they formed into a cross, like the form of a noughts and crosses grid, then when two of the younger girls entered the grid the poles were rhythmically clashed together and separated whilst the dancers stepped intricate patterns amongst the poles, the beat of the music and the pitch of the song rising steadily as the poles were banged back and forth with ever-increasing speed and the dancers sprang agilely away from each closing trap until eventually one was caught by her ankle and the whole group disintegrated into a giggling fit of laughter and grinning happy faces.

At three o'clock the following morning we set out up the mountain road in our Jeep, following a large tipper truck, fitted with rows of seats beneath a damaged billowing canopy, that appeared to be completely overflowing with tourists! We came eventually to the end of the road and stepped out into the chill morning air of the mountainside where several men who had hitched a ride on the truck attempted to sell everyone cups of over-sweetened coffee from large thermos flasks. The group of tourists set off up the pathway with great speed and I trundled along in company of the coffee sellers in the complete blackness of the pre-dawn with not even a hint of the moon. I cautiously picked my way amongst the broken stones of the pathway, judging my route by the dark shadow of the man in front and the now feeble beam of my torch. On each side was thick vegetation, and when we eventually surfaced onto what appeared to be the summit it was only a boulder-strewn plateau that had to be traversed before the real climb of several hundred concrete steps took you to the viewing point situated between the three lakes at the very highest point of the crumbling crater walls. Despite the coffee sellers shouting directions the large group of tourists disappeared up a flight of dark steps and sticking with the local knowledge I continued the lung-bursting climb to the summit where I collapsed gratefully onto the steps of a cross monument.

The three lakes of Kelimutu are currently turquoise, olive-green and black, but they have been known to change colour over the years, being blue, maroon and black a short time ago and blue, red-brown and coffee in the sixties. It is rather satisfying to know that science has not yet been able to adequately explain the colour changes except to speculate on the various mineral contents of each basin. The locals believe that the souls of the dead go to these lakes; the young to the warmth of the green, old people to the cold milky turquoise and those of thieves and murderers to the black! Puffing for breath in the thin air of the mountain-top I wondered where the souls of expired tourists went. I had complied with the local instructions that I must see the lakes at sunrise and now while I sat and stared out over the unbroken blanket of white cloud several hundred feet below me I was amazed at the incredible feeling of spaciousness and the calm windless atmosphere where varied birdsong and monkey calls rang out clearly from the unseen jungle so far beneath. The large group of tourists arrived sweating and red-faced from their detour in time to see the bright orange and amber streaks of daylight cut the far horizon, but the sun rose exceedingly slowly and did not illuminate the lakes as I had expected but crept ever so gently towards me on the flat upper surface of the clouds until it eventually reached the turquoise lake some two hours after its initial appearance. The deep milky colour of the lake became evident when the sun struck it and the perfect flat stillness of the water made it appear like a large glazed plate that had been laid in the exploded rock crater. As I returned down the pathway to the lower slopes and the car park I was quietly amused to see large numbers of Indonesian tourists happily working their way up the steps; they passed me in chattering merry groups and I took pleasure in exercising my hastily learnt Indonesian phrases of 'good morning' and 'how are you today?' much to their amusement; they, sensible people that they no doubt were, had obviously not felt compelled to rise in the early hours for the pilgrimage to see the sunrise, and arriving now they would be able to view all three lakes in full sunlight. It was a lesson well learnt, and still brings a smile to my face now.

Sunday morning saw us ready to leave and head back west along the daunting snake-like highway to Lauban Bajo. As we left Moni I was highly impressed by the large procession of residents that snaked alongside the road from the local church, men and women walking hand in hand, groups of young men and women chatting lazily, all dressed in their Sunday finery, and I saw most of the dance group, still wearing their distinctive pink blouses. The return journey was no more comfortable than the outward leg but Sunday made for a definite change in the scenery; on this Christian island the day of rest appears to be taken most seriously: there were no workers in the fields, people were gathered on doorsteps or garden gates and we passed village after village where great crowds had assembled to watch games of soccer or volleyball, spilling out on to the road so that we had to slowly negotiate our way through the crowds whilst receiving a thousand greetings of 'Hello, where do you come from?' through the open windows.

So it was I came back to Bali, and despite my original misgivings about this holiday resort destination I was to find that it was something very unexpected indeed. There are of course the beach resorts, huge sprawling towns of massive hotels with every amenity and indulgence you could ever wish for; massive high-class golf courses and country clubs where hundreds of gardeners labour over the manicured lawns and gardens in livery uniforms akin to those worn by regency footmen. There is the night club Mecca of Kuta, populated with thousands of young people, mostly British or Australian, who want nothing more than to dance and drink themselves into senseless oblivion every night; here the streets are packed with designer shops selling labelled goods for a tiny fraction of the price charged in Western Europe; dozens of surfing shops and tattoo parlours vie with elaborately carved temples and multiple seafood restaurants where great fish swim mournfully in tanks awaiting their turn to be dispatched and cooked on the open grills at the pavement side, piles of fresh lobsters, clams and squid are heaped so high that the waiters heave themselves up on their toes to reach those at the very top and the crackle of hard carapace shells being broken apart and the sizzle of the cooking pans is a constant repetitive melody amongst the stifling humid heat of the evenings. The pavements are a rollercoaster of high kerbs and open manholes, gaping holes and ditches that beckon you to break a leg or an ankle in a moment of distraction. Every street is populated with large numbers of ragged flea-bitten dogs, almost all of which bear noticeable wounds and injuries. The wide beaches of golden white sand stretch away as far as the eye can see and in the early mornings they are host to an endless stream of joggers and walkers who seem to have agreed their own arrangement of one-way traffic along the surf's edge. Later in the day when the sun is high these beaches sprout a thousand mushroom-like sunshades, and hundreds of fit young men and women ride the pummelling ridges and funnels of surf thrown against the shore from the Indian Ocean; when the day is done you may see them relieving their abused and battered bodies with therapeutic massages delivered on the beach by old women dressed in turbans and great flapping skirts who apply the oils and labour the skin with passive disinterested faces.

Away from Kuta and clear of the endless urban blight that is Denpesar one enters a world of quiet engaging beauty where the wind whispers gently through the long stems of the vibrant flowing rice stalks and the crisp blue sky reaches down to caress the incredible mantle of multiple greens that dominates the countryside in every direction. In some of the more ancient remnants of forest, colonies of macaque monkeys thrive in decaying temples under the benevolent care of local communities that regard them as honoured guests. Elaborately carved pagodas, kiosks and towers, crumbling now after centuries of weather, are covered in great thick blankets of damp moss, and in a scene from Kipling's *Jungle Book* troops of soft grey monkeys saunter amongst the ancient structures, tiny infants clinging to the backs or beneath the bellies of mothers while the large and frighteningly aggressive troop leaders swagger their arrogant importance amongst the tourists, offering bags of peanuts or bananas. It is a serious mistake to enter these monkey forests with anything in your pockets or on your head or neck; sunglasses, hats, jewellery, even false teeth are likely to be snatched away and lost forever in the heights of the giant trees. In one of the more famous temples that is home to large numbers of these monkeys I was amazed to find a whole company of guides equipped with Polaroid cameras and sporting tee-shirts that proclaimed sponsorship by Kodak; however what was more amazing was that each guide also carried a small catapult tucked in his belt, and exceptionally aggressive or troublesome monkeys had only to be shown a brief flash of the brightly coloured red elastic on this item to ensure a hasty retreat from whatever mischief they were engaged in!

In other small towns or villages the long-standing cultural history of Bali as a centre of excellence for artisans is overwhelming; wood carvings of unimaginable intricacy are arrayed by tens of thousands in hundreds of shops where every known animal from the natural and mythological world is represented in ascending size and quality. You may purchase tiny turtles or dolphins carved from bone or horn, or life-size komodo dragons hewn from giant hardwood tree trunks. Kites are sold from large galleries where spectacularly coloured and vividly imagined dragons, phoenix birds and devils wait patiently to take to the skies. Above most towns the skies are dotted with hundreds of kites which are tied to the houses and left to fly constantly in the ever-present ocean breezes. Silver is prized in Bali more than gold, and beautifully worked bangles and necklaces, chains and anklets are presented in bewildering combinations; sale prices are bargained in weights, a confusing system for those of us used to controlled and fixed prices. If more up-to-date purchases are your taste you may choose from any amount of fake luxury goods; whether it be pirated CDs, Gucci shoes or imitation Rolex watches, the Balinese have truly spanned the centuries in their tradition of craftsmanship!

In the town of Ubund I attended the nightly performance of the Barong dance in the walled gardens of the Palace. The Barong is a fascinating character found only in Bali; he is a little akin to the Chinese dragons that dance during the oriental New Year festivities. The closest thing I can describe it as is a cross between a large dog, a dragon and a lion; it is a benevolent character much loved by the Balinese peoples and has a whole history of widely known fable surrounding its mythical existence. The Barong guards over the people, attacking malevolent spirits which would cause them harm; the Barong dance is the story of his repeated conflicts with a yeti-type character. The costume is worn by two men who manipulate the limbs, head, rolling eyes and snapping wooden jaws in a perfect imitation of animal behaviour that is quite astonishing to watch. The tempo of the performance is a correlation between the dancers and the lead drummer of the musicians; the fantastic jangling, almost discordant temple music which they play for these dances has an almost hypnotic quality which sweeps you along in its embrace so that you become totally focused on the conflict of these magical beasts.

Some time later I was to have a further brush with both the Barong and this lovely seductive music. Amazed by the minimal prices ,I decided to indulge my predilection for souvenir tattoos. I made firm friends with one particular artist and his large staff whilst I had several new designs added to my collection of travel memories that I carry on my skin. Most impressive of the bunch, taking almost six hours to complete, was the large komodo dragon which he designed over my left shoulder, a remarkably lifelike representation produced from a collection of dragon photographs which I provided from David Attenborough's book *Zoo Quest for a Dragon*. Eventually, after I had sat looking at the design on the studio wall for so many hours, I decided that the best possible souvenir of Bali would be a tattoo of the Barong; the whole company were delighted, they are enormously proud of their culture and mythology and a long discussion was entered into as to the correct and most respectful place to position this holy image on the body! I was quite amazed; these were all young men, not one of them older than thirty, but they obviously held their religion very dear despite their taste for hard rock music, surfing and tattoos! Each day small offerings of food, flowers and incense were placed at the door of the premises in order that the gods might smile favourably on the business and provide the team with customers! A second item of education which they enlightened me with was the fondness with which the average Balinese person regards the common cockerel! Komick, the boss of the shop, owned six large rather striking individuals which he intended to train and use for cock fighting; each day they were placed outside the shop beneath separate large wicker cages where they strutted and kicked and generally proclaimed their importance to the world. Their repeated crowing, whether it be in broad daylight or the dead of night, is apparently regarded as a comforting presence which is welcomed by all who reside within earshot. Komick told me his grandfather had taught him to value the birds and the crowing soothed the mind and reassured the older generation that their house was well-watched and protected! These people were a constant source of amazement to me; when we gathered together for a party the night before I was to fly home we feasted on a roasted suckling pig and Arac palm wine which was drunk from one small shot glass passed in strict rotation like after-dinner port whilst the whole group sat cross-legged on the floor. As the night wore on and the group became merrier, a large drum, a rack of temple gongs and a glockenspiel were produced and to my astonishment they began to improvise tunes that were very close to the temple music for the Barong! A red and white chequered sash appeared, and tying this about their waists in turn, the more extrovert members of the group danced in hilarious imitation of the temple girls. I was given a large gong and hammer, and so whilst Korea played Portugal in the World Cup semi-finals and bets flew back and forth across the room we improvised thunderous music to each attempted rush on the goal, and I wondered if anyone would ever believe me!

I have driven in many countries around the world; some are very easy, delightful places to use a car, others are stressful in the extreme, dangerous and expensive. For a while I had believed that Lima in Peru was the worst for aggressive traffic and corrupt policemen, but Bali has Peru completely outclassed. The streets of Denpersar are a total confusion of indescribable chaos where vehicles of every nature pay not the slightest heed to traffic signs and signals; red lights are ignored completely, cars will force their way out from side streets without any attempt to avoid colliding with the oncoming stream of traffic, the direction of the road appears to be wholly dependent on the number of cars attempting to use it at any given moment and you might easily find whole streams of vehicles barrelling towards you on what you believe is your side of the carriageway. Motorbikes and scooters outnumber cars and trucks by ten to one and great swarms of them converge around you whenever the flow slackens for the slightest period. Horse-drawn carriages race against massive trucks belching vile clouds of black exhaust gases and street vendors teeter alarmingly on their cycles, impossibly overloaded with piles of boxes, hats, shoes or even portable stoves and pots of curry and rice which they set up on the pavement when a hungry customer flags them down. Most amazing of all, amidst all of this potential for death and injury you will encounter old women patiently sweeping the debris and dust from the road with short straw brushes whist the maelstrom surges around them in its roaring, fume-choked ear-splitting chaos.

To drive a vehicle in Bali it is necessary to be in possession of an International Driving Permit. Whilst I usually have such a licence I had neglected to actually take it with me on this trip; this was to prove an expensive and irritating mistake. The hire car companies will rent you a vehicle on production of just your national licence but the traffic police seem to have caught on that the majority of tourists driving in Bali do not have the required extra permit. The first time I was pulled over and questioned and politely asked to pay the "on-the-spot fine" of about sixteen pounds I took it in my stride, accepting that this was the system. I remember thinking at the time that it was rather odd that having paid the so-called "fine" I was allowed to continue to drive without the permit. During the following days when this same charade was played out on repeated occasions, the fine increasing substantially each time, I became aware that any vehicle being driven by a white European face was obviously regarded as fair game by all traffic cops. I also eventually caught onto the fact that the usual preliminary questions of "Where do you come from?" and "What is your profession?" were polite systems of assessing how much they might be able to fleece from you. It was an expensive lesson, one that I am never likely to forget should I ever return to Indonesia; the whole business of knowing that you are being robbed and the police officer knowing that you know he is robbing you all adds to the lesson. Compared in similar terms to my encounters with our "usually" unbribable traffic police it makes the whole situation more than a little incredible! Most absurd of all was the officer who with a courteous smile provided me with a seat from his office whilst he examined all my documents, made polite enquiries as to whether I was enjoying my stay in Bali, and having taken his bribe proceeded to give me his brother's business card and suggest that I should secure his services as a tour guide! I found it rather hard to imagine a British policeman, having found me driving with no valid licence, acting in a similar way; one can live in hope I suppose? Perhaps I should have taken him up on the offer, I expect it may well have been the cheapest option in the long run!!

fig 14.   Komodo Dragon, Rinca Island, Indonesia

8. *Slave Forts and Elephants*

Ghana is a happy country! Or perhaps it is more correct to say that its people are happy. Despite the crushing unending poverty that pervades every corner of this magnificent land the human spirit appears to have triumphed: there are no warlords or acts of tribal genocide, there are no brutal massacres or battalions of child solders, no death squads or political executions.

It is possible that this country, enveloped as it is in the staggering history of brutality, suffering and inhumanity of the colonial slave trade, has passed through a unique cathartic gate where compassion and peace are now the predominant motivations. It's also possible that this stability and tolerance are merely a lull in the ever-repeating cycles of vicious unfathomable human behaviour; the newspapers daily report acts of government fraud and complicity and there are a great many visible injustices; however one has only to look east to Nigeria or west to the Ivory Coast to see that things could be very much worse. Here in a country that acted as port of departure for an estimated twenty million slaves you will now find reception centres full to overflowing with terrorised refugees fleeing the torture, death and destruction of the almost continual civil war that plagues Liberia.

Like many of the countries that I visit, Ghana was completely unknown to me; I had a vague shadowy recollection that it had once been called something else but beyond that I had no knowledge of what to expect. In hindsight I doubt that any amount of prior reading or website research could have prepared me for the genuinely friendly and effusive people residing in this oblong chunk of land that faces out onto the windy surf-beaten Gulf of Guinea.

There is, of course, the ever-present burden of extreme poverty, and child labour with its attendant abuses is quite prevalent, but the people here do not appear crushed by their lack of wealth and resource. There is an evident strength of spirit and a massive dignity which I felt displayed by even the poorest individuals that I met. If one can generalise about any continent with accuracy I might be forgiven for saying that, like most Africans, the Ghanaians value education, but actually that would certainly be a giant understatement. The ability of education to act as a tool in providing a wider scope of career opportunities and thus a better standard of living appears innate amongst the population. Academic achievement is lauded for the multiple fiscal and social benefits it may bring to one's life, and not merely for the abstract acquisition of knowledge. If you pass through any town or village in the mid-morning you will see hordes of happily animated children dressed in various combinations of brightly coloured, simple uniforms, converging on school buildings with eager faces and quickened step, and one cannot help but compare the gruelling, and often futile, battles fought between despairing parents and reluctant children here in the UK.

Arriving in Accra is the usual disorientating and somewhat threatening experience akin to landing in any new country. The magnificent new airport terminals are out of bounds to all but passengers and authorised persons and so when you finally exit the front door you are immediately adrift in an ocean of swarming curious people. Thankfully the usual predators and villainous characters that you may encounter in similar situations throughout the world are generally absent and the airport is staggeringly close into the capital so that you may very quickly fix your bearings.

I can't say that Accra held any real interest for me; it is a huge sprawling mass of seemingly endless suburbs with darkened streets and mundane features. The administrative centre has its usual clutch of high-rise governmental accommodation contained in the square Marxist architecture so beloved of African politicians, and the main boulevards are expressively wide like those of Moscow or Buenos Aires. The main central shopping area is crammed with clean and shiny designer label shops, expensive emporiums and American-style fast food restaurants. Here amongst the Gucci handbags and the Rolex watch displays you may find the occasional group of highly westernised, obviously wealthy young Ghanaians but for the most part this area is populated by expatriate individuals from all corners of the globe and it could be mistaken for any such shopping and entertainment venue in a hundred different countries. This tiny isolated anomaly of western culture is anchored dubiously amongst the ocean of more typical African commerce which supplies its customers provisions and goods of a less exalted nature from rickety wooden stalls and dusty steel-shuttered lock-ups.

There is one particular form of retail outlet which appears quite unique to Accra, however, and these are the wonderful coffin shops that are scattered along the edge of town on a wide dusty road that parallels the beach. Here in large open-sided showrooms covered with rusting corrugated iron, talented carpenters and painters produce the most astonishing and eclectic range of caskets for your final repository. You may choose from amongst the brightly coloured and carefully styled representations of giant bewhiskered lobsters, grinning sharks and menacing tigers, you can be encased in Jumbo Jets, tipper trucks, Cadillacs or fighter planes, there are medieval castles, charging elephants, nonchalant rhinos and bug-eyed orange goldfish. There is no limit to the imagination brought to bear upon this subject by these inventive craftsmen, and you may go to burial contained in lacquered wooden finery as elegant and lavish as that of the ancient Egyptians, except that your sarcophagus is more likely to be in the shape of a giant mobile telephone or a monumental beer bottle than a royal effigy.

Much of the wild game has been destroyed in Ghana by poaching and deforestation, but there remain a few remarkable pockets of wildlife protected in undeveloped national parks and reserves. In the extreme north of the country, some fourteen bone-crunching hours from Accra, you will find the impressively large Mole National Park. Covering a huge expanse of wilderness the park has little infrastructure and the miniscule amount of road hacked into the bush means that if you wish to see animals up close and personal it will involve tracking on foot rather than riding in the usual four-wheel-drive Land Cruisers.

The park is a patchwork of open savannah and dense low-level scrub; there are large areas of lush tropical forest torn with the red and orange smears of churned dust and sloppy mud that sucks at your boots with hungry anticipation as you try to step lightly on the thin sun-baked crust. Herds of sinuous gazelle stalk fretfully amongst the long sage grasses, their twitching ears and flicking tails a constant indication of the ever-present danger the bush conceals. Stocky mellow red water buck graze unhurriedly amongst the deeper pools of shade and great tribes of dark threatening baboons skitter about the twisted fallen branches of huge withered trees. Family groups of serious-faced warthogs advance upon their knees with tusks and mouths pressed closely to the ground as they crop the tender new grass shoots, their irregular columns and shuffling gait a vague imitation of commando troops dragging themselves forward by the elbows beneath the barbed wire tracery of an obstacle course. You may find the occasional indifferent, immobile crocodile basking in the fierce sunlight on the ramp of a muddy slipway close by quiet bug-ridden water holes, its hooded reptilian eyes and faint enigmatic smile a thin façade of passive disinterest that barely covers the violent intent and agonising death that will erupt lightning-fast upon your person if you venture too near. Picking your way through the tangled prickly brush and placing your feet carefully to avoid snakes amongst the carpet of tinder-dry vegetation, you may encounter massive excavation works engineered by that most elusive of nocturnal marauders, the giant aardvark. You might stumble across the perfect imprinted spoor of a stealthy leopard, or if you are particularly lucky, when the enveloping black shroud of a moonless night descends upon the jungle you may be fortunate enough to hear the king of beasts sing his resonating guttural challenge out over the miles of darkened reverent kingdom.

Perhaps the greatest attraction of Mole, however, are the large elephant herds that wander the idyllic reserve, protected from poachers by units of dedicated government rangers. The only formal accommodation and camp ground in the park sits on a high bluff of crumbling red clay overlooking the deep muddy expanse of an elongated water hole where each morning with clockwork regularity groups of elephants bathe and socialise with complete careless abandon. In the many trips I have made to Africa I have never observed a similar spectacle of elephants to match this daily ritual of play and relaxation. Trumpeting loudly as they approach the water, the herds would quicken their step into a jogging gait of happy anticipation and slide down time-worn gullies into the cooling waters with as much dignity and aplomb as a four ton beast can muster in such situations. The group that I watched for four days in succession were all males; perhaps this explains why they were so carefree and easygoing; with no pregnant cows or babies to defend their worries must be few and the pleasures of the long day an endless round of bathing, sleeping and grazing midst the lush tropical vegetation. The members of the herd ranged between ancient wrinkled and time-beaten grandfathers with torn ears and almost toothless imploding gums down to adolescent youngsters with clean, unscarred hides and impudent playful faces. There were giant tuskers in prime condition with huge ivory sabres that almost touched the ground, the enormous weight seeming to bow the heads of those bearing such tremendous loads, and emergent challengers with the notable streaks of musk and the arrogant bloom of sexual maturity. The larger animals walked on the bottom of the lake whilst the smaller individuals swam with their deeply lashed eyes barely above the water and wavering trunks raised high to act as a breathing snorkel. Here in the cool and murky water these intensely magical creatures were as at home as when standing on dry land; pairs or even groups would engage in mock battles, rearing upwards to place tusks and trunk above the backs and heads of their opponent before rolling easily back on their sides into the cushioning murky depths with obvious resplendent happiness. These play fights would continue for an hour or more, each thrust and parry accompanied by great bursts of thrown spray that sparkled momentarily in the harsh sunlight like a thousand scattered diamonds. Often the fake protagonists would entwine their trunks in swirling coils like giant anaconda snakes encircling their prey, each slippery prehensile tube grasping for purchase on the other whilst the sensitive tips often gently explored the eyes and mouth of their adversary. Although we are unable to hear the low frequency sonic communication that passes between these magnificent creatures, the social bonds and emotional intelligence are blatantly obvious. Engaged in play activity like this there can be no doubt these are clearly sentient beings, with massive capability for those higher feelings which we arrogant humans often regard as ours alone.

It is quite unbelievable how quiet these gigantic beasts may be when progressing through the bush. I had a somewhat unnerving first-hand experience of this ability early one morning when perched on the bank of the water hole watching the bathing bachelors; engrossed in the ablutionary antics a mere ten feet distant I turned to find two very large bulls approaching stealthily less than twenty feet behind me, ears flapping dauntingly and trunks waving as they tasted my scent. I beat a hasty sideways retreat only to find another group closing in from that direction, perhaps sixty feet distant. Standing very still and close to a thorny acacia tree I waited anxiously whilst the groups, now indifferent to my presence, slumped ponderously into the water down muddy gouged slipways like newly launched rotund grey barges.

There is one exceptional elephant in this locality who vividly demonstrates the close, if sometimes invisible, shared bond that exists between mammals; a huge old bull with ragged ears and musk-streaked wrinkled cheeks visits the park headquarters and barracks daily. Known as "people's friend" he is a gentle creature who willingly shares the living space of his human cousins and walks amongst the houses, vehicles and playing children with insouciant ease. Often he will drink from the mains water supply using the tip of his trunk to delicately turn on the standpipe taps so that he may quench his thirst without descending the steep hillside to the shared water hole. Observing elephants in close proximity is truly one of the great joys of Africa. I recently read an article that claimed that you had not "lived" until you had seen the protective behaviours displayed by elephant herds towards their infants; I am not sure that this is an absolute necessity of fulfilment during one's life but it certainly is a remarkable and endearing experience which fills your heart with tender joy and gladness for the existence of such incredible animals.

Close by the southern entrance to Mole is the village of Larabanga, a relatively large Muslim community that maintains stewardship of the most ancient medieval mosque in Africa. Dated provisionally at around 1421 the structure is the usual primitive architecture of curvaceous adobe walls bristling with wooden spars and beams that protrude from almost every surface beneath the rounded crenellations so that the whole building, coated in brilliant reflective whitewash, resembles a giant milk jelly turned out onto a plate and spiked with numerous chocolate flake sticks. It is doubtful that much, if any, of the original building still exists, its fragile earthen construction must have been renewed many times over, beaten by torrential rains and baked by relentless sunshine, but the edifice has an air of mystery and noble continuity. The community charges for brief uninformative tours around the outside of the mosque which facilitate photography, the monies going toward minor improvement projects and maintenance of the mosque itself. The chief of the village, propped in regal horizontal splendour beneath the shade of a large baobab tree, hauls himself unsteadily to his feet to weakly shake hands and accept his cash tribute over and above the official charge, but as the National Park provides no support to the village it seems appropriate that they should exploit their single notable asset in this way.

It was disappointing to find that there was no effective involvement for the locals in the existence of Mole National Park; if poaching and deforestation are to be controlled the only effective means is to actively involve the communities in close proximity to the park boundaries; these are after all the very people who so often engage in the plunder of the animal and forest resource for food, timber and ivory. Tourists visit Mole in large numbers but little if any of the generated cash seems to make it back into the struggling nearby communities, and the local schoolteacher still finds it necessary to beg for pens, crayons and toys for the numerous children she teaches.

An example of how it can be done exists some four or five hours to the northeast of Mole, close by the border with Ivory Coast in the village of Wechiau. Large colonies of common hippos live in the rivers that thread through this region, and the local community leaders have developed an eco-tourist programme that shines like a beacon amongst the many African countries I have visited. Finding hippopotamus in this area is not like visiting other traditional reserves where you may drive up to the river bank and view the animals from the comfort of your air-conditioned Land Cruiser. Here, after you reach the end of the beaten dirt road, you must hike to the river and then perch precariously, balanced in narrow dugout canoes whilst sweating paddlemen drive you through the twisting currents and reed banks with deft silent strokes of primitive wooden oars. The river is a paradise of undisturbed wildlife; delicate giant butterflies flitter above the gentle streaming water, their magnificent iridescent wings sparkling with multiple rainbow colours like jewelled Fabergé masterpieces. Lissom metallic blue and orange swallows dive-bomb unsuspecting insects disturbed by the canoe with astonishing high speed aerobatic skills, the vortex of their tiny wingbeats washing onto your face in the warm sultry air as they skim past mere inches from your head. The unbroken tangle of thick vegetation sagging with dense creeper and vine forms impenetrable walls along each bank, heavily laden branches sweep down to touch the flowing waters and as you pass beneath their dark and gloomy shade the slippery mud banks are dotted with kingfisher holes and hidden trails that provide access to the water for the multitude of small fauna that reside safely obscured therein.

When you reach the sandbanks which the hippo prefer you are immediately aware of the fragile nature of the vessel that you have arrived in; the giant liquid-polished red and grey heads of these massive ton weight beasts break the water's surface with flicking ears and snorting guttural barks of alarm whilst they regard you with watchful mistrusting eyes. It is impossible to know accurately how many animals are in any one group as they repeatedly surface and submerge with indifferent ease in constantly changing locations around your boat with bewildering irregularity. The money raised from the boat hire and guiding is clearly visible in the village: dozens of shiny new galvanised water pumps are set into concrete well heads on almost every corner of the litter free streets and a large visitor centre provides information on the area along with locally made items offered for sale in a relaxed atmosphere completely devoid of any pressure to buy. It is a masterpiece of sensitive and appropriate development where an excellent balance has been achieved, seemingly without effort.

Remarkably Ghana has two other excellent examples of carefully managed eco-tourism which the world would do well to observe and replicate. In the central west region of Brong Ahafo midst the secondary growth of lush tropical rainforest that covers the entire area you will find the twin villages of Boabeng and Fiema. Here amongst the high canopy of giant mahogany trees and twisted strangler fig you may visit groups of magnificent black and white colobus monkeys, startling primate beauties wrapped in skeins of carefully groomed long hair that falls from the shoulder to form a regal anthracite cloak equal to those worn by any emperor or Zulu king. Also contained within this forest reserve is a thriving colony of five hundred mona monkeys. Delicately coloured with brindle backs and clean white fronts, these agile and elegant creatures have enchanting faces surrounded with large ruffs of fawn and white whiskers; topped above the eyes with a cap of faded yellow they appear as if they were wearing handkerchiefs drawn across their lower face like bandits about to rob an express train in old El Paso. This resemblance to masked robbers is quite apt, for the people of the two villages, bound by a taboo of over one hundred years, regard these creatures as sacred individuals equal in stature and rank to the human members of the community. The monkeys assembling in the trees on the edge of the villages in the early afternoon have learnt that they may plunder the foodstuff being prepared by the women for the evening meals with impunity, for no person involved in this astonishing compact will ever harm any of their sacred simian cousins. There are several contradictory legends relating to the taboo status of the monkeys: one suggests that an early chief who was able to perform magic acts, transforming people into monkeys, died before he could reinstate some of his changelings back to their rightful human incarnation. Whatever the truth behind the origin of the taboo the strength of feeling is demonstrated clearly in the grief displayed when a monkey dies, and the funerary rights of burial observed when placing the creature to rest amongst the graves of its brethren and traditional priests in a tiny forest glade cemetery.

The third and most famous of these exceptional nature sites is the Kakum National Park. This is a relatively small area of dense primary rainforest close by Cape Coast. Fiercely protected and preserved, it is a tiny remnant of the massive jungle that once covered the entire width of the country and a constituent part of the greater equatorial belt sweeping across the whole continent. Kakum is famous for its canopy walkways, a thousand feet of swaying catwalks and viewing platforms suspended between giant trees a hundred feet above the forest floor where you may walk in the very treetops in the frontier between earth and sky. It is an enchanting and delightful realm, home to hundreds of vibrantly coloured high-flying birds, skittering bats and a myriad of dazzling butterflies. There are bush babies and potto, palm civet and hyrax unmolested by the pressures of deforestation here amongst their realm of thin shaking branches and timorous emergent leaves. In the darkened forest below amidst the shadows and piled decaying vegetation there are over forty species of large mammal, and although you are unlikely ever to see them there is one of the world's last remaining colonies of forest elephant! Smaller and darker than its savannah counterparts, with less expansive tusks to facilitate its passage through the deep undergrowth, these animals, despite their bulk, are masters of forest camouflage and there are many stories of trackers who have failed to recognise the giant beasts standing mere feet away, silent and still among the dark shadowy underworld. Kakum is one of only five such canopy walks in the entire world and the first of its kind in Africa; access to the canopy walk has only been open since 1995, since when some three hundred thousand people have visited. Pilgrims to this vast natural cathedral may only enter the park under the control of a ranger, and numbers are strictly regulated on the walkways during each day. Although there are the usual European tourist demographics amongst the visitors it was pleasing to see how many Ghanaians were enjoying this exceptional site and how many large groups of excited schoolchildren were being welcomed at the visitor centre.

Away from Accra the population centres are the usual massive stains of ad hoc construction styles hemmed in by dreadful crumbling and rusted shanty communities. The avenues are wide but the traffic is horrendous and the exhaust fumes even worse. There are legions of hairdressing salons and mobile telephone sales rooms and little of interest except for the gigantic central markets. These huge spaces swarming with busy crowds of brightly dressed people extend over literally acres of land; uncountable tables and stalls are piled high with local produce and the cheap exported wares of China and Taiwan. Around the congested edges of these vibrant circus rings, battered minibuses and taxis churn in a constant irritation of evasive manoeuvre and nudging aggression, vying for customers like Red Indian war parties circling the wagons of beleaguered settlers. The Ashanti capital of Kumasi, however, contains a cultural park and museum complex which is an oasis of protected calm and studious endeavour. Here you may browse the shops of fifty or so carvers, artists and weavers or, if your timing is good, enjoy the performance of a local choir or dance group. The delightfully decrepit museum of the Ashanti is the fascinating jewel at the centre of this particular educational crown. The small building centred upon an open square no bigger than a normal detached house is surrounded by large wooden display cabinets filled with dusty relics of Ashanti culture: there are decaying personal artefacts from the various kings and queens, exquisite hand-worked golden jewellery and magnificent carved ceremonial staffs, each topped with a symbolic animal or bird that represents the power of the associated tribe. There are elegantly carved throne chairs and biers, for the feet of an Ashanti king may never touch the ground, and centre stage is given over to the royal golden stool, the symbol of Ashanti power and the item of regalia so desperately sought by the colonial powers whilst trying to suppress and control the

Ashanti nation during battles in the early nineteenth century. Most impressive to me were the drums amidst the assembled musical instruments; these ingenious items were weapons of psychological warfare; used by besieged or encamped armies they could replicate perfectly the roar of a lion when the taut skin was scraped in a circular motion with a clawed wooden stick!

Travelling in Ghana is a pleasurable if hazardous experience: there are huge numbers of road deaths every year and as there are as many, if not more, pedestrians using the roads as cars near misses occur with alarming frequency during any journey over any distance. Cows, goats and even pigs are regularly driven onto the roads in front of oncoming traffic, and bicycles teeter alarmingly beneath impossibly large loads of firewood and cut grasses as their riders try to avoid being crushed by equally overloaded enormous trucks belching choking clouds of acid diesel fumes. Rice, maize and millet are dried on plastic sheets atop the heated tarmac surface and barely a mile is free of some broken-down vehicle undergoing repairs with its wheels or engine parts scattered about it. The drivers of these disabled vehicles, attempting to warn oncoming traffic of the hazard ahead, and no doubt to protect themselves, cut large branches from trees and bushes and lay them on the approaching carriageway along with large stones and chunks of mud. These improvised traffic calming devices do work but are almost always left in place once the vehicle has been repaired and left the location, and consequently one is forever swerving between multiple obstacles of some sort as if one were on a giant dodgem track. Police checkpoints are common and courteous traffic officers check your documents without any requirement for the bribes that one might expect.

At one of these checkpoints, where I stopped behind a single red car with a policeman leaning in at the open door, I was astonished to see the vehicle take off at high speed with the terrified officer clinging tightly to the open door! The car roared on for perhaps four hundred yards, swerving wildly from side to side as the driver tried to shake the unwelcome passenger from the wide-open door before it flipped completely over and landed upside-down in a large roadside ditch! I was even more amazed to then see the driver exit the vehicle at high speed, apparently unharmed, and disappear into nearby cornfields. One reads in Dickens novels of a "hue and cry" but I can truthfully say that until that time I had never actually seen one! It was quite incredible to see the many people who had been calmly going about their business walking to and fro along the road suddenly animated into a righteous and vocal mob hot on the heels of the rapidly disappearing miscreant. I don't know if they caught up with the absconding driver but I certainly didn't fancy his chances if the policeman's colleagues managed to lay hands upon him. As I had been following the fleeing car at a safe distance during its acrobatic getaway I was first to arrive at the upturned vehicle, completely convinced that the officer was mortally squashed beneath it. I was once again amazed to find that the car had flipped completely over him and he lay with just one arm trapped beneath the vehicle on the opposite side to where he had started! I managed to heave the vehicle up sufficiently for him to free his arm and crawl out from the ditch, at which point his colleagues arrived and bundled him into a police car! Thankfully this sort of occurrence doesn't happen to me too frequently and there are more often than not many delightful things to be seen along the sides of any African road rather than violent police pursuits.

You may purchase almost anything from the roadside; tiny stalls will sell you succulent fruit or vegetables, charcoal or woven baskets. There is dodgy-looking petrol in old Coca Cola bottles, worn spare tyres and sawn timber or even fancy coloured awnings to attach to your Jeep or Land Rover, but what fascinated me most were the giant cane rats held up by numerous hopeful vendors squatting on the dusty verges or lazing in the long grass and soft vegetation of the more rural areas. Known locally as grass cutters these large rodents, about the size of a Jack Russell terrier, are much sought after for food; they have blunt muzzles and resemble giant guinea pigs or the South American capybara but have long rat-like tails and shiny fur like the pelt of a beaver. I am told that the meat is delicious but was certainly not inclined to eat it as the resemblance to a rat is all too disconcerting; however they are certainly regarded as a bush meat delicacy, as large numbers are reputedly smuggled into England in suitcases and haversacks each week to meet the demand from the thriving West African communities there.

The Atlantic coastline of Ghana is all that one expects of a tropical paradise, with endless white sand beaches, swaying palm trees and sparkling crystal-clear waters. The numerous fishing villages daily send forth great flotillas of wooden boats piled high with mounds of green nylon fishing net and decorated with brightly coloured flags and tatty sails. Some store their catch in large chest freezers that stand amidships, visibly stark and cubist, out of place in these traditional and aged vessels, like sterile monolithic icons left by visiting alien cultures. Along the shoreline amidst the fallen coconuts and crackling palm fronds, large teams of morose looking children heave arduously on great hemp ropes attached to heavily laden nets hidden deep beneath the pounding surf. Child labour is rife here in Ghana and the newspapers carry daily reports and horror stories of families who have been tricked into handing over their offspring to unscrupulous and abusive middlemen who eagerly meet the unquenchable demand. Close by there are walled luxury resorts with five star accommodation facilities complete with liveried staff, icy air-conditioning, elegant lawns, clean swimming pools and tennis courts. There is no doubt that these costly high-class establishments provide work for some small portion of the local population; however this seems to be the limit of the local benefit and the cosseted and refined sumptuousness within is in depressingly strict counterpoint to the poverty that abounds directly outside of the gates.

In some of these coastal communities and in Anomabu in particular there are

Posuban shrines belonging to local Asafo companies. These philanthropic groups are a cross between the Masons and the Round Table; originating as Fante or Ashanti military organisations, they were the reserve of warriors and something similar to the Territorial Army. Nowadays they are charitable groups which collect money and instigate much needed local improvements in roads, community facilities, schools and other public infrastructure. One of their primary sources of fundraising is their striking and unique shrines. These elaborate concrete structures are lavishly decorated with naive stylised animals and tribal figures; painted in vibrant colours, the decorative figures range from posed leopards and bongos to smiling whales, cheeky pied crows and local historical characters. Each shrine revolves around a central structure relevant to its geographical significance: there are giant crowns, clock towers and one in the shape of a large tugboat. Bright, eye-catching and eminently photogenic; a small charge is levied against each visitor wishing to snap a shot of these amazing structures although sometimes it is hard to tell if you are paying the toll to the official collector or to some quick-witted, plausible opportunist.

Whilst the coast is home to some of Ghana's most beautiful locations and inspiring attractions it is also the location of the dismal relics of its darkest and most horrendous chapter of history. Scattered along the coast at intervals of less than twenty miles are dozens of ancient and often crumbling forts. Constructed by Portuguese, Dutch, Swedish and British explorers as trading ports, the earliest date back to 1471 and have changed hands many times between the various warring European nations intent upon plundering the massive resources of the famous "Dark Continent". Local gold mining activity was the primary target for these traders, which created the colonial name for the country of Gold Coast. The free trade relationship based on a non-currency barter system operated peacefully for one hundred and fifty years before it was replaced by the brutality of the slave trade, and by 1700 the country might easily have changed its name to "Slave Coast"!

The forts that had been constructed around large subterranean warehouse chambers then expanded quickly to accommodate the massive quantities of starving, shocked and brutalised humanity that were required to fuel the economic growth of the New World with its booming cotton and tobacco plantations. An estimated twenty million slaves were forced out of Africa via these vile portals of misery and suffering and at least half of that number died before they ever reached America or the Caribbean on the infamous Middle Passage of the slave triangle. I had read the various historical books and seen the documentaries with the harrowing photographic evidence of the evil that this trade in humankind had propagated, but none of that had made an impact upon my consciousness equal to standing in those harrowing dungeons. The former warehouses were converted into giant holding cells; their dark and forbidding interiors running with water and coated with slime were often completely devoid of daylight or fresh air. Men and women were separated when they arrived at the forts and packed into these foul pits, many hundreds to each appalling space where they were kept for weeks, swarming in their own faeces, shackled to the dead bodies of those that could no longer stand the ordeal and gasping for every breath of foul and foetid air. Resistance amongst the slaves was crushed mercilessly in death cells where troublesome or aggressive slaves were held until starvation killed them, none of the bodies being removed until the last inmate had expired. Food and drinking water were restricted deliberately to lower the potential for resistance; access to daylight, fresh air or bathing water was impossible and denied as part of the systematic destruction of the human spirit. In the fort at Elmina, one of the gloomiest and most depressing places I have ever visited, the sergeants' mess was directly above the men's dungeon so that the soldiers ate their plentiful meals to the wailing accompaniment of the hunger-mad slaves six feet beneath them.

For the women slaves the ordeal often included the added barbarity of rape. Naked above the waist they were often paraded in a closed courtyard at Elmina so that the governor of the fort might select the most desirable for his forced intentions. There was even a special trapdoor in the balcony overlooking the women's courtyard to facilitate the selection process. Those unfortunate women picked from the crowd would be brought from the courtyard, forcibly washed by soldiers and given a small amount of food before being dressed in European gowns and taken to the governor's bedroom. This large room on the upper floor of the castle is now known as the rape room; no figures exist for the numbers of women who suffered this further degrading violation, however, and often, when the governor was finished, he would dismiss the unfortunate woman into the care of the troops, where she would be raped to death and her broken body discarded like refuse into the sea from atop the stained battlements.

The largest of the forts stands at Cape Coast; a giant rambling pile with high mildewed walls and open battlements. There are expansive triangular courtyards which contain the formal graves of various governors and other colonial dignitaries who suffered agonising deaths from malarial infection, so prevalent in white Caucasian settlers that it inspired the nickname for the country of "the white man's grave". Each fort contains a "door of no return", the exit used to remove close-shackled slaves from the dungeons to the ships waiting to transport them to a further living hell on the Middle Passage. The larger forts such as Cape Coast are designated UNESCO World Heritage Sites and contain excellent detailed museum exhibits on this barbaric chapter of heinous development. They receive considerable funding from the former slave trading colonial nations to maintain the structures so besieged by the damaging tropical climate, and welcome thousands of visitors and pilgrimage tours every year. Many of the smaller forts however are decaying and derelict, with fallen roofs and broken walls, but they offer enthralling opportunities for unhindered personal exploration. At Anomabu you may wander unimpeded along the tiny shadow rich alleys and dank musty dungeon rooms, feel the rusted iron rings set into the mould-covered walls and breathe the fresh salt air as it washes in off the ocean above the unsteady battlements where rotten cannons shed their concentric layers of perished iron like the skins of a giant onion. In Fort Amsterdam, one of the most ancient and most derelict, you may find small colonies of tiny bats suspended sleepily from the vaulted ceiling of an open store room, and rectangular goose baths set into the stone floors of the courtyards to accommodate these avian guard dogs as part of the castle's defences. Many famous Americans have been able to trace their ancestry back to fateful departures made from these depressing forts, and in 1992 the widow of Louis Armstrong, who had visited previously, returned to scatter his ashes here in this crumbling fortress high above the tiny fishing village of Kormantse.

The feelings that one experiences here in these dreadful places are hard to describe, the enormity of the crimes against humanity perpetrated here in these awful locations is a tangible heavy presence, a weight of sorrow and suffering that seeps through the crumbling fabric of these ghastly structures. Cloying and sickly, it challenges your perceptions and induces a dread sinking in the stomach and creeping skin on your neck and arms distinctly similar to the feelings you will experience if you should ever visit the former concentration camps at Belsen or Dachau. Disturbingly, although Ghana seems to have progressed exceptionally from this horrific experience, the United Nations claims that there are an estimated one million slaves still in bondage today throughout various countries of the world. It seems that as a species we may well be incapable of actually learning from past experience and benefiting from the inherited wisdom of our ancestors. For me personally, that inability was demonstrated most clearly and effectively by the malaria which I contracted and suffered from for two weeks after my return. Despite all of the resource and medical knowledge available to me I still managed to convince myself that I would avoid infection without taking any prophylactic treatments! What a fool, eh?

fig 15. Juvenile elephants at play, Mole National Park, Ghana

9. *Penguins in Minefields*

In 1982 I was eighteen years old, the Falklands war was in full swing and I was extremely conscious that I had missed being there by the narrowest of margins. A few years earlier, whilst still at school, I had attended the Navy careers office in Chelmsford and successfully passed the entrance examinations, only to be told that there were no positions available for me.

This was the late seventies and the Navy was undergoing stringent cutbacks, unaware of the huge demands that would be placed upon them in the near future. I had intended to sign up for twenty-five years, and I have often tried to imagine how different my life would have been but for that one rejected application. These days I am firmly convinced that it was truly a blessing in disguise; as the whirlwind events of that spring and summer unfolded in the press I was vaguely aware of the fact that I might easily have been on HMS *Sheffield* or *Coventry* had things worked out differently. Twenty-two years later, when I stood in front of the huge polished granite memorial on the wind-battered and rainswept harbour of Stanley I was intensely sensitive of the sacrifice made by so many young men who had been lucky enough to have their applications accepted.

My knowledge of the Falklands was limited to an old linen map I had once possessed which outlined the division of the islands into various sheep farms. I had actually always preferred the idea of visiting South Georgia; the lure of Shackleton's epic crossing enticed me, along with its claim to have some of the largest breeding colonies of marine mammals in the world, but access is strictly controlled and permission to land is only granted by the Governor. To add to this hurdle, one can only reach South Georgia by ship, which requires a very open and flexible timetable. Then one September morning as Debbie and I waited in the queue to enter Westminster Abbey for the annual Battle of Britain memorial service we chatted with David Cox, a decorated Spitfire pilot from 1940, and his eldest son Ian, and an idea was planted in my mind. Ian had been in the Falklands for some time after the war, working with the Development Corporation, and he informed me that not only did the Falklands possess its own quota of exceptional wildlife sites but it was also less difficult to gain entry.

So here I was, some eighteen months later, dropping down rapidly through a low cloud base and peering curiously out at my first glimpse of the islands. It is so very true to say that first impressions count; they are so often the basis upon which you make subsequent decisions, and my first impressions now were of a much larger area of land than I had imagined. There was no indication of the height of the mountains and hills, and the flat brown shapes of the numerous islands with their craggy coastlines of multiple bays and headlands sat like spilt tea stains on the calm blue tablecloth of the South Atlantic.

There are two ways to fly to the Falklands; one can take an RAF Tri-Star from Brize Norton for a mind-numbing twenty-hour direct flight or you can take a more fragmented trip via Chile, stopping off in Santiago and then hopping down to Stanley through Puerto Montt and Punta Arenas in southern Patagonia. It used to be a little more direct than this, but Argentina has recently taken to restricting any flights over its airspace which are bound for the islands; this is thought to be an attempt to force the island government into reopening the airspace to Argentine aircraft. For non-RAF personnel the Tri-Star is horribly expensive and so I opted for the LAN Chile flight pass, which is about half the price of the RAF and allowed me the chance to reacquaint myself with the vibrant city of Santiago. I have always liked Chile; the people are the most friendly of all the South American countries I have visited; it is difficult to explain the average Chilean person but I have always found them to be completely relaxed and accepting of foreign visitors; easy to smile and ready to chat in English or Spanish, they are very easy to approach. I have often felt that they have a depth of humanity to them which is less evident in certain other Latin countries. Santiago is a huge urban sprawl of massive boulevards choked with madly racing traffic, and tiny streets jammed with thronging crowds. There are no really great public buildings but it has a charm which is ephemeral and pleasant in its own unique way. In the markets you may find groups of young girls singing beautiful a capella harmonies and elegant Spanish versions of European Christmas carols. Students twist long strands of silver into intricate items of jewellery whilst they sit on public benches sheltered from the sun by panels of hessian netting fixed between the shops, and ragged feral cats can be seen marching to and fro on these aerial highways with huge, corpulent rats clamped firmly in their jaws.

The centre of the city is the Plaza Des Armes, a large dusty square bordered on one side by the grand edifice of the main post office and on another by the huge cathedral. In the tradition of all plazas this is a place to see and be seen; it is an eclectic mix of upmarket café life and grimy tramps, of hot-dog sellers and lively street entertainers; there are hugely overloaded bicycles from which you may purchase any conceivable item of manufactured plastic supplied from Taiwan and exceptional portrait artists who will represent you in oils stood arm in arm with your favourite film or football star; for a small fee you may view the moon through powerful telescopes or have your fortune told complete with ancient chipped and tarnished crystal ball! Amongst the huge grimy trunks of the long-established palm trees the numerous dilapidated benches and fountain pedestals are populated with young couples in tight embraces and passionate clinches and large wolf-like dogs loiter with simmering murderous intent which occasionally erupts into vicious snarling fights barely registered by the busy crowds intent on pleasure. It is a place of pleasant sociability where people smile and laugh unrestrainedly and where, even at midnight when most everyone has wandered off to bed, there is no feeling of danger or threat.

When I boarded my flight to Stanley from Santiago I was completely amazed at the huge amount of people travelling; the flight schedule is once weekly, I admit, and it was Christmas and there were no doubt a few people going to and from families, etc. and there was also a fair percentage of military personnel, but I could hardly believe that there was really such a tourist industry in these tiny remote islands! There was a very distinct social class and age group to which the majority of these visitors clearly belonged; the uniqueness of the islands appears to appeal to those who crave the prestige of the remotest locations or those who seek unusual wildlife phenomena, either grouping containing a hugely disproportionate number in genteel middle-age with an apparent excess of disposable income, although, from my own observations, one cannot say that extra wealth appears to make them any more disposed to behaving in a polite and courteous manner in airport baggage halls and immigration! The International Airport of Mount Pleasant is some thirty miles from Stanley, a massive military establishment constructed after the war to provide an adequate base for the thousands of troops and airmen shipped down here to act as a permanent deterrent against any further attempts at seizure by the Argentineans. It is a huge field with lots of ominous black-painted hangars, miles of rusted razor band wire and more than a few noticeably strange looking bumps in the windswept grass that may or may not contain military hardware!

It may well be some twenty-two years since the war but the level of security and paranoia displayed on and around this base was remarkable; photography is strictly forbidden despite the fact that almost everyone had been merrily snapping off aerial shots from the aircraft on its approach, some even stopping on the tarmac to frame a picture of the RAF Tri-Star parked in front of the terminal building.

The civilian customs and immigration officials are perhaps the most suspicious and unwelcoming that I have ever had the misfortune to encounter, pummelling me with a barrage of questions relating to my reason for visiting the islands and how I had arranged my accommodation and who I knew in the location; they begrudgingly stamped me in for one week only. I shouldn't complain as it was reasonably painless for me, unlike one particularly irritating chap who turned out to be a former British Consul of somewhere or other, who became loudly indignant when his Polish travelling companion was told she could not enter without a visa and that he would also be sent back to Chile unless he could provide documented evidence of pre-booked accommodation. It really does seem that the Falkland Islands are not prepared to accept anyone just turning up and spending time there as and when they see fit! You must have either an onward ticket or pre-arranged employment, and if you are a tourist, you must also have adequate funds and pre-booked accommodation arranged through an "officially recognised" agent! I couldn't help remembering that it was marginally easier to gain entry to the former USSR!

Leaving the islands is no easy task either; all luggage is scanned in x-ray machines but not just for the usual security considerations; it seems that the metal minefield signs which are scattered around much of East Falkland are often removed by souvenir hunters, and in addition to these any items of military hardware such as shell cases or spent small arms rounds are also prohibited from being exported. Having passed through the departure formalities, I was asked to enter the hangar area where all the bags were being loaded and invited to explain what the square metal items in my bag were; the small tins of cigars I had bought in Chile projected on the x-ray like rifle magazines or small anti-personnel mines! The LAN Chile staff working at the airport appear to have only one crew which deals with both incoming and outgoing traffic, which makes sense if you only have two international flights per week but which makes life difficult when they are slow checking everyone in for a departing flight and then lock the doors to the departure area because they are rushing to direct arriving passengers into immigration! I think I might still have been waiting to leave were it not for the Governor of the islands, whom I had met the night before, coming to my rescue. He was there seeing off his own guests who had been staying for Christmas and insisted the ground staff reopen the doors to allow us through. On top of all this, there is also a whopping great twenty pounds departure tax for non-residents, payable in either FI pounds or sterling!

Thirty-five minutes' drive from Mount Pleasant is Darwin, a huge estate of land that once rivalled Stanley in population but now has only four permanent residents. This huge sheep farm once used for cattle rearing was named after Charles Darwin who stopped here at various times during his travels on the *Beagle*. Most of the settlement which once stood at Darwin has been moved to nearby Goose Green and the few farm buildings that remain are used now primarily for tourist accommodation; it is a charming place that tries to nestle down into a small hollow close by the water's edge to avoid the enormous winds that bellow across Choisel Sound in frantic battering gusts that beat your face and thump your chest with hammering fists. The horizon is uncut as far as the eye can see and the deeply blue sky with its fast racing billows of white cloud reaches down firmly to the bright yellow and green blanket of undulating gauze which drapes itself over the landscape like a giant carelessly thrown duvet cover. This blanket of prickly wire like bushes is riven with dozens of tiny streams that are cut so deep beneath the overhanging bushes that their presence is defined only by the soft tinkling of water and the discernible crease of adjoining foliage where the plants on either bank meet above the hidden watercourse. Elsewhere you may follow the narrow beaten tracks of rabbit and geese that wind and wander between the enormous bushes in endless twists and turns like a huge maze set amidst elegant topiary trimmed hedgerows, black chinned siskins and Falkland pipits the size of thrushes twitter amongst the yellow blooms, displaying complete confidence and a lack of fear in the presence of a human intruder. The gorse pushes down to the very edge of the water in the sound and occasionally you might chance upon an unwary hare feeding amongst the littered pebbles of the narrow beach before he darts away at top speed into the labyrinth of slender sunken roads and incommodious switchbacks. Everywhere you are surrounded by geese and when there are no geese you progress over closely cropped grass that is littered on almost every square foot with copious goose droppings, the thick grey and white worms of guano decaying nitrate fertiliser directly back into the lush green turf.

Close by Darwin is the village of Goose Green, immortalised during 1982 as the scene of a fierce battle between men of the 2nd Battalion, the Parachute Regiment and the Argentine land forces. As you walk up the hill away from Darwin your eyes quickly come to rest on the small stone obelisk memorial that sits atop the highest ridge between the two communities: the weathered bronze plaque records the twenty paratroopers killed in the action to liberate the civilian population of Goose Green who had been held captive in the small community centre for two months. At the head of the list is the name of Lieutenant-Colonel H. Jones, killed during the firefight and posthumously awarded a Victoria Cross; much has subsequently been written about this action; some have called into question the wisdom of a commanding officer being so far forward on the battlefield, the tactics of the engagement and the award of the VC, but whatever your feelings about the controversy the small stone cairn that marks the site where Jones was killed, situated on the steep slope of a bare wind-driven and water-sodden valley, evokes a deep sorrow for the loss of these brave soldiers.

Later in my trip, whilst visiting another battlefield close to Stanley, my guide told me that he had met the two paras who had been closest to Colonel Jones when he was wounded; rushing to assist, they had found him flat on his back but were unable to decide where the colonel had been hit due to the huge amount of expensive battle kit festooned on his combat jacket; a moment of shocked indecision was followed quickly by some world-class squaddie wit, when one is reported to have said to the other, 'Okay, you take his compass, and I'll have his watch!'

As you leave the Para memorial and start down the deeply grassed slope, the settlement of Goose Green is clearly visible a mile or two distant, the green and brown painted roofs of the small buildings silhouetted against the white-flecked blue of the wind-driven sea. At the bottom of the slope your passage will be halted by a barbed wire fence which contains one of the many minefields laid by the Argentineans, unremarkable areas of deep tussock grass where beautiful long-tailed meadowlarks sing loud warbling mating calls, their magnificent crimson breasts matched only by the skull and crossbones' signs that jangle softly on the swinging wire, the only indication of the sudden violent death awaiting you amongst the quiet clumps of coarse brown sedge.

The village of Goose Green is a dreary place of mismatched architecture and dilapidated housing where rusted Land Rovers sit amidst piles of household debris; overgrown vegetable patches and mounds of desiccated cut peat, and piles of discarded beer cans are visible beneath the raised foundations of dismantled barns and weary galvanised steel sheds are stained with streams of oxide corrosion; dusty packets of tea and large bales of toilet rolls can be glimpsed through the grimy windows of the single shop and bottles of HP sauce sit on the blue and red plastic chequered table cloths of the silent café. There are one or two original white and green painted stone cottages from the eighteen-hundreds that sit close to the harbour quay sheltered by wind-distorted trees that lean away from the billowing gusts that drive violently in from the deep-cut Choiseul Sound. A decaying wooden sailing hulk leans drunkenly against the curving jetty, its ancient weathered timber a beautiful tapestry of mosses and lichens, the gentle green, orange and yellow pastels blending in a living canvas equal to the tones of an impressionist watercolour. Colourful Magellanic oyster catchers wade in an elegant ballet amongst the odorous pools of sewage discharging onto the grubby pebble beach; the large piles of wet brown kelp and dark stones are littered with sheep vertebrae and broken glass bottles and amidst the softly lapping shallow water the larger clean white bones from cattle are clearly visible on the sandy seabed.

Aside from the large "POW" painted on the side of the huge shearing shed used to house Argentine prisoners after the liberation, there appeared to be few indicators of the combat which had taken place here. The famous community centre where the one hundred and fourteen villagers had been incarcerated for over sixty days has no commemorative plaque or memorial and in fact the only signs of the inhabitants that I encountered during the whole of this visit was a large scraggy ginger cat who stalked out of the grass as I sat on the jetty and solicited some affection by nudging his clean white head heavily against my arm and sinking his claws painfully into my leg!

Later whilst staying on Pebble Island, I met a pleasant lady who had been just fourteen when she, along with her mother and father and the rest of the Goose Green residents, had been herded into the confinement of the small community centre. When I managed to corner her in the lounge of her guest house one evening she spoke with an easy confidence and obvious humour about the experience; unlike certain other islanders who had been absent from their homes during the occupation she exhibited

119

no animosity for the Argentineans; this, I was to note, was a relatively common feature amongst those who had been present throughout the conflict.

The worst privations of those imprisoned at Goose Green appear to have been the lack of bathing facilities; there were only two toilets available in the hall and she told me how when she had met with members of her family and friends after the paras had released them she had been told how much she was missed and loved but also how bad she smelt! She also related how the Argentine commander at Goose Bay had allowed some of the women to leave the community centre each day to prepare food for the prisoners and that this had been the cause of two strange situations, the first being that as the duty rotated through various pairs of women the menu became more and more exotic and upmarket as each new set of cooks tried their hardest to outdo the meals provided previously. The second situation was a great deal more personal and urgent for this particular girl and occurred when she was helping her mother to fetch food to the centre and they encountered her uncle under arrest by the Argentine forces. He had been using his boat to ferry children away from the community and had been intercepted and was being treated as a spy by the nervous Argentine forces who had him surrounded in the village centre. The girl, seeing his plight, screamed at the officer that this was her uncle and that they should 'bloody well leave him alone'. The now partner of the girl told me that her mother had always maintained that this action had saved the uncle from summary execution!

The primary method of travel between the major islands is by air; there are some limited ferry services usually run during the summertime but almost everyone uses FIGAS, or the Falkland Island Government Air Service. The robust islander aircraft used for the service are flown by clean, fit-looking young men who swagger with the usual confidence that commercial pilots display. But there are no shiny airport lounges or attractive flight attendants here; aside from the passengers hopping between islands, the cargo consists of piles of mail, local newspapers, fresh eggs and canned provisions, tractor spares and birthday cakes! The islands are dotted with grass and gravel air-strips and many of the larger farms possess their own runways. FIGAS pilots are only permitted to fly solo when they have completed a tour of every single strip within the islands and the Chief Pilot has assessed their ability to cope with the varied nature of the many differing fields. The farmers or landowners act as ground crew for the serv-ice, communicating local weather conditions directly to the pilots via air band radio and erecting windsocks prior to each arrival; grazing livestock and indignant geese are chased from the runway with Land Rovers and emergency firefighting trailers are hitched to the vehicles to comply with the civil aviation regulations. Approaches to any field in the Falklands appear to be completely ad hoc; there are no circuits with downwind and base legs and all eyes search the sky for the first signs of the aircraft midst the low cloud and driving wind. Conditions are far from ideal and aircraft are often thumped down onto muddy grass strips with an almost tangible sense of relief; the farmers hurry forward to meet the taxiing aircraft and both cargo and local gossip are exchanged in the briefest of moments whilst each new passenger and suitcase is weighed precariously on a set of tatty old bathroom scales!

Leaving Darwin we stopped briefly at Port Howard and I was amazed that the aircraft managed to avoid the huge bump and water filled hollow that sat in the very centre of the runway, but upon arriving at Pebble Island I was even more astonished to see the troop of black and white saddleback pigs that galloped out happily to meet the arriving plane with pendulous flapping ears and inquisitive muddy snouts raised in hopeful food seeking supplication. The settlement on Pebble Island is tiny, populated by only four or five people, two of whom run the single tourist accommodation. The island takes its name from a curios phenomenon which occurs on one or two of its more isolated beaches where transparent black pebbles are formed amid the tumbling waves; they are much sought after by visitors and even locals. It is a long serrated island covered in tough brown grass and numerous ponds that teem with exotic bird life; tumbling rocky mountains rear up from the higher western side of the island, their massive grey stone ramparts decorated with tough bushes of gorse and diddle dee on the protected lower faces. Pebble sits to the north of the two main islands of the Falklands and was involved in some of the 1982 conflict; the simple wooden cross which commemorates the loss of HMS *Coventry* sits atop a low ridge of First Mountain where, on a calm day at least, you may gaze across many miles of blue sunlit water where all indication of the fierce destruction that rained down from the Argentine Mirage fighters is completely invisible. The island is also able to claim the first engagement of Argentine land forces in the famous Pebble Raid by members of the SAS. The tiny size of the airfield in Stanley had meant that the Argentine forces had occupied the strip on Pebble and were holding large contingents of aircraft on the island. The action was a classic SAS raid, with forty-nine members of the regiment being crammed into two Sea King helicopters and dropped onto the beaches at Pebble; having fixed delayed action explosives to many of the aircraft around the field, they then stormed down the hill into the village where the Argentineans were billeted. The farmer, who still works the island, was present during the raid, he and his family sheltering in the basement of their house during the attack. There is little remaining now in the way of evidence of the raid; there are some fragments of Sky Van and helicopter aircraft wreckage strewn along the edges of the runway and the remnants of a machine gun nest on the low slope of the cliff looking out over the dull waters of the sound. There is a small concrete marker set into the grass of the airfield which gives a minimal amount of information and no indication whatsoever that barely one month later all of those soldiers who had taken part were killed when their helicopters crashed whilst transporting them into a further action.

Pebble Island has magnificent wildlife colonies that rival most other locations throughout the Falklands; huge southern sea lions loll nonchalantly on spray covered rock shelves beneath slippery crumbling cliffs, the thick fur manes of the dominant males ripped and scarred from numerous battles for mating privileges. In the skies you may view elegant peregrine falcons, red-backed hawks or the brazenly bold crested caracara, and the many deep ponds of fresh water set amongst the low-lying boggy peat of the inland pastures and moorlands are a birdwatcher's paradise. Large upland geese strut in the shallow water, their magnificent white plumage enhanced with narrow zebra-like black stripes, steamer ducks, grebes, swans and speckled teal all vie for feeding positions amid the black mirrored waters of each pool and the tussock grass plantations teem with colourful chattering finches and pipits.

Most impressive of all of Pebble Island's features, however, are the penguins! There are huge breeding colonies of gentoo and rock-hoppers on the island and the more common Magellanic or jackass penguin can be found around almost the entire coastline. These odd little black and white birds with raw looking pink stripes above their eyes nest in excavated burrows amid the carpets of crumbling goose droppings and may often be seen popping up from amongst the sheep and lambs in fields of spongy fresh grass. The smaller rock-hopper penguins that feature vivid yellow tufts above each small red eye and comical Mohican-like crests of oily black feathers on the head, are engagingly bold and curious. The young adolescents cannot contain their inquisitive nature, approaching you with such obvious scrutinising intent that they will actually peck at your clothing before they retreat back into the colony with amusing hops and flapping wings, akin to the swaggering confidence of a child who has successfully completed a schoolyard dare. Some of the colonies in close proximity to the edge of the cliffs contain a mixture of penguins and elegant king cormorants, and hovering always within striking distance are the awesome giant skuas; huge predator gulls with dull brown plumage and fearsome beaks, they raid the nests of the penguins with merciless persistence, swooping down into the shrieking, alarmed mass of penguins and rising again on easy beats of their massive wings with the tiny brown feathered bodies of the defenceless chicks clamped between their razor sharp mandibles. If you spend any time at all observing the penguins you very quickly become amazed that any offspring ever actually make it through to adulthood; the mortality rate is punishing, with the skuas averaging ten or more chicks per hour! These are very aggressive birds and whilst I was on a deserted beach on another island later in the trip I managed to scare a skua away from a baby penguin that it had just plundered; as I examined the small, warm but lifeless body in my hand, the fluffy brown down stained with fresh blood and visceral fluid, the indignant skua stomped up to me with conspicuous violent intent to demand the return of its meal!

At another rock-hopper location on the north coast of Pebble Island where the colony numbers some twelve thousand birds there was a nearby skua feeding station where the remains of hundreds of white penguin eggs lay littered amongst the low diddle dee berry bushes; many of the large shells the size of goose eggs were almost complete with just one large puncture hole. I carefully packaged some of these empty shells and posted them home to myself, intrigued by the curiosity value of owning a penguin egg from the Falklands; they passed through our customs successfully and arrived intact, only to be stolen from my desk and eaten by our largest dog one afternoon whilst my attention was distracted. I shall never forget his blissful expression as he chomped merrily on the remaining fragments of this most expensive vitamin supplement provided at great expense from a source some eight thousand miles distant!

Many people are often greatly surprised to find that penguins like to nest far from the sea; they are in fact most accomplished mountaineers, climbing precipitous rock faces with only the sharp claws on their grubby webbed feet, and the largest of the gentoo penguin colonies on Pebble is some two miles inland from the sea; a constant stream of waddling, hopping or belly sliding figures can be seen progressing purposefully in a two-way traffic pattern on time-worn trails that traverse the low scrubby bushes and pebble strewn ground. The gentoo is perhaps the most classic looking of all the penguin species: it stands about two feet tall with a bright white breast and black frock coat and hood which is split by a horseshoe of white eyebrows that meet on its brow; it has a deeply orange beak which is matched by its large rubbery looking webbed feet. The gentoo is often referred to as the brush tail penguin as it has long rigid tail feathers that protrude in a fan from its rear and are often used as a third leg for balancing when the bird is at rest; its nesting colonies, like all penguin nest sites, are awash with the stench of ammonia from the copious amounts of fish rich faeces which the birds deposit. Gentoos build shallow nests with low ramparts of collected stones and pebbles and the surrounding ground is picked clean of every available object; the nests are often surrounded with a spoke like decoration of spattered faeces of varying colour depending on what the individual bird has been feeding on, and some unfortunate birds who have nested in the line of fire for several adjacent broods are thickly coated in a multicoloured nose stinging cover of noxious guano. Despite the execrable odour that surrounds them, the newly arrived chicks appear to flourish; many nests contain pairs of infants and large fluffy bundles can be seen snuggling beneath the breasts of almost every adult. Birds returning to the colony from the sea stumble through the crowded nests and numerous squabbling adults, where beaks are often clattered together in aggressive confrontation and raucous calls are thrown skywards from craning necks and back-stretched heads. Hungry young chicks force their complete craniums into the gaping mouths of mothers and fathers as the oily predigested contents of the stomach are regurgitated in a succession of quickly repeated and rather painful looking spasms. On the wide sandy beaches of the island, where huge rollers of thundering surf crash into the shore, you may see these fascinating birds surging along inside the fearsome barrel of the rolling waves, their dark bullet-like shapes speeding through the crashing white water with infinite, skilful grace and astonishing unchecked aquatic velocity; released from the swell with tremendous projectile force they skim through the shallow bubbling surf, rising to their feet on the hard packed sand in one effortless movement as the effervescent spray retreats rapidly in shimmering fluid skins from the beach.

Fifteen minutes' flight time from Pebble brings you to the magnificent Saunders Island, a huge place of some thirty thousand acres which has been run as a sheep farm continuously since the nineteenth century. The island was the site of the very first British settlement in the Falklands as early as 1765, and a Union Jack is still flown above the tumbled stone ruins of the tiny Port Egmont garrison. Even during the seventeenth century ownership of these obscure islands was hotly contested and a number of marines who were killed when the settlement was attacked and occupied by Spanish naval forces are buried close by. I had originally intended to spend Christmas in Stanley, thinking that this would be the best option available, but I was so taken with Saunders that I discarded both plans and reservations and spent a wonderful three days in this fantastic and inspiring location. The island is owned by a tremendous couple who are quite typical of the islanders who live outside of Stanley or in "camp" as it is known locally. They are hard working farmers with common sense attitudes and a welcoming hospitality. The husband is something of a local celebrity, a huge man of enormous strength who lives his life with an air of freedom and control so notable that even the Governor of the islands remarked on him being 'a law unto himself' when I mentioned I had been staying out on Saunders. The ramshackle farm is untidy and dilapidated, populated with friendly pet goats and numerous sheepdogs and cross breed mongrels that loiter around the main yard. For someone who loves nature and animals, these people are a breath of fresh air; they understand the natural world, farming and livestock, and their lives revolve around the cycle of lambing, shearing and slaughter; shoes and boots are kicked off in the crowded wooden porch onto cheap lino mats identical to those that my mother had in our kitchen when I was a child, and should you find that your coat or trousers are soiled with animal dung not an eyebrow is raised or a comment made. Of the native people that I met on the islands, these and the couple on Pebble were certainly the ones who were easiest to get along with; elsewhere my general feeling was that the islanders were aloof and haughty, some verging on arrogant, and almost all displayed what I can only describe as indifference to anything other than island people or island issues; they display little interest in the outside world but remain immensely proud of all local institutions. Perhaps the easiest way to sum up this attitude is to say that even persons who have worked and lived in the communities for over fifteen years are regarded as non-native!

Saunders contains a truly inspiring wildlife phenomenon in that it is home to over forty thousand black-browed albatross which have colonised almost the entire north coast of the island where it faces out onto the empty, desolate expanse of the South Atlantic. The breeding colony is a magnificent spectacle with an estimated twenty-two thousand pairs returning each year in order to rear a single chick on their own particular mud pot nest. These mud nests are reminiscent of small tree stumps or the hollowed wooden bowls that are used in Africa to pound corn free from its husk; they stretch along the contours of the grassy cliff like rows of dark brown traffic bollards or miniature earthen tank traps, each one topped with a giant feathered sentry. Each of these enormous birds, roughly the size of a Labrador dog, has a pristine coat of elegant black and white plumage; their inquisitive eyes, topped by a brief sooty smudge that strokes backwards like a softly pencilled eyebrow, provides their distinctive genus name. Beneath each bird is a fluffy clump of grey down with beady black eyes and a curving black bill that resembles a grizzly bear claw; tucked below the wide protective breast of their parent they struggle for space in the toughened mud bowl, and forcing their entire heads into the gaping beaks of the adults, receive regurgitated portions of oily fish captured perhaps several hundred miles distant from the nest site.

Albatross are known to be monogamous, mating for life and returning to a specific nest each year in order to raise their young; their mating ritual is an exquisite ballet of caressing gesture and formal manoeuvre which may last for several days; the obvious tenderness and joy in companionship which the birds display toward each other during these hours of carefully scripted dance is astonishing and uplifting. Webbed feet are lifted slowly in a softly swaying step, and deep bows and careful bobs, accompanied by a sonorous rumbling from far down in the throat, are followed by a tactile jousting of the beaks, each bird repositioning its bill with gentle compassionate clacks until the required perfect crossed-sword position is achieved and the body stiffens with the resplendent fan of stumpy tail feathers held rigid, and a raucous drawn out cry is thrown out by both partners with obvious amicable delight.

Elsewhere amidst the crowded nests pairs of birds continue the incessant ritual of tender mutual grooming, the padded spongy feathers being carefully cleaned and repositioned with intimate sensuous oblivion amidst the tumult of chattering birds and pummelling wind. Most charming of all are the birds which settle close against the toughened sides of the nest below the elevated ledge of the pot to be reassured with gentle repeated caresses from the partner sheltering their offspring. Arriving birds swoop in along the edge of the cliff with perfect aerodynamical control; their large webbed feet lowered for final approach they land in impossibly short distances and immediately retract their massive articulated wings; feathers are checked briefly with a toss of the head and then with a quivering shake of the tail they set forth in a slow determined waddle amongst the low forest of nests where they run a belligerent gauntlet of swiftly slashing beaks and dissonant protests from their many indignant, fussy neighbours. Once the returning partner has located its nest and completed its formal protocol of greeting and grooming, the carefully slow process of exchanging position upon the nest is accomplished with watchful delicate manoeuvres, the vulnerable and precious infant being exposed for the briefest possible moment. Along the complete expanse of the cliff edge you are exposed to hundreds of soaring albatrosses, their enormous wings held rigid and motionless as they sweep past in a tremendous swoosh of disturbed air barely inches from your head, each new bird that surges towards you creating a swirling vortex in your own personal atmosphere, an indescribable delight of sensory anticipation which holds you transfixed for hours.

My accommodation for this festive season was a steel ship's container converted into a cabin; set amongst an area of thick gorse and fern it was furnished with two beds, a small table and chair and an ancient Aga stove in which I burnt clumps of peat and dried branches of diddle dee plants; the toilet was a traditional "country seat" located a suitable distance from the living quarters. Water was fed to the rear of the container via a plastic hosepipe connected to a natural spring somewhere on the adjacent Rookery Mountain, and lighting was provided by hurricane oil lamps, but on Christmas morning when I opened the door to bright sunshine and blue skies there were some two hundred or more albatrosses soaring in calm unhurried circles above my temporary home and I couldn't imagine a more unique way to celebrate my Christmas. That evening I dined on fresh lamb chops and new potatoes produced on the island and supplemented this with tasty wild mushrooms that I'd picked from amongst the springy resilient grass and low-lying scrub. Much of the day I spent flat down on my belly in stinking piles of desiccated foul smelling penguin shit whilst I photographed the magnificent residents of the Neck; this is a small isthmus of wide sandy beaches about a mile long between two large hills; it contains perhaps the best of all wildlife sites in the whole of the Falklands: there are huge colonies of gentoo, rock-hopper and Magallenic penguins and occasionally you may even find an odd chinstrap or a frowning low-browed macaroni amongst the colourful, bustling denizens. High on the steep grassy hills tiny rock-hoppers clamber up worn and crumbling penguin highways, scrabbling on the dangerous ledges and furrows until they reach the massive breeding sites high above the sea, a home shared with hundreds of sleek black and metallic blue king shags. These upper colonies are a noisy turmoil of constant muddled agitation with the shags barrelling in on violent gusts of wind, their mouths agape with clumps of seaweed and other foliage collected for repairs to their untidy nests which are constantly plundered by the pilfering rock-hoppers. Tiny streams of tumbling fresh water trickle in winding circuitous patterns between the many nests, the water bubbling out from springs still higher on the cliff, and as with all such breeding grounds, pugnacious groups of giant petrels and skuas hover in an ever-present plundering vigil above the clamorous stinking community. In fact, the whole of the Neck is bathed in the same stringent stink of ammonia, the wide expanse of each inspiring beach is fringed with great piles of decaying kelp which crunches like ripe lettuce beneath your feet and releases yet more foul smelling sulphurous gases as you sink into its squashy elastic depths. Amongst this putrid mass of tangled brown fronds you may find a sleepy southern sea lion or a snoozing juvenile sea elephant; nestled comfortably amid the putrefying mass of slimy vegetation, their bellies turned up to the warming sun, they snore loudly with smacking lips and occasional contented belches or loud farts, and when they wake from their heavenly slumber they will raise a slow flipper to scratch idly at a nose or a cheek before they turn their wide doe eyes onto you with a soft enquiring gaze so anthropomorphic that it is truly difficult to believe that this is a sea-dwelling creature, and one can readily see how the sailors of ancient times were convinced the oceans were populated with alluring mermaids!

At the base of the cliff are a multitude of sparkling natural pools where excited rock-hoppers frolic and cavort in splashing abandon, spinning and rolling in the shallow water with chattering enthusiasm. Many pools appear to be owned by a dominant fussy bird who repeatedly chases each successive bunch of ecstatic gatecrashers from his hydrous domain with pinching snaps to the head and crests. At low tide flat shelves of shiny black rock are exposed to the sun and create perfect landing decks where these small agile creatures catapult from the stinging surf in a coat of frothing spray and glistening droplets; out in the surging sea small black shapes dart amongst the frothing turquoise water judging the capacity and strength of each new roller until the perfect approach configuration is achieved; they appear on the ledge as if thrown from the sea, a giant unseen hand bowling compact underhand balls which transform into live penguins as they touch down with unhurried casual confidence on the slick wet surface. Brightly coloured oyster catchers and upland geese stalk slowly amongst the arriving crowds and out on the flat windswept beach huddled groups of penguins sleeping flat on their bellies appear like multiple cylinder-shaped weather vanes, their narrow heads pointed away from the abrasive flying sand particles; they sleep so soundly in this haven from predators that you may walk right up to them before they eventually register your presence. Large well-fed thrushes twitter from amongst the grass and bushes far away on the edges of the hills and the occasional group of unconcerned sheep wander amongst the penguins with barely a glance for their squabbling noisy neighbours, whilst littered amongst the tangled seaweed and poking from the soft sand dunes are the sun-bleached bones of a thousand birds; whole penguin skeletons lie in the sheltering lee of grassy ridges, the sightless eye sockets and long thin mandibles silent witness to the poisonous red tide which sweeps through these colonies at regular destructive intervals.

Appropriately, the most impressive of all the groups of birds and animals on the Neck are the huge king penguins; this small breeding colony has only been established since the late eighties and whilst there are currently only twenty birds the viewing experience is exceptional. Unlike the massive colonies on East Falkland which contain many hundreds of birds nesting amongst the minefields and barbed wire adjacent to Stanley, here you may sit close by the birds and observe them for as long as you like; occasionally a bird returning from the sea may waddle stiffly past the very tips of your outstretched feet as it takes up its unmarked place amongst the small irregular circle of magnificent monarchs. The colour and texture of these elegant birds is truly captivating so that your eyes linger endlessly on the dense waterproof plumage, a magnificent vestment of pristine white on the long flat breast, and a perfectly fitted morning coat of shining blue-grey that neatly covers the flanks and tapering back, the dense velvet-like surface of short down on the head accentuated by the glorious yellow and flaring orange necklet that sweeps across the breast and passes up each side of the face like a carelessly tied cravat or vivid painted earmuffs. About half of the birds in this tiny group can be observed incubating eggs, each supporting a single massive white shell balanced in the crook of their leathery upturned feet; this precious resource is covered with a retractable fold of skin and silky white feathers which appears like a small pot belly when it is lowered protectively over the future offspring. Poised like small statues, their weight distributed through their heels and the stumpy tail feathers, the birds maintain a silent observant vigil, moving only to chastise those birds returning to the group from fishing expeditions; with straining necks, snapping beaks and serpentine tosses of the head the group quickly re-establish their community hierarchy in loud bursts of jarring protestation and settle back into their previous immobile positions. Occasionally you may be lucky enough to witness the exchange of an egg between partners, the careful transfer of the delicate progeny achieved with gentle considerate control as the egg is nudged slowly across the small area of open ground between the two sets of feet and nestled smartly into its warming cocoon of deep protective feathers. Whilst I sat watching these incredible birds the group was approached by a striated caracara, or johnny rook, as he is known affectionately amongst the locals. These rare birds of prey which survive only in certain areas of the islands and small parts of South America are extremely tame and incredibly inquisitive; they are regularly reported to steal hats, gloves and stray pieces of camera equipment, and now as this one stalked purposefully toward the Kings crouched low over his long gangly legs his appearance was troll-like and furtive and it was obvious he had designs on the cherished eggs. I was amazed by his boldness in attempting to steal from such enormous birds but more amazed by the static defence which the penguins raised as he entered their close proximity; not a single bird moved from its spot, all heads were thrust toward him with loud alarm calls and a swarm of sharply snapping beaks clattered with menacingly hostile coordination until the caracara retreated. No eggs were surrendered and no casualties sustained! Later I saw this same bird searching methodically amongst the Magellanic burrows, the bulging bright yellow skin of his crop extended like a half-filled child's balloon amongst the brown feathers of the breast, indicating that his scavenging had been at least partially successful. On Christmas morning I saw one pair of Kings mating, the gentle caressing of necks with the long black bill interspersed with periods of delicate mutual grooming and occasional ecstatic calls from a bobbing upturned head and trembling neck eventually culminated in the male restraining the female in a kind of loving half nelson clamp between his wings and his beak whilst he quickly trod the lower portions of her back, the assembled group appearing to be discreetly oblivious of the carnal act taking place in their midst.

Eventually, at the very end of my time in the islands, I came to Stanley, a tiny microcosm of English traditions and establishment transplanted to this distant and remote location as if by surgical implantation. Coloured light bulbs are strung between the cast iron lampposts along the windswept waterfront, small flocks of sparrows flutter amongst the grass verges and huge skuas patrol the water's edge on massive sweeping wings, gliding slowly above the distorted and disabled trees. Carefully trimmed gorse bushes spattered with yellow blooms mark the garden boundaries of small white-painted bungalows where house plants are displayed in the glass windowed conservatories and passive gnomes stand guard amongst the lupins and heathers, similar in almost every detail to those you might find in Eastbourne or Hove. Red telephone and post boxes sit staunchly outside the huge pillbox architecture of the general post office and the massive decaying mizzen mast of the SS *Great Britain* is perched on concrete plinths like a giant ceremonial sabre resting on carved ivory stands above a mantled fireplace. Many of the whitewashed houses are topped with galvanised steel sheeting in varying degrees of faded red, blue or green and at the far end of the jetty close by the "Globe Tavern" are the Jubilee Villas, a row of archetypical British terrace houses, their large bay windows screened with net curtains and closely adjoining front doors framed in carefully laid yellow stocks. Elsewhere you may find wartime Nissen huts thickly layered in heavy coats of British Racing Green, and unkempt allotments littered with broken cold frames and fragile wooden trellises supporting straggling withered vines. There is a "Thatcher Drive" honouring their guardian angel and a "Holdfast Lane" commemorating the point where the advancing British forces were ordered to restrain their pursuit of the fleeing Argentine troops during the assault on the capital. On the waterfront there are the two huge memorials, one of decorated colonial splendour that commemorates the massive naval engagement of British and German fleets during the distant First World War, and the second, a sombre and functional granite composition which records the more recent events of 1982. The two items on the liberation memorial which leap out forcefully at you are the massive number of ships engaged in the task force and the three civilian residents of Stanley who were killed during naval shelling from battle cruisers far out to sea; some of the houses still bear the painted DAP insignia daubed on their façades by the Argentines to indicate a concrete basement capable of withstanding bombardment. You rarely see anyone walking in the streets of Stanley and when you do you may be perfectly certain that they are tourists! The locals seem to prefer the isolated comfort of their many vehicles for even the shortest of trips and traffic on the narrow roads is a constant variation of numerous shiny new Land Rovers. There are one or two pretentious restaurants, staffed, like almost every establishment in the town, with Chileans, Brazilians or the more exotic natives of Saint Helena known amongst the locals as "Saints"; shipped in from their equally remote island they serve out contracted periods of employment with travel and lodging expenses provided before they return home with their hard-won nest egg. The pubs are depressingly tacky, carbon copies of those you find in garrison or naval ports like Plymouth or Southsea, populated with extremely young, baby faced solders, sailors and airmen who bellow loudly above the thunderous vibrating music in the sharp nasal tones of Glasgow, Tyneside and Liverpool. Huge plasma screen televisions show various sporting extravaganzas played out to uncaring customers whilst miserable looking locals sip their English beer and crunch their Walkers' potato crisps in companionable silence, all but the most violently shouted conversation precluded amid the furious volume of the combined entertainment. At closing time the packed bars churn out their disgruntled boisterous patrons and the streets are thronged with crowds of unsteady young men; full of beer and bravado they are watched carefully by aggressive looking redcaps as they slowly disperse back to private lodgings or the barracks at Mount Pleasant Airbase.

The Christmas period in Stanley is celebrated with annual sports days and race fixtures the soggy race course with its single, shabby wooden stand is packed with locals milling amongst the various burger vans and fast food caravans, a packed portacabin houses the purely functional bar and the odds chalked up on the blackboards of the Tote are examined with serious intent before the huge queue for the betting windows is joined. The races are a mixture of magnificent high-stepping thoroughbred racers with finely groomed coats, their riders dressed in professional silks and the more down-to-earth owners in flat caps, jeans and windcheaters on short stubby ponies or thickly rounded slow plodding horses. Between the sweepstake runs, the local children are invited onto the waterlogged course to compete in traditional schoolday foot races and the whole event appears to be an annual stage for mating displays amongst the teenage population of the islands. Ruddy-faced and thickset youngsters sporting huge Mohican hairstyles or conspicuous facial piercing parade in front of assembled groups of podgy adolescent girls in an ostentatious show equal to those produced by any albatross or king penguin!

Close by Stanley are the many mountains which gave their names to the final and often bloody engagements of the war back in 1982; they are massive surging ramparts of granite, their craggy ridges and furrows buttressed with great piles of loose boulders and shale where the approaching troops must have been hard-pressed to maintain their orders of silent approach. The infamous Mount Tumbledown looms out of the plain, ominous and stern, impassive towards the lives lost and the blood shed upon her slopes. The impossible angles of the crumbling faces of Mount Williams, where the Gurkhas stormed heavily fortified Argentine defences, leave you in complete wonderment that victory was ever forthcoming, and the long and narrow crest of Wireless Ridge is littered with debris from the last and decisive battle. Mountings from heavy machine-guns rust quietly amongst the boggy soil and shell craters, and the giant parallel plates of granite that furrow the ridge like the backs of massive slumbering dinosaurs are littered with the jumbled steel, wood and canvas of Argentine entrenchments and command posts. As you gaze down into Stanley from this vantage point and ponder the loss of life on both sides and the ridiculous geographical quandary of the whole episode it is hard not to feel that the war was an unnecessary conflict. How does one justify the massive costs, both fiscal and emotional, that were paid to liberate these tiny colonial islands? It seems a lifetime past now, a brief fleeting memory of a summer long ago when the fleet was waved off from Portsmouth, the people flew flags from their homes and cars and the press rattled the national sabre for all it was worth. Perhaps the only real way to understand if it was all justified or worth the price is to be a Falkland Islander!

fig 16. Black-browed albatross chick, Saunders Islands, Falklands

fig 17.   Black-browed albatross, the Falkland Islands

fig 18.   Black-browed albatross, the Falkland Islands

fig 19. Juvenile sea elephant, Saunders Island, Falklands

fig 20. King Penguin pair, Saunders Islands, Falklands

fig 21. King Penguin pair, Saunders Islands, Falklands

10. *A Photo to Die For*

Some years ago I travelled to the town of Churchill in Manitoba so that I might see polar bears in their wild environment. The result of this trip was over one thousand photographs of polar bears fighting, walking, sleeping, and rolling playfully in the snow. Some of the photographs were quite good and a few, very few, were remarkable. That Christmas I had numerous enlargements made and, framing them carefully, I was really rather impressed with the resulting professional looking product. It has to be said that very few of the friends and family who received these pictures as gifts that Christmas actually ever put them up on their walls! However, I was soon back in Alaska and the Yukon where I was again lucky enough to take some rather good pictures. I didn't make Christmas gifts of them but an idea was shaping in my mind, and when I was again in Churchill and managed some further good close-up shots of polar bears I looked at the often published photographs of long-standing professionals like Tom Mangleson and thought, "I can do that!"

That was some eight years ago and whilst I am pleased to say that I still manage to take the odd exceptionally good wildlife photograph I have long since realised that I will never make my fortune at it; I usually average about one really good photo per thousand shots taken. What I have realised is that no matter how good your photos may be there will always, without doubt, be a better one coming along soon, there will always be someone who has more capital than you, someone with a bigger and better camera than you, and, where wildlife photography is concerned, someone with more time available to them! When you realise these truths your attitude towards wildlife photography changes, for the better I think, at least for the better in my case anyway. You begin to wonder just how big the world market for wildlife photography is, who it is that buys all these wonderful photos that are taken by their millions each year? You start to think about all the people that you know and all the homes that you have been in and you wonder where are all the pictures? Amongst my own personal acquaintances I can think of no more than two or three who actually have a real wildlife photograph on their walls, discounting of course the family pets and children! So where do all the photos go? Into albums? Into files? Onto computer disks? Did you ever try to show someone your holiday or travel pictures? The average friend will flick through an album of your best photographic efforts in a matter of moments, devoting all of a

138

second or less to the majority of the images! So you begin to wonder what keeps your finger clicking on the camera?

Is it that you need the photograph to prove to yourself your friends and family that you have actually seen the grizzly bear or the Komodo dragon? Would your personal experience be diminished by NOT having the photographs? When you see the astonishingly dangerous behaviour that people will indulge in (myself included) to get "the shot", can it really be such an important and necessary prize? The signs erected at the massive roaring falls in Jasper National Park recording the young man who fell to his death in the rushing, pummelling torrent of water as he positioned himself on the slippery rock ledge outside of the protective fences (his body has yet to be recovered) made me wonder if there really is a picture "to die for"! The man who brought his car to a screeching halt on the remote country road and nearly broke his neck dashing down the loose shale of the bank in his hurry to photograph a giant bull elk swimming a sunlit river certainly seemed to have little concern for his own welfare as he tumbled forward, cameras and equipment swinging about him! The man who loudly proclaimed to his travelling companions that he was 'not even going to bother setting up his gear' and promptly returned to his car as we watched a large grizzly bear through binoculars whilst it was digging for roots high on a hillside in Yellowstone National Park made me wonder why animals are not worth watching if one cannot get a decent photograph? Are we such that we really must have that square of glossy paper to make it all worthwhile?

The competitive nature of committed photographers is quite disturbing; the looks of utter contempt and disgust that Debbie and I were greeted with when we quietly walked across some open grassland to a large stand of trees where we hoped to get a better view of the wolf pack assembled on the far bank of the Lamar River in Yellowstone were undisguised and hostile in the extreme. It appears that the larger the camera and lens that you can deploy the more right you feel you have to be the only persons allowed to be taking pictures. The parallel with those aggressive drivers of long phallic shaped sports cars who feel no one else should impede their progress on the public highway was more than evident! Perhaps the most inexplicable manifestation of this whole phenomenon is that no matter how good your camera, or how big your lens equipment, there never seems to be a position that is adequately close to the animal which ensures that the photographer will be satisfied with the result! Large and potentially aggressive wildlife like moose and bears are approached step by step, shutter snapping at each increasing position until the cameraman is in a position of complete danger; no doubt these individuals have never seen the speed that a bear can achieve in a determined charge? The more docile animals such as deer and pronghorn antelope, mountain goats or marmosets, are stalked relentlessly with disposable cameras that are all but thrust into the animals' faces before the photographer is satiated.

There is undoubtedly a huge amount of joy to be gained from capturing a perfectly clear and crisp image of a beautiful animal in its wild home, the satisfied thought that "I did that"; these days my observations of the many hundreds of devoted photographers that I have seen around the world makes me feel that there is also something lost along the way, or pushed aside in the rush and competition to get the "best shot", the "ultimate shot", and as I have been caught up in it too I am aware that the real truth behind the ultimate shot is quite forgotten. A photograph is primarily a means of recording an image, a means of remembering a moment in time, an event or an action, and whilst you may be lucky enough to actually release the shutter at that exact moment when the lion roars or the bear yawns I can assure you that you won't have been paying much attention to the event in the meantime. Your eye will have been glued to the viewfinder and you will have been constantly edging back and forth in an attempt to keep the very best angle and the very best play of light on the subject; your finger will have been tensed on the shutter release button awaiting that split second when you can breathe out and take the shot. Although it sounds rather odd, the one thing you won't have been doing is actually watching the animal! You will have been looking at it, looking over it at the background at the sky, the branches of trees on the fringe of the frame, but you won't have been truly looking at the beast! In all that concentration and effort to get "the ultimate shot" actually looking at the animals is something of a secondary issue. When you stop worrying about getting "the picture" you start to see a whole world of detail and activity that had previously passed you by and the enjoyment that you gain from actually just watching the creatures is doubled.

fig 22. Playful polar bears, Churchill, Manitoba

11. *Taking a Wrong Turn*

I was told by one native Afrikaner that I'd met that Namibia was to South Africa what Scotland is to the British Isles! A remote, wild and unforgiving land populated by strange and exotic tribes, teeming with magnificent wildlife and battered by a relentless grinding climate. It was, he said, a place where people went on adventurous holidays but where few would choose a permanent home!

To date I have never visited Scotland and so I am unqualified to judge whether the comparison is valid but the description certainly sat snugly over the experience I was about to enjoy and endure amid the burning deserts and parched lands of this former German colony.

This large, generally unknown country, is swept along its entire western coastline by the pummelling Atlantic Ocean and is enclosed rigidly on its other three borders by Angola, Botswana and The Republic of South Africa. Three quarters of the land mass is buried beneath massive deserts swarming with gigantic red and yellow sand dunes, huge expanses of ruptured volcanic rocks, endless gravel fields and interminable tracts of vicious thorn bush scrub. The whole eastern side of the country slides unrelentingly into the savage wilderness of the Kalahari, a desert landscape so ferocious and unparalleled in its deprivations, that even today much of it still remains physically unexplored.

This obscure and cryptic land, like so many other African countries, has passed through the tortuous crucible of tribal warfare, forced missionary enlightenment, white settlement and colonial possession. Claimed, owned or administrated variously by the Boers, the Germans, the British and most recently the South Africans, it has struggled hard and long to achieve its final independence. Today it is a country slowly building its national identity, shrugging off the long burden of its varied usurping cultures and embracing its future promise with heartfelt determination. It is remarkably secure for a country that so recently suffered through a freedom struggle; one does not perceive any great threat or danger on the streets of Windhoek, the capital city; the people are friendly and open, easy to talk with and quick to smile. There are none of the overbearing and clamorous salesmen so incessant in certain other African countries. Neither was I approached with offers of golden investment opportunities or requests for my address or my contact details in the UK. Despite the obvious poverty of some sections of the population I never once saw any beggars and the most I was ever asked for was to provide medicine for Himba tribes in the very remote Kaokoland, or roadside assistance to travellers in distress!

Windhoek has little to commend it except for its remarkably clean and uncrowded streets; there are some fine examples of Colonial German architecture but for the most part it is nondescript and unenthusiastic, a strange conglomeration of would-be skyscrapers and large retail outlets that seem to have been dropped from the sky at random into this hostile landscape.

It takes a few minutes only to leave the confines of the city and head out into the beckoning vistas of endless sky and distant horizon. No matter which direction you choose from Windhoek you pass quickly out from beneath the wafer thin veneer of civilisation into astonishing primeval landscapes of ceaseless ridges, valleys and plateaus, each cloaked beneath delicate tracery quilts of thin yellow grass that waves and rolls amid heated torrents of swirling low-level breeze as it sweeps up infinite billowing clouds of stinging dust and sand.

In the mountain passes to the south of Rehoboth the barren green and black rock, suffused with pyrite crystals, reflects the savage sunlight in glimmering sheets, the thousands of facets shimmering like gigantic mirror tiles. Great gnarled camel's thorn trees sag beneath the enormous burden of multiple weaver bird nests, each individual woven grass domicile combining into a giant golden haystack which hangs heavily amongst the stout branches like a carelessly discarded straw mattress. The tremendous weight in these intriguing structures is unnervingly palpable and the tumbling mass of shaggy thatch appears as if suspended in free-fall animation, constantly about to crash earthwards!

Heading south, the trees soon give way to the barren rock and sand on the fringes of the gigantic Namib Desert. At the tiny settlement of Solitaire the single desiccated stump of the dead tree from which the farm takes its name is forlorn amongst the tourist camp accommodation where a relatively constant stream of four-wheel-drive vehicles churns in and out of the archaic gas station and bakery. Assuming that you have completed the tiresome ever-present bureaucratic procedure and obtained the appropriate permit, you may strike out from here into the awesome beauty of the Namib Naukluft National Park. The pan floor of the Sossusvlei Valley is surrounded by desert dunes of staggering proportions, with billions of tons of fine amber sand driven by the wind into enormous pyramids stretching out for a hundred miles, an unceasing three-dimensional chequerboard of precipitous slopes dark with dramatic shade or shimmering in harsh stinging sunlight. The few rare thorn trees that nestle against the lowest creases of these mighty dunes are scorched and wizened, twisted and bludgeoned into tortuous arabesque shapes; they fight for life amid the stranglehold of choking sand that slithers over them in greedy relentless torrents.

Like almost all desert landscapes the Namib is far from lifeless and the briefest excursion amongst the boiling hot sand will reveal a wealth of adapted wildlife; impatient scarab beetles commute busily back and forth on urgent untold errands, their beautiful carapace shells shimmering with blue and green luminescence, the toil of their journeys marked upon the sand in meandering ticker tapes of tiny opposing dents, each holding its own miniscule pool of shadow. Magnificent oryx stride with majestic unhurried grace amid the burning landscape, their scintillating velvet-like coats of black and grey topped with glorious pikestaff horns more than a metre in length. In the rare stands of trees that exist around some unseen subterranean water source there are flocks of chattering Cape sparrows who will mob your unattended water bottle in an instant and who will remain there, pecking fruitlessly at the clear plastic until scattered by the wheeling shadow of an approaching sparrowhawk. All around amid the sand and stone are tiny burrow entrances and plentiful desiccated droppings of foxes and other nocturnal visitors.

On Christmas Day the influx of tourists to this great desert pan was quite staggering; busloads of eager travellers bumped and slithered to the extremity of the sand road and disgorged frantically out into the gigantic dunes. Later you could view their ant-like figures staggering up the knife-edge ridges of the most massive dunes, slithering and sliding backwards as the sand disintegrated beneath each tortuous footstep. I cannot say that I was at all driven to attempt such punishing exercise in the forty-degree heat, but the goal of the highest point on the highest ridge certainly seemed like the lure of the Holy Grail to most of these flagellant visitors.

Travelling north away from the Martian ochre landscapes of the Namib but still within the confines of the Naukluft park you progress through equally alien landscapes of eerie wind-eroded stone and river cut passes where giant folded layers of volcanic rock thrust and swirl, trapped in frozen animation from times many millions of years distant. You cross the Tropic of Capricorn on a high empty plateau where ferocious winds whip clouds of grey stinging dust into your face and obscure the horizon, and here you begin a descent to the coastal lowlands around Walvis Bay. Should you ever find yourself on this desert road you may hopefully encounter a lone Eskimo Innuksuk statue. Tempted by the piles of large angular stone scattered along the roadside I constructed my own Arctic messenger, the standing man of Inuit culture who marks the route for fellow travellers in territory devoid of trees.

The barren desert land that borders the Atlantic Ocean north of Swakopmund and stretches up as far as Angola is known infamously as the Skeleton Coast; this huge strip of desolate and unforgiving wilderness takes its name from the dozens of decaying shipwrecks that litter its upper reaches. Huge rotten hulks of long-forgotten vessels which, having floundered on rocks amongst treacherous waters, were driven ashore to decompose amid the savage arid beauty, their rusted steel plates twisted and bent, exposing sharp steel ribs like the giant desecrated carcass of a mighty defeated Leviathan. The subplot of the name Skeleton Coast lies also in the fate of any sailors who were lucky enough to survive the initial trauma of being wrecked here; thrown ashore in this giant wind-torn desert, the nearest fresh water hundreds of miles distant, there was little hope of survival. Today the skeletons strewn among the deep sand beaches no longer belong to unfortunate seamen but to thousands of desiccated sea lions. Hundreds of porcelain white sun-bleached scapular plates lie amid the piles of storm-tossed debris two hundred yards in from the water's edge and dozens of angular feline skulls grimace with fearsome canine teeth in mummified remains still bearing whiskers and scabby salt-hardened fur. Every few metres dry, clean white bones peep from the grey and yellow sand, a mute undeniable testimony to the constant brutal cycle of nature played out upon this most inhospitable and merciless shore.

Each morning great banks of water-laden mist roll sluggishly in off the cold grey ocean and hang listlessly over the desert, depositing diamond-like droplets of life-sustaining dew upon the tiny lichens that cling with resilient disregard to the parched sand and stones. The tough filigree mantles of these miniscule multicoloured plants coat whole swathes of desert in splashes of vibrant orange, yellow and green like the spillage of giant pots of powder paint knocked carelessly onto a roughened yellow parchment. Silver and tan jackals patrol with disdainful grace amongst these tinted fields of Lilliputian verdure, spraying musk heavy urine on the invisible signposts and markers that proclaim the boundaries of their giant territories. On the gently sloping beaches of Cape Cross there are gigantic colonies of Cape fur seals. Tens of thousands of these sleek and agile marine predators crowd the beaches in a compelling mass of heaving black bodies. The colony proclaims it existence with a dual assault on the senses, the clamorous tumult of raucous dissonant braying overshadowed only by the incredible, almost overpowering stench of ammonia which violently storms the sinus cavity at every breath. In December the beaches are doubly crowded with thousands of tiny infant pups; herded together into nursery groups they squirm and tumble constantly against each other, forming a pulsating carpet of tiny black water slick and oily bodies. Astonishingly, these tiny infants, many less than forty-eight hours old, duplicate exactly the cry of newborn lambs and the combined calls of many thousands of hungry, quarrelsome babies unite into a pandemonium of noise equal to the adult hullabaloo! The infants, just as with almost all mammal species, are engagingly curious and will approach closely and even climb onto your legs or chew tentatively at your boots if you sit still and quiet in the stinking urine soaked sand. They gaze at you with infinite wonder through immature eyes running with sticky mucus before taking fright and scuttling off at high speed, often tripping over their own gangly flippers and crashing head first onto the ground. These colonies must suffer an enormous mortality rate for everywhere amongst the sand are the bleached remains of tiny emergent skulls, and hovering ever-watchful on the fringes of the beach, hungry jackals pace with murderous dark intent.

The Skeleton Coast is divided into two areas, the southernmost region being labelled as a site for recreational activities, and it completely lives up to its descriptive designation, the sand swarming with four-wheel-drive vehicles, quad bikes and tented barbeque camps. Surf fishing in the heavily populated Atlantic water is the primary attraction and as you progress northwards on the single winding road you pass an endless procession of huge station wagons and Jeeps; each adorned with numerous gigantic fishing poles fastened upright into racks on the front bumpers, they resemble giant antennae of massive land travelling armour-plated catfish.

The upper or northern half of the coastal area is a more formal national park with heavy restrictions and massive bureaucracy; no road exists in the extreme northern limits and visitors may enter only on pre-arranged fly-in safaris; it is a place for those with significant wealth alone. Below this section, permits to enter are issued only after fractious interrogation on the status of your itinerary, accommodation and petrol reserves; there are no services and entry to the two fishing camps at Mowe and Terrace Bay is strictly regulated. If you manage to circumvent the red tape and obtain your precious day permit you enter the confines of the park through large iron gates with dramatic skull and crossbones' symbols welded onto them and the clock begins to tick against your carefully monitored time in this severe but magical wilderness.

It is a place of contradictions and anomalies, a desert where delicate bright pink flamingos wade in shallow salt water lagoons and where groups of impossibly beautiful ibis nest amongst the rusted, torn and twisted ruins of a fallen oil drilling platform. There are great red and brown boulder fields and massive tattered stone cliffs thrusting vertically into the sky like battle scarred ramparts of ancient long-forgotten castles attacked with cannon and catapult. Huge welwitschia plants sprawl their great wind-torn leaves out across the parched sand like the tentacles of a monstrous stranded octopus; the giant central bloom surrounded with the lollipop stalks of tiny seed pods creates an image of miniature ornamental gardens lined with topiary laurel bushes. Occasionally you may pass beneath a lone harrier hawk wheeling lazily on turbulent currents of heated air rising invisibly from the land, or pass by small groups of earth-coloured sparrow larks that flit with curious agitated indignation between the heat riven rocks and dusty grasses. If you are lucky you may spot a solitary oryx immobile and watchful amongst the curtains of precious shade cast down by the higher bluffs and crags and if you are supremely fortunate you may actually glimpse the acclaimed and elusive desert elephants, magnificent creatures that march these wastelands on extra long legs adapted to carry them the huge distances between viable water sources perhaps two weeks apart.

Past the eastern gates of the Skeleton Coast you may venture into an equally des-

146

olate and water-starved landscape surrounding the Brandeberg or fire mountain. Home of the legendary "Bushmen", this circular range of orange peaks and shadowy deep valleys is decorated with one of the world's greatest concentrations of rock paintings. Here, after strenuous walking in sandy river beds and scrabbling over loose rocks and winding through narrow water-worn passageways, you may view the exquisite artwork of the Bushmen, much of it produced in periods of prehistory, the dates of which we are only able to make feeble approximations. The paintings have a delicate, ethereal quality; the lithe stick-like figures, although fixed upon the rock, surge with elegant sensuous grace, the exertions of the pursuit captured for a moment in eternity as if the hunter were about to loose his bow or plunge the spear into the giant eland the very moment one looked away. All the beasts of the veldt are recorded with the same discerning sensitivity; giraffe and kudu gallop purposefully across the gritty stone canvas chased by determined trackers, their bows and quivers carried across their backs, and herds of hartebeest and gemsbok are surrounded with the petite ancient handprints of the talented artist. These paintings are truly remarkable; for me they carry the same vicarious resonance that Lowry produced in his matchstick men, a fascinating tangible record of the lives of these long-dead individuals and families. Brandeberg is home to perhaps the most famous rock painting in the entire world, known by the continuing misnomer of the "white lady"; we are now sufficiently educated in the ways of the Bushmen to recognise that the single white painted figure amongst the many brown and ochre bodies is in fact a shaman or medicine man decorated with mud and ash for ceremonial ritual. The original and erroneous identification of the figure as a white Grecian-style woman caused years of fruitless speculation over whether the Bushman's artistic capabilities had been induced or even motivated by Mediterranean influence. Sadly there are few Bushmen left today; the straggling remnants of this incredible race which scratched a living with stone age technology from the searing Kalahari desert have all but gone; occasionally you may see faint evidence of the exceptional bloodline in the yellow tinged skin or miniscule frame of the children who beg for water along the roadside, presenting crumpled plastic bottles and beseeching eyes to every approaching vehicle.

To the north of Brandeberg you pass through the animal control fence, a seemingly weak and ineffectual structure deployed across the entire width of the country to prevent the spread of the devastating and virulent Rinderpest virus, and pass onwards into Palmweg reserve. Here you may stumble upon small groups of beautifully pale reticulated giraffes or sit enthralled beneath the swishing frantic wingbeats of graceful iridescent swallows, the disturbed turbulence of their passage washing down on your face like tiny zephyr winds as they skim tiny insects from the air barely inches above your head. In this region you will encounter Damara tribespeople; one of the oldest ethnic groups in Namibia, they are tall and noble with magnificent fine-boned

Neil Pepper MBE, FRGS

facial features reminiscent of the chiselled marble elegance of classic Greek statues, their language suffused with a cryptic symphony of strange glottal clicks like a secret ancient cipher.

At Sesfontein the peeling white walls of the German-built fort are a pure 1920s' Hollywood image. It is a magnificent piece of atmospheric colonial architecture, built to dominate the area and press controls on the gun running and poaching activities of the early century; it possesses a genuine theatrical ambience and one expects to see the square crenellated battlements lined with the posed corpses of dead Legionnaires, weapons propped in their hands to fool the besieging forces. Instead, the cool shaded courtyards with their carefully watered lawns and sagging palm trees are home to hundreds of industrious bright yellow weaver birds and the occasional dust-covered tourist.

As you head north from Sesfontein you enter a magical area known as Kaokoland, a truly remote wilderness devoid of proper roads or signposts where no bridges have been built and where maps are unreliable, misleading and near defunct and travel is achieved from GPS coordinates. It is a threatening place on which guidebooks are either deliberately vague or outright discouraging, attempting to deter would-be travellers from venturing out into this magnificent rugged territory.

This awesome place is populated by nomadic Himba tribes, the most exotic and photogenic of all the peoples of Namibia. The Himba maintain for the most part the traditional lifestyle that was once common to all peoples of the world; dependent upon their cattle and goats they move in seasonal patterns between effective grazing areas, taking up temporary residence in ancestral kraals, the proprietary rights of which are respected by all, even during the long periods of abandonment. The mud huts in which the Himba live are prehistoric in their appearance, the sun-baked wattle and daub construction offering a perfectly adapted rainproof structure which provides a surprisingly cool, almost insulated interior. Food caches are stored in miniature versions of the houses; raised on stout timber boughs they are almost identical to those used by Saxon and Viking cultures of the twelfth and thirteenth centuries. The Himba continue the ancient pagan religion of ancestor worship and there are strict codes of etiquette to observe when visiting their homes; one should never enter the Kraal uninvited and it is forbidden to pass through the space between the main hut and the sacred fire, although this can be extremely confusing as it is often far from clear which of the several fires actually represents the spiritual flame! The most striking aspect of the Himba culture however is the incredible decorated appearance of the women and some of the older generations of men. The women are magnificently beautiful, their skin dyed an ethereal dark orange by a cream of crushed ochre, cow dung and milk which is never washed off. Applied twice daily it produces an exquisite toned velvet texture far superior to any spa treatment available in western cul-

148

tures. The traditional cowskin apron and bustle is still worn by all women, its carefully shaped edges curled and ruffled into frills resembling piped icing on an elegant wedding cake, while heavy wire bracelets adorn each wrist and ankle and above their bare breasts, great collections of decorative necklaces are often surmounted by the polished cones of large seashells. The hair is braided and drawn back tightly from the face, each plait coated with a thick application of the ochre cream which is never combed out or rinsed in water.

Considering the extreme remoteness of their environment, the Himba are very easy people to interact with; you will receive requests for sugar and salt and sometimes tobacco or even water but most commonly you will be asked to dispense medicine. Isolated as they are from any external support or assistance, they will often seek medical aid from passing travellers and should you venture here you will be called upon with regularity to provide diagnosis and treatment for all manner of ailments and illness ranging from respiratory congestion to broken limbs. My large and well stocked medical kit was quickly depleted, and on one dark night I was flagged down on a deserted sand road by people in obvious distress and my vehicle became an impromptu ambulance for a shamefully feeble pensioner racked with dysentery and close to death. Wrapped in plastic sheeting, he was bundled into the back seats of the car and supported by his anxious children whilst we thumped and bumped through the night to the only hospital in the region at Opuwo. Once we were granted access through the barbed wire security gates the staff of the hospital were supremely indifferent and left us to transfer the weakened father from vehicle to ward on a soiled and unstable theatre trolley. Family groups of Himba sat on the floors of the corridors and stared curiously at us as we passed, and with the vocal prayers and repeated thanks of the children raining down on me, I left the hospital feeling ashamed at my initial selfish reluctance to assist these desperate people in their hour of need.

Opuwo is a place of glaring anomalies; the only service centre for the entire region, it is home to fancy western-style supermarkets where fresh, clean vegetables and fruit lie decoratively arranged beneath fluorescent lights and angled mirrors, while herds of scrawny cattle or bellicose goats are driven through the potholed streets protesting with loud indignation, where internet cafés with shiny new computer terminals sit close by the rusty galvanised sheeting of foetid shanty towns and where the primitive Himba step with elegant disregard amongst the jeans, sweatshirts and mobile phones of the insidious trampling invasion of western consumer culture.

From Opuwo the vast wilderness of Kaokoland stretches out north to the Angola border and west to the Skeleton Coast and if you have supplies and nerve enough to ignore the dire warnings of the guidebooks, adventure beckons, although I didn't quite bargain on the unexpected version that awaited me in a moment of careless navigational error. Nestling amongst the four huge mountain ranges of the region is Van Zyl`s Pass, a staggering feat of surveying and engineering completed by bullock cart at the turn of the century, it is now one of the toughest and most dangerous four-wheel-drive tracks in the world. Its inclines are so steep that it is only passable driving east to west, so that you may inch down the steepest grades, nursing the axles over the deepest ruts and holes with infinite care, although the rises are not any easier and the car scrabbles for traction, lurching and bouncing fearfully as it tears at the loose shale and stone, fighting for grip and purchase, tilted fearfully on the sharp slopes. It was only after I had traversed the first and most staggeringly vicious slope of all of the thirty miles of rollercoaster track that I realised my mistake! The entrance to the pass, like all tracks in the area, has no signs, and choosing the deepest amongst the multiple tyre depressions in the sand as the most likely route, I had blundered into Van Zyl's and now had no choice but to continue westwards as, even if there had been sufficient room to turn around, the car was certainly incapable of climbing back up the precipitous incline behind me. So I pushed forward slowly, nursing the car gently down each successive slope, feeling every individual inch that it travelled deep in the pit of my stomach and forcing it with punishing urgency up each subsequent rise, the engine screaming loudly in first gear and plumes of noxious blue exhaust smoke billowing through the open windows. On the worst sections it was necessary to walk forward on foot and judge the best course over the most treacherous spikes and ridges that would shred the tyres or puncture the tank; sometimes I had to lay rocks into the deepest of the cavernous potholes that would swallow the wheels and ground the axles. For the entire transit of the pass the vehicle was never more than inches from the blasted crumbling edges of the track, the two and three hundred foot drops tugging with hungry anticipation at the preposterous tilted angles of the car, and in my mind ran the constant repetitive mantra of calculations around the available petrol, distance and daylight.

I expect that the huge surge of relief and accomplishment that sweeps over you as you roll forward onto the flat sandy river bed at the far side of the pass is the same for those who actively choose to drive this challenging route but I doubt that many do it alone and even fewer would admit to doing it by mistake! Here at the foot of the mountain a lone stunted tree is surrounded by dozens of flat stones decorated with the Tippex or felt tip inscriptions recording the details of the numerous travellers who have successfully negotiated the pass. It resembles a miniature graveyard with cluttered rough-hewn tombstones, and is perhaps appropriate for the level of risk involved in such an adventurous enterprise. I scribbled my details on a business card and left it hanging in the tree on a bathplug chain and headed off out into the flat yellow grasslands, conscious that my adventure was far from over.

After the narrow constrictions of Van Zyl's Pass with its threatening ominous aspect the open flat plains of waist-high yellow grasses are a cathartic experience, which lifts the spirit and floods the senses with delightful anticipation. Navigating now only by compass and the position of the sun, I set off to find my way back west and then southwards to sweep in a huge wide arc around the mountains that barrier this vague and unknown paradise from all but the most determined or, as in my particular case, most lost travellers! The few vehicle tracks in the soft red sand soon petered out into nothingness and I took to following the wide dry river beds that swept in meandering loops in the rough direction I needed to travel. Like many trips that one makes in a state of anxiety or nervousness you are only really able to appreciate it once it is behind you, and following the great sweeps of this river course low beneath the parapet of the steeply cut banks, I travelled in what I now remember as an enchanted realm to which I am almost certain never to return. Sleepy groups of oryx sheltering in the deep shade of the overhanging trees never even rose to their feet as I passed by, and slinking jackals that crossed my track with lazy, unhurried strides shot curious, dirty looks over their shoulders at the intruder in their realm. Velvet grey geese and shiny metallic peacocks raised their heads from amongst the brittle dry grass to observe my passage, and great flocks of ostrich, twenty or thirty strong, took to their feet in indignant startled ruffles of feathers and dust as the car rounded bends, running almost silently against the wind on the cushioned surface of crystal sand. In some of the deeper gorges where I found myself backtracking and feeling my way for an exit, I encountered menacing troops of swaggering aggressive baboons that shouted their territorial defiance at me with piercing sharp screams, their lips drawn tight back to expose threatening massive canines. The complete lack of any sign of human habitation tested my nerve further and as the sunset began to colour the sky with deep reds and orange my confidence was faltering, the mileage travelled seemed endless, the direction I knew was correct but the geographic features only vaguely resembled the features on the map, and then I stumbled onto a small group of skinny malnourished cows walking purposefully in a straggling line. I knew immediately they were my saviours and I followed their unswerving direction with growing confidence, for the Himba cattle men of the region water their herds at sunset and where the cattle were headed there would surely be people! My theory held true and eventually I found a young man wrestling with a starting handle, attempting to enliven an ancient diesel powered pump tapped into some deep unseen water source; he spoke no English and I spoke no Bantu but within minutes my car was surrounded by a group of nervous Himba, including the chief of the community, although the village remained completely invisible to me. Depositing the last of my medical supplies with the chief and distributing toys and balloons amongst the children, I headed off again with detailed instructions memorised from a map drawn with a crooked walking stick in the dusty earth. Some hours later I picked up a road that actually seemed to exist on the map and climbed again through a series of narrow trails laid in broken rough stone, some as challenging as the worst of Van Zyl's, before I finally descended again into a tiny hamlet I recognised from some days earlier. The only shop, constructed from battered galvanised metal sheets, had a noisy old freezer which was half full of large bottles of strong beer and I treated myself to a celebratory drink. I thought I deserved one!

I hauled myself reluctantly from the incredible delight of Kaokoland and passed northwards to the Ruacana and the narrow strip of land along the top of the country which claims the highest population density. Here the main road that parallels the border with Angola is magnificently paved and the towns are abundant and familiar; full to overflowing with people and western luxury they teem with cars, buses and giant freight trucks, bars, supermarkets and gas stations. Travel on the road to Ondangwa is an endless and tedious procession of police checkpoints where your documents are subjected to perfunctory examination but where quite astonishingly no bribes or baksheesh are solicited. Water is plentiful, fed into the land via concrete sluiceways from the huge Kunene River which flows east-west along the border and out into the Atlantic, and children swim joyously in the manmade rivers while mothers toil with the never-ceasing drudgery of repetitive laundry. Eventually the road sweeps southwards and the people, towns and infrastructure thin out quickly as you approach the enormous plain of Etosha National Park.

The tremendous game reserve at Etosha covers an area of land roughly equivalent to the size of Wales; it is equal in stature to the more commonly known Serengeti and Masai Mara, containing a staggering five hundred and sixty-four mammal, bird and reptile species, but unlike the parks and reserves in East Africa it is completely fenced and provides no great migration spectacles. The wildlife viewing opportunities are quite incredible. Roaming free within its confines is one of the largest populations of endangered black rhino in the whole of Africa, and these along with the more common white variety may be seen trotting with their distinctive armoured contempt across the flat grasslands and low scrub. Few other animals maintain such a prehistoric appearance, the plates of their magnificent battledress worn like an enormous thick overcoat draped upon their backs and shoulders, the haughty toss of the head and contemptuous nasal expiration a confident bellicose challenge to all would-be champions. The central feature of the park is the enormous Etosha Salt Pan, a gigantic kidney-shaped depression which in years of exceptional rain becomes a shallow lake where zebra and wildebeest splash in ankle-deep water, appearing from a distance to be levitating upon the surface. More commonly it is a massive glaring white stain of parched and broken clay shimmering with glittering mineral deposits that make it clearly visible from the depths of outer space.

Animal life abounds here; great prides of nonchalant sleepy lions sprawl in the drowsy sunlight beneath the thorn trees, the spots and dapples of the infants shimmering on their golden coats like blown leaves floating on a still water pond. Huge herds of graceful impala, springbok and roan drift in careless patterns foraging the tinder-dry growth for tender young shoots and lush new grasses. Excitable pale grey wildebeest with jet black masks skitter, spring and kick amongst the mud and debris of the pan and hundreds of Burchell's zebra cluster together, forming large psychedelic displays of ever-changing geometric shapes and combinations. Serious-looking warthogs snuffle amongst brush and scrub searching constantly for edible substances, the high-frequency squeals of their tiny infant bands emanating loudly from amongst deeper thickets, and busy mongoose and meerkat communities scuttle with industrious intent around the boundaries of their burrow colonies. At the waterholes you may find twenty or more reticulated giraffe bowing their impossibly long necks to the water with gangly fragile legs outstretched in a necessary but comedic and venerable courtesy. Massive bull elephants with ancient torn and battle-scarred appearance spray themselves in thick clay-laden water until they are ghostly white with sun-dried sediment like penitent pilgrims smeared with ashes. Testosterone laden gemsbok joust with murderous fury, turning in sharp circles similar to the patterns of aerial combat, their heads held low as they expertly fence with viciously sharp sabres. Pedantic looking secretary birds make high careful steps whilst hunting amongst the bush for snakes and frogs, their decorative frock-coats and knee-breeches a solemn badge of office amongst the overwhelming bird life. Marshall eagles, marabou storks, guinea fowl and the giant Kori bustard all stalk the grass and scrub, and ever-present are the vulture hordes patiently circling high above the grand theatre stage awaiting their subtle cue for their curtain appearance. If you are lucky you may glimpse the rarities of primitive wild dogs or even leopard as they pass on silent padded feet along time-worn trails searching for their opportunity to dispense immediate, merciless death.

Between the grand Etosha Plain and the eternal acacia bushveld surrounding Windhoek is the impressive Waterburg Plateau. This huge table mountain is the tiny remnant of a previous sedimentary land mass eroded over millennia into its current curious isolation. The gigantic perpendicular ramparts of red and ochre sandstone thrust upwards in fissured and crumbling columns for six hundred feet from the surrounding plain, creating a formidable natural redoubt. Atop this ancient fortress, lush subtropical woodland overflows with high grass, elegant ferns and an estimated two hundred bird species. In my mind it equated to the tremendous and foreboding plateau of Sir Arthur Conan Doyle's *Lost World*, that giant forgotten land where dinosaurs roamed and pterodactyls soared above gigantic impassable forest, and in its own way it is indeed similar. Designated as a park in 1972 it is now a sanctuary for endangered wildlife where both black and white rhinoceros claim monarchs' rights on the high kingdom, and leopard, giraffe, hyena and kudu all roam the precincts of their idyllic walled citadel. South of the plateau there are several private game reserves, large fenced areas centred on luxury rest camps stocked with easy-to-view game, chilled wines and gourmet foods. But if you are prepared to seek them out you will also find delightful remote farms where the analogy to Doyle's *Lost World* is further reinforced amongst groups of perfectly defined fossilised dinosaur footprints. At Otji-haenamparero you may track the progress of awesome three-toed giants, their paths criss-crossed in the sandstone with tiny clawed prints of creatures that scurried on hind legs amongst soft mud and sediment a hundred and ninety million years previously.

Amongst its ownership of some of the world's most incredible natural sights, Namibia is also home to the most significant extraterrestrial attraction known to man. The giant sixty ton Hoba Meteorite slammed into the planet slightly to the west of what is now Grootfontein; this massive block of iron and nickel roughly nine feet square is the single largest meteorite on earth and it is believed that it may actually be just a fragment of an even larger missile which broke up during its passage through our atmosphere. Since its discovery in 1920 souvenir hunters have hacked various pieces from its rusted exterior and despite having been designated a national monument in the mid-fifties and having its own warden, one can still see the shiny new scratches of hacksaw blades upon its pitted edges.

All in all, Namibia may well be one of the most fascinating places I have ever visited, but then Debbie and I are due to go to Scotland this Christmas so who knows …

fig 23.   Etosha National Park, Namibia

fig 24.   Himba girl, Kaokoland, Namibia

fig 25. Juvenile Sea Elephant, the Skeleton Coast, Namibia

12. *Missing all the Bears*

There are an estimated four thousand polar bears in, on, or around the peninsula of Svalbard and I can say with absolute certainty that I managed to see not a single one during my stay!

I had been thinking about making a visit to Svalbard, or Spitzbergen as it is often called, since my first visits to Alaska. Apart from the almost magnetic attraction that areas of isolated frozen tundra exert on my mind, I had visited the tiny Eskimo settlement of Teller Alaska where Amundsen and Nobile had eventually managed to land the airship *Norge* thus completing the first ever Trans-Polar flight. Having seen the terminating location of this most romantic of polar explorations I felt it would be appropriate to see the staring point!

The town of Longyear, named after the American mining engineer who founded it, is like most Arctic settlements, rather an odd place. The population is obviously small and appears to be dominated by people from just about everywhere other than Spitzbergen! The brightly painted timber houses sit in ordered rows; their red, green and yellow fronts splash brief squares of colour out towards the relentless whiteness of the massive valley walls. The cliffs rise on both sides of the town; interrupted at regular intervals with zigzag bands and outcrops of loose grey shale, they thrust upwards almost vertically, terminating abruptly in a completely flat plateau as if some giant carpenter had planed off the rough tops. In the windows of almost every house there are tier upon tier of carefully tended vibrant houseplants, miniature rainforests with hanging creepers and giant leaves that beckon the eye with welcome remembrance of warmer places. In many houses lights are left to burn all night as if the people wish to reassure one another that they are not alone, that there is warmth and shelter at hand.

All services, water, sewage etc run on the surface in giant rust-covered heated pipes supported well above the frozen ground so that the short-legged and barrel-like Svalbard Reindeer which wander freely about the town can pass easily beneath, searching for the tiny lichens and moss which they dig from beneath the deep snow. On the flat mountain-tops giant radar dishes point heavenwards, continually measuring the Arctic atmosphere and the cosmic light show of the aurora.

Snowmobile routes wend tortuously through the town and on the pathways locals pass you on skis or pushing shopping bags on small wooden sleds that resemble walking frames used by the elderly. But most memorable of all are the roads, which are in the most literal sense paved with coal!

Longyear was founded on coal! Shallow horizontal seams pass through the mountains high above the valley floors like a vast layer of chocolate sandwiched between iced cakes. It is quite amazing, surrounded by endless snow and ice, to consider the enormous tropical forests and swamps that must once have covered this area. During the war the islands became a battleground for the Allies and the Germans, both sides wishing to establish weather stations in order to provide accurate forecasts for the Arctic convoys and bomber fleets. The town was all but obliterated by shelling from the *Scharnhorst* and *Tirpitz*; one mine struck with high explosive continued to burn until the late 1960s!

There are seven separate mines of which only the newest and most remote, number seven, is still active; the coal is transported to the loading dock on the frozen ice fjord by large trucks which hurtle endlessly back and forth every day, the heaped contents spilling out onto the road at every turn or junction; the ice is spotted in every direction with gleaming particles of anthracite. At the loading dock, where the coal is stockpiled to await the summer thaw and the arrival of the colliery ships, the huge winds rushing out of the Advent Valley scatter great clouds of it seaward until the frozen, contorted and twisted ice is decorated with a perfect black fan opening out for many miles from the shore.

In the past when the mines were working at full capacity the coal was transported to the water's edge by an intricate system of cable cars. Huge bathtub-like containers were swung along on stout wires supported between massive wooden trestles. Loaded tubs from all the mines were pulled into the town by the central powerhouse of the system, an octopus-like building which stands sentinel on a ridge above the town. It swallowed the loaded tubs at one of several entry points and magically sent them out at another to be tipped out on the dock and shuttled back to the mines for never-ending further loads. It must have been a fascinating sight in its heyday.

Now however the system is defunct and decaying, the hundreds of almost tree-like wooden gantries stand stout and resolute, their symmetrical apex shapes march outwards across the white frozen tundra like columns of milkmaids burdened with loaded wooden yokes across their shoulders. The cables are mostly broken and hang rusting and rimed with ice; some support the frozen carcasses of ring seals hung there high above the reach of inquisitive polar bears by hunters who feed the stripped, blackened meat to their dogs. The few tubs that remain in place are empty and still and on calm evenings when the sun sets flaring deeply red and orange in the clear unpolluted air it burnishes their lead-painted sides in shimmering vivid ochre.

There are other mines still working in the Russian settlements of Barentsburg and Pyramiden. Here you walk in deeply snow-laden streets among typically Russian-built houses that appear to have been transported from the mainland, their filigree fretwork battered and desiccated by the biting wind and frost. For me it was a step back to pre-Glasnost Russia, decay and dirt, dilapidated and unkempt at every turn. The statue of Lenin still stands proudly intact in the main square and portraits of miners with exceptional production quotas are framed on billboards outside the swimming hall. Stocky men carrying the ever-present canvas bag step by you without acknowledgement or interest and occasionally a young woman with the high cheekbones and fair hair of the Ukraine passes you by, wrapped in an elegant ankle-length fur coat.

The company canteen maintains a twenty-four-hour meal service for all residents in the town; they do not have the benefit of cooking facilities or refrigerators in the barrack blocks and bags of frozen food hang outside many of the grime-laden windows. Perhaps the most interesting item in the town is the mine entrance; situated on the main street it is an ornate wooden block complete with decorated frieze which you might easily take as the municipal hall or library!

There are no connecting roads between the few towns and to reach Barentsburg you must travel by snowmobile for three and a half hours; for the vast majority of visitors this speedy pastime is the primary reason for coming. Hundreds of these machines roar out of Longyear daily in long snaking lines that disperse off to all points of the compass. It must be said that there is a definite adrenaline rush when driving such a vehicle; roaring over the concrete-hard snow and ice produces an illusion of freedom that infuses your mind despite the ear-splitting noise and the physical effort required to stay on board. A fair percentage of people are injured, usually when descending precariously from the high reaches of glaciers; it is no easy feat to control the scooter, winding downwards through the moraine at an acute angle where normal application of the brake will ensure that you skid sideways in an alarming manner. Thankfully for me, unlike Yellowstone National Park, there are no trees with which to collide!

The weather on Svalbard is an education in localised conditions; the nature of the mountains ensures that whilst you may be battling in storm-driven snow in one valley, all perspective lost and the driver in front a vague dark smudge, in the next valley there can be bright sunshine and blue skies. When I arrived in Longyear the huge expanse of the ice fjord was completely frozen across its whole expanse; large circular pans of ice, their serrated edges impacted together and raised like china saucers, stretched away into the far distance with a repetitive geometry that reminded me of chickenwire mesh. A week later this solid mass of ice had been totally destroyed and scattered, dismantled by a violent gale driving down onto the water off the valley sides. Now there was open sea; darkly green against the white snow-capped ridges and deposited along the coast were great piled discs of ice, each circular section a foot thick, stacked upon each other in untidy confusion like massive casino gambling chips thrown carelessly on the roulette table. Once the water was freed the bird life in the area became evident and beautiful, and cloud-white fulmars cruised along the water's edge in lazy unhurried glides that produced elegant shadows on the glittering tumbled circles of ice.

Driving the fast snowmobile is fun but for me it will never compare to the joy of a dog team and sled. For me this is the reason to be on Svalbard. Spending almost every day with the dog teams, I was able to improve my mushing skills and provide memories that will delight me for the rest of my life, such moments as you draw upon when you have a bad day at work or life just seems to be against you!

I have such enormous respect for these animals; they astound me with their intelligence and devotion. They are wondrous, beautiful creatures that live to run, and driving them is a much more complex deal than turning the key on a snowmobile. There is daily food to be prepared and distributed, great cans of steaming mush that is more water than solids set out in dented bowls in front of each kennel box in strict order of team hierarchy, and they bolt it down in moments before it freezes immovably into the bowl.

The preparation for a trip is a strict protocol of procedure and tradition and you release each dog from its half-buried kennel box, and clamping its hind quarters between your legs you fit the running harness while they squirm and writhe in eager excitement. The more docile ones lift each front leg in turn to be passed through the straps, their dense knotted coats which have never known a brush are harsh and gritty against the fingers, and skin is easily lost, frozen onto the metal clips of the collar or harness. When the dog is ready you walk it to the sledge, holding the cross straps behind its shoulders, and in their impatience to precede you they walk upright on back legs, springing forward like trained circus horses. The lead dog is always attached to the sledge first and then you work your way back, fitting each dog in turn to the traces and attaching the neck line between each matched pair until all six are in place, the strongest most powerful two at the rear of the team; now the collective anxious baying reaches a fever pitch, their whole reason for being straining in the harness, eyes bright with anticipation, their excitement is almost uncontrollable; they leap forward, throwing their full weight against the ice anchor, howling their impatience or thrashing on their backs in joyous exhilaration for the trail ahead. When you release the brake and shoot forward from the dog yard those animals left behind secured on their chains set up a great chorus of mournful wolf-like howls in protest at their wrongful exclusion.

There is no intrusive noise with a dog team, just the gentle swish of the sled runners on the snow and the soft padding of the dogs' feet; the ancient Inuit commands require only a gentle voice and when the temperature is warm enough and you can go without a hood or fur hat the rush of the wind past your ears is almost soporific.

You very quickly learn the individual personalities of the team, those that are content to run straight, or those that are easily distracted. When you stop to rest those that require reassurance and affection make their feelings abundantly clear. There are the mischievous ones who bite through their neck lines and run out to the side of the team, snapping up pellets of frozen reindeer dung to be chomped up greedily on the hoof, or those who only pretend to pull whilst searching around them with keen noses, their inattention betrayed by the slackness of their trace.

When the snow packs up hard in between their pads they rake at it angrily with their teeth with barely a pause to their stride. Even the bowels are emptied on the trot, usually within the first ten minutes or so of every journey. In this completely odour-free, sterilised, frozen landscape where nothing has any discernible smell, this can come as quite a shock to the unsuspecting senses! Running with the dogs can be extremely hard work and co-operation is required if you are to make progress on some of the steeper gradients; what appears to be hard-packed snow will swallow your legs above the knees when you step off the runners to assist the dogs by pushing the sled. Climbing in steps to a thousand feet or more on a glacier with eye-searing sunlight and frozen air that stings the face and burns the lungs leaves you sweating hard and breathless from exertion but the reward is a thousandfold and the descent, where the dogs dash headlong down the slopes, freed from the weight of the sled, is breathtaking in its turn.

The only unbreakable rule is to never let go of the sled! If you topple over on such a gradient and find yourself being dragged along face down in the snow the team will eventually stop, anchored by the drag of your body; if you let go of the sled, you can be assured that this will be the last you will see of your team; at best this can mean a long walk home; at worst, well, this is a very easy place to die in, which is why you always carry your rifle slung on the shoulder and not in the sled! The experience of driving a good team is fantastically rewarding, the bond between you and the dogs even in a short time is remarkable. The slow speed and quiet nature of the travel has various rewards: you may pass within a few feet of a baby reindeer curled up tightly, its great dark eyes staring dolefully from beneath its blanket of blown snow, and when the sun sets and the obliquely cast light sheds tender pastel tints of pink and orange on the snow caps and your eyes water with the delicate transient beauty of the colour; but most memorable is when the wind whips up the ground snow and creates a fast-moving soft blanket of gentle wisping white a foot above the surface; it is as if you are travelling on a surf of silent billowing cotton wool where the dogs' backs and heads plough forward like dolphins riding a bow wave.

I had a young Norwegian boy ride as passenger in my sled one day when the wind was driving hard; at just twelve years old Eric was the stereotypical Scandinavian, well-built, with a mop of blond hair, bright blue eyes and an engaging smile. He was on holiday with his parents and sister, and the whole family were kitted out in specially fitted snow suits that are mandatory for just about everyone living north of the Arctic Circle. Despite his attire, after a couple of hours in the sled, bumping and bouncing on stone-littered ice, he was frozen to the core: noticeably blue and chattering, he expressed his feelings to me in heavily accented but perfect English: 'I am totavlly froven'. We thawed him out with chocolate and cups of steaming Ribena, and on the homeward trip he disappeared into the sled, curling up in a great reindeer skin and zipping up the Gore-Tex cover so that he was protected completely inside. He never surfaced once for even the briefest of peeks but I knew him still to be alive by the muffled cries of bruised pain as we thumped over some of the deeper ridges and ruts! And when we eventually halted again in Longyear he had to be coaxed out of his vaguely warm cocoon. I saw him again later in the week, on an equally chilled day with the racing wind whipping up snow clouds; his parents had signed him up to partake of some riding on Icelandic ponies. Approaching him from behind I recognised his snow suit and waved enthusiastically as I passed, only to be met with his frozen and miserable frost-reddened face squinting in suffering endurance!

It is difficult to explain the fascination of Arctic wastes to people who have no desire to venture there; it is an almost magical atmosphere of indescribable pristine purity where one feels that the earth is fresh, unspoilt, dominating, tender and awesome at the same moment. The air has a clarity that leaves you breathless and invigorated and the cold, stinging embrace of the chilled wind is like the caress of nature herself. You are filled constantly with an air of expectancy as if something remarkable were about to spark and explode around you. Stood high above sea level atop the massive and ancient depths of glacial ice you survey the endless expanses of unbroken diamond-sparkling brilliant white snow surmounted with clear deeply blue sky that burns the eye and you are conscious of your insignificant tiny mortality in a way that frightens and excites you simultaneously. No wonder, then, that people are drawn back to such places over and over. It has been called the "draw of the North" or "song of the North"; on Svalbard they call it "Svalbard Bug", an infection of the mind and blood that fills your thoughts when you are returned and warmly safe in your home and work. You feel a melancholy hunger for the enveloping cold and exquisitely harsh beauty of the snow and ice. It's at this juncture that you usually part company with the understanding or comprehension of family and friends and words are woefully inadequate to explain the siren-like calling of the North. But then most of them already think I am rather mad anyway!

13. *Off the Map*

We were back in America; actually we ended up spending half our time in Canada but our plan was to trundle around between national parks and monuments and generally see where the road took us. As any soldier will tell you, even the best plan survives only seconds after contact with the enemy, and that holds true of road trips. The hours spent poring over maps, judging routes, times and distances, can all be waylaid in an instant by an intriguing roadsign, an interesting back route or a glimpsed moose or bear. One plain truth that I have learnt is that there are no such things as definitive maps; no matter how many you buy or how up to date they may purport to be, there are always places of interest and wonderment that spring out at you unannounced, distracting you from your intended destination with joyous and unpredictable irregularity. This trip was to be no exception.

We flew into Seattle on a bright sunlit afternoon when the massive, straining, snow-capped peaks of the Rockies looked like giant ploughed furrows of rich carrot cake decorated along their ridges with pristine white folds of fondant icing. The beautiful clarity of the air foreshortened the thousands of feet of altitude and made it seem as if one might reach out from the aircraft and touch their shimmering, icy snow-caps.

As always, we left the city immediately, heading south on highly congested freeways that eventually released us onto the Olympic Peninsula. The following morning we boarded the ferry in Port Angeles and sailed across the straits of Juan de Fuca to the marvellously colonial city of Victoria in British Columbia. This beautiful town, centred on its large harbour, is one of the most pleasant parts of Canada that I have ever visited; finely clipped lawns and colourful flowerbeds line the streets where native Indians produce and sell carefully carved totems or intricately beaded bags and necklaces. Quiet and well-behaved horses pull open white carriages on the remarkably vehicle-free roads, and huge hotels and the legislature building glower down on the assembled scene with their thundering Victorian architecture of spires, gargoyles and green copper roofs.

From Victoria we rode out onto Puget Sound in a high-speed rubber Zodiac launch; wrapped in cumbersome survival suits which resemble the Michelin Man, and beaten mercilessly by the raging wind, you clench your jaw with gritted teeth against

164

spine-jarring thuds of the hull as it roars, bangs and shudders across the water's surface at almost forty knots. Your reward at the termination of this numbing torture is, hopefully, an encounter with one or more of the pods of killer whales that frequent these waters.

The last time I had taken this ride some five years earlier I had been incredibly lucky, seeing two resident pods, those that pursue and eat only salmon. At that time, much to my amazement, they had swum within touching distance of the boat and passed directly beneath it in graceful unhurried dives that left one in breathless contemplation of such magnificent creatures. Things had certainly changed: there were no resident pods within striking distance of Victoria but far out on the sound a pod of itinerants had been spotted and a flotilla of assembled whale-watching boats homed in on them with relentless intent.

Itinerant killer whales are often referred to as the wolves of the sea; they do not pursue salmon in regular feeding grounds but hunt marine mammals such as porpoise and sea lion. This particular pod was very obviously not happy with the attention they were receiving from the dozen or so assembled boats. Unlike the residents' behaviour that I had previously observed, they did not approach the boats and deliberately avoided them, swimming in irregular patterns and continually attempting to distance themselves from their unwelcome spectators. The pod was dominated by an absolutely huge male; his massive dorsal fin towered above his back as he broke the surface and expelled the air from his lungs with that rushing spray-laden whoosh that is so unique to whales and so delightful to hear.

The whole group stayed in a tight formation, their ebony skin glistening in the weak sunlight like the rubber of a diver's wetsuit as they surged forward with the infants close in at the mothers' flanks. They are a truly awe-inspiring sight; the sense of freedom that attaches to their passage through the water is remarkable; they are the masters of their domain, roaming at will and completely at one with their environment and your heart is filled with a swelling joy for the fact that they exist.

Surprisingly, despite the presence of such a formidable group of predators, there were a number of Dall's porpoise who were quite happy to ride the bow of the boat, flashing in and out of the foaming white spray with loud slaps and splashes on either side; they have you twisting your head back and forth as if you were watching a demented tennis match. Their speed is astonishing: beneath the water's surface they are blurred speeding forms distorted by the refracted light and in the instant that they burst into the daylight the eye is far too slow to register anything more than a sleek flash of shining grey skin streaming water from its latex-like surface.

We crossed back into the United States on the same ferry and headed off into the Olympic National Park. Olympic lays claim to the highest level of biodiversity found anywhere in the North American continent. It is a huge circular area of temperate rainforest centred on the eight-thousand-foot Mount Olympus. Rain is the consistent and overpowering factor in this magnificent wilderness, it averages between twelve and fourteen feet each year! The ancient forest is a dripping, sodden, twilight labyrinth of towering giant spruce trees coated in dense mouldering blankets of velveteen moss that undulates on every available surface. Liquorice ferns and lichens tumble from the spur of every branch and dividing trunk and large discs of fungus protrude horizontally from the bark like porcelain dinner plates fired in vivid Clarice Cliff orange and ochre glaze. Tiny rivulets of water snake lazily between the sorrel plants, joining together to scour small streambeds and eventually tumble into the roaring creeks and rivers that rush over the lips of polished rock in thunderous, mist-laden waterfalls.

In places where the water has excavated deep ravine-like crevices along fault lines in the bedrock the bellowing tumult of foaming water is bridged completely by fallen tree trunks, decaying in the moisture-laden air so that eventually they will fall into the water and be borne out to massive tangles of driftwood and flotsam that decorate the wind-torn, storm-ravaged beaches of grey sand and tussock grass.

On the very edge of one such beach we found a grove of cedar trees with huge boles growing on their trunks and branches; these spherical tumours that form around areas of damage ranged from the size of a football to that of a large dustbin; they were so numerous that they totally changed the shape of the forest so that it appeared that one was looking through a massive beaded curtain hung there by the largest of giants. Olympic naturally has its share of giant trees: they are not as well preserved as the huge Californian Redwoods or the New Zealand Kauri, but they are magnificently ancient, gnarled and split; hollowed in the centre by centuries of rot and regrowth, their massive trunks divide into dozens of giant cords draped with vines and ferns; their bases are a huge softened pad of released decaying vegetation permeated by the astringent odour of cedar; they generate an almost tangible sense of life as if a heartbeat within their ancient depths, their continued presence in the rainforest a solemn and silent rebuke to your tiny human insignificance.

We turned north again and headed for the Canadian border by way of the North Cascades National Park, which turned out to be an unexpected jewel of mountain scenery - massive forested mountains that surround huge lakes of mineral-filled water shimmering in the most exquisite turquoise blue. This is said to be one of the homes of the legendary Big Foot; multiple sightings have been recorded, and gazing down onto the dense unending canopy of trees from one mountain peak, it is easy to believe that creatures unknown could survive in such an environment. We didn't see any Sasquatch, but we did spot an equally unusual and rather rare species.

On the road through the very highest pass we crept up steep gradients and switchbacks in low gear, where much to our complete astonishment we passed several dozen cyclists of quite obvious pensionable age, gamely pedalling upwards on magnificent lightweight racing bikes. At one scenic lay-by where we watched groups of chattering and inquisitive chipmunks searching manically in the shattered rocks for seeds and begging for tourist fast food, these cyclists caught us up and I was able to observe them more closely: they certainly were all over sixty years of age and some considerably so, but these were a much more exotic bunch than those we find at home. They were all deeply tanned with skin the texture of worked calves' leather, they were all remarkably thin and healthy and dressed in stretchy Lycra riding apparel that is usually best suited to twenty-year-old fitness instructors. Whilst Debbie lit a cigarette and I wandered about puffing heavily in the high altitude I was moved to wonder if it wasn't perhaps something in the water.

We blundered by pure chance into the town of Winthrop and were so delighted with its preserved charm that we stayed to explore. A tiny mining settlement that had once been a Gold Rush boomtown, it is now a museum town where almost every shop has displays of contemporary memorabilia on display and the boardwalks barely keep the dust off your shoes. Here you may purchase anything from coyote skulls to six-shooters, and on the corner on Main Street you may indulge yourself in an orgy of chocolate: marshmallow and toffee that transports you magically back to childhood. Chocolate Bears Paws and treacle tart are sold by the pound; honey is made on site by bees which enter their transparent hive through glass tunnels that run across the length of the shop. A beautiful mahogany counter is laden with trays of cake and chocolate-dipped treats, and the overwhelming aroma of coffee, cinnamon and sugar has your mouth salivating before you have walked two steps onto the polished sprung floorboards.

We crossed into Canada at a tiny run-down town called Osovoos, a quiet dusty backwater where the evening was warm and the sunset slow; the local women's guild were meeting in the rather grubby back room of the only café, and on the main street a man was camping out for the night guarding the contents of his yard sale, several tables full of old glass jars, paperback books, garden implements and carved walking sticks.

We passed quickly through the Okanagan Valley with its elongated lake and numerous fruit stalls and headed up into the Rocky Mountains. A sign for Mount Revelstoke waylaid us, and some hours later we rejoined the highway, lost in wonder at the beauty of this tiny National Park which we had almost passed by. The Alpine meadows on Mount Revelstoke are painfully beautiful: perched amongst the hollows of the mountain close to its peak the tree line falls away and large expanses of spongy rock-strewn grass and moss are interspersed with clear pools of crystal-like water; amongst the grasses are a multitude of delicate Alpine flowers; scarlet, purple and yellow blooms push their startling petals above the meadow in riotous confusion as if the very ground were infected with some exotic natural measles or chickenpox. In the higher reaches where the grass gives way to the jumbled piles of shattered grey rock, the darting shapes and high-pitched whistling calls of pika accompany you as you pick your way ever upwards. The perfect clarity of the air exhilarates your lungs and your eyes are incapable of taking in the endless vista of ridges and valleys that stretches away to eventually become the Columbian Ice Fields.

Continuing into Glacier National Park, I was rather disappointed with the contrast to Revelstoke; in Rogers Pass you may view the tumbling choked rivers of ice that cut down the valleys like huge frozen tidal waves, their upper surfaces split and cracked in a million ominous fissures and dirt-laden pressure ridges.

Of Yoho I can recall very little except that it took us into the truly awe-inspiring scenery of the Banff and Jasper National Parks and the very heart of the Canadian Rockies. I am at a loss to find words to adequately describe this place. The magnificent snow-capped pinnacles and rugged stone massifs repeat themselves at every turn in the road; there is no break in the sensory overload you receive in this humbling landscape. At every glance there are perfect blue skies and soaring mountains thrusting upwards with immense bygone power; crashing waterfalls gouge the rocks in thundering white torrents, and where the bases of the mountains are visible there are millions of tons of shale and fallen rock piled against the slopes, decorated with zigzagging layers of opposing colour like the sand-filled ornaments that used to be offered for sale at the seaside.

The Columbian Ice Fields nestle in the very centre of these parks, their immeasurable bulk of ice and snow tumbling over the leading bowl where the excess folds out over the lip and falls away. You may see deep ice caves and hanging tongues of frozen snow as it is forced towards the edge of the precipice and occasionally you may witness great building-size chunks calving from the weakened face.

At Lake Louise Glacier, ice hangs precariously from the lip of the mountain high above the deep azure blue of the lake, which is completely encompassed by the mountains, in a scene of such stereotypical picture book clarity that it is no wonder this luxury holiday resort has developed into a massive tourist destination with all the associated industries.

In the Rockies, people standing at the roadside usually means they have spotted some form of wildlife. We joined two men on a steep embankment and in the cool evening air with the pastel-washed colours of the sunset fading rapidly in the sky and the backlit mountains shimmering in polished silver outline, we watched a huge female moose and her baby feeding on water plants. Standing knee-deep in the silent darkening water, she dipped her massive head below the surface, securing large mouthfuls of weed and succulent stems which she chewed unhurriedly as the water streamed from her gigantic antlers and carpet-like fur. The two guys turned out to be singers and described themselves as 'Canada's most up and coming country and western band'; they were just returning to the east coast after having attended the country and western awards ceremony in Calgary. They questioned us closely on our knowledge of Canadian country singers and the popularity of such music here in England, pondering whether there might be a possible outlet for their records. When we parted again Debbie and I were considerably more knowledgeable on matters of country singing, and they were, I suspect, unimpressed and rather indignant at our ungrateful incomprehension of the exported talent displayed by Celine Dion!

When night falls into the valleys and ice fields of the Jasper National Park you are very quickly overtaken by an ominous sense of isolation. There is an almost overpowering sense of threatening abandonment and the tail lights of a lone car far ahead on the tortuous road become a point of distant human companionship, a tiny intermittent light in the darkness that your eye will automatically seek and which reassures you that you are still in contact with your fellow species and have not actually fallen off the edge of the earth into the endless deepening black void of space.

We arrived eventually in the small town of Jasper and found that our faith in the symbolism of those lights would not extend past the edges of the wilderness; there was not a single spare room or bed to be had in the town and reluctantly we plunged back into the darkness again, heading towards the next settlement some thirty miles distant where we might find accommodation for the rapidly diminishing night. Eventually we chanced upon what appeared to be a truckers' roadside motel and spent the night in a log cabin where signs warning of bears raiding the rubbish bins were posted at every turn. Like so many other situations that arise when one is travelling, this forced extension of our route had some exceptional consequences.

The following morning, not long after daybreak, while cold banks of mist hugged the trees and rain swept down off the cloud-covered ridges, we headed off into the depths of the Jasper National Park, and there on a turn of the road we chanced upon three young bull moose sparring and challenging in preparation for the rut. Engaging each other with the great sweep of their impressive antlers, pushing forward with their long stilt-like legs, the impact of the bones has an astonishing sound quality, the smaller clashes like loud castanets clattering in brief staccato bursts, but the full-blown attacks had the resonance of splitting wood or an axe thumping into a heavy tree trunk. We were also completely amazed at the vanishing act which these giant creatures could achieve: stepping unhurriedly into the trees with measured, elegant grace they would become invisible within seconds; their camouflage is so complete and the trees so dense they were swallowed in moments and although they were less than six feet away, only the most intense scrutiny would reveal their presence, and only then if they deigned to move from their position of silent watchfulness.

A few minutes later we were to find an infant mountain goat gingerly picking

169

its way down a near-vertical cliff face with anxious nervous glances whilst calling in alarmed bleats to its parents standing patiently at the foot of the rock. The highlight of our unexpected trip that early morning was awaiting just a mile or two further on, and had we not been denied a bed in Jasper we would most certainly have not experienced one of these wildlife encounters.

On the edge of the Athabasca River we chanced upon a herd of female and infant elk just as they had decided to cross the fast flowing waters. They stepped out into the swirling current with elegant long-legged steps and were quickly embraced by the muddy grey torrent; holding their heads above the deluge they beat their way forward despite the heavy drift of iced water; the babies struggling to keep pace with their mothers were soon visibly tired from their exertions.

When all were safely across and up onto the far bank our attention was drawn by a long and piercing, almost bugle-like cry from a truly massive bull standing close into the foot of the bank below us. He had stood there unobserved by us, no doubt keeping careful watch on his subjects as they made their crossing. I had never heard an elk call until that moment and I would certainly not have believed that this strange vocalisation came from that particular beast if I had not witnessed it myself. Thrusting his giant head forward and tilting his awesome rack of antlers back against his shoulders, his thick neck strained as he released a high-pitched trailing whistle that one might expect from a soaring eagle; his harem on the far bank stopped in obedience to his call and after several more high octave notes he stalked into the water with a sturdy, dominant assurance. The charging water was no obstacle for this tremendous creature, his gigantic antlers that must have weighed forty pounds or more were held erect in defiance of the tumult and he continued to call to his family as he swam. We crossed a nearby bridge and were within twenty feet of him when he emerged from the trees that skirted the river: he stepped past us in a swaggering tiptoe gait, head held high with the haughty disdain that only noble breed monarchy can display. The top of his head was easily nine feet above the ground and the stretch to the tip of the highest antler point must have been four feet above that; the deep russet of his blanket-textured coat was even and unblemished and there was not the slightest indication that he had so recently been immersed in the Arctic river water.

We crossed the continental divide, and leaving the Banff National Park we headed south into Kootenay, an elongated park that borders one of the original roads driven through the Rockies; it was quiet and obviously a backwater compared with the huge volume of visitors that the other larger national parks attract. Infrared sensors situated along the roadside detect the movement of animals in the tree line and alert passing motorists with flashing red lights in an attempt to minimise the high numbers that are struck and killed by vehicles each year.

Kootenay holds a tiny but unique attraction, a well-kept secret with an amazing visual impact that delights and mystifies you if you take the time to hike the brief trail to its location. The Paint Pots are iron rich cold water mineral springs that rise up imperceptibly from the earth through still circular pools that provide perfect mirror images of the tall fir trees surrounding them; they deposit their heavy minerals on the slopes and creeks, staining the whole landscape a deep and vivid ochre.

Falling tree trunks, scattered rocks, wiry grass and exposed, tangled roots are all encrusted and stained in this orange and yellow pigment as if a massive overloaded paintbrush had been applied in careless daubs and swipes against every surface. In some places there are large conical mounds where the springs have become choked by the build-up of the iron and clogged with debris so that the rising water has sought another outlet, leaving the abandoned dome like a giant inflamed and pus-filled boil on abraded skin. The huge iron content in the water is like a blistering tart sherbet on your tongue and would certainly be best avoided if you have dental fillings!

These springs were visited for thousands of years by aboriginal tribes that prized the natural paint for ceremonial and medicinal rituals; the wet clay substance would be collected and shaped into cakes baked in fires for ease of transportation and consumed in carefully rationed quantities until the next migratory visit to the area. Eventually, like so many other natural resources, it was exploited by white European settlers and mined with industrial machinery, the remains of which lie abandoned, scattered and rusting in the long grass.

At the foot of Kootenay is the town of Radium Hot Springs, a manufactured Santa Claus village that twinkles with fairy lights, where holidaymakers sit neck-deep in bubbling superheated pools of natural mineral water that condenses into great clouds of steam above their heads in the cool surrounding air. Here there was no lack of bed space; the town boasts over fifty motels and boarding houses!

To the south east of Radium we passed through the "Frank Slide", a huge tumbled mass of mountain that had plummeted down onto a booming mining town, destroying all but the few homes and buildings that were on the very outskirts, where the rush of sliding rock had finally exhausted its catastrophic progress. The great, undulating, black and grey blanket of shattered rock has now been cut open to allow the road to pass through, and it is astonishing to contemplate that the huge twenty-foot high walls of stone that fence the highway on either side were once suspended high above on the mountainside.

We passed on eastwards through the sleepy town of Cowley so that I might post some cards to a good friend who owns the same name and who is a great collector of stamps. Far out on a high ridge of the horizon was a great marching column of giant wind turbines, the huge blades tuning in slow unsequenced revolutions high above their narrow steel stems. These quiet forgotten prairie towns are an endless source of fascination to me; they seem to cling to the very edge of existence, defying the economic forces which should have long ago consigned them to the dust and vague memories of old men. There are many hundreds of such towns in the great grasslands, each with its overgrown railroad siding adjacent to the decaying wooden towers of defunct grain elevators, their weatherboarded sides flaking paint and their ropes and tackle tapping mournfully in the gentle wind. Rusted farm machinery stands forlornly on the untended grass verges of the dust-blown gravel roads, small birds twitter softly and a million crickets chirrup in the long stems of dried golden grass, no voices intrude, no car engines rumble, and the still, unbroken solitude settles on your shoulders like a heavy backpack of expectant anxiety so that your mind feels as if it has been dipped into thick tar or molasses.

On the road to "Head Smashed in Buffalo Jump" we passed a huge wolf plodding along slowly on the edge of the road; at the time, despite the total lack of habitation in the area, I mistook him for a very large and unkempt dog, but thirty minutes later I was confronted with an exact replica model of the animal in the Indian museum at the Buffalo Jump. I had been to a Buffalo Jump in Saskatchewan before, and although I was enchanted with the name I was not expecting a great deal and was therefore completely surprised at the fantastic history of this World Heritage Site.

In prehistoric times, before the horse was imported to the North American continent, Indian tribes hunted bison by driving the herds over the edge of a cliff. One thinks of the prairies as endless flat expanses of grassland that have no distinctive features, let alone cliffs. However this is far from the truth; the land is often scoured by deeply cut coulees or riverbeds and broken fissures that provide adequately high drops. Successful hunting in this manner was a feat of ingenuity and skill that far outweighs the later horseback hunting style. The ground approaching the cliff face must be sloping upwards so that the bison would not be alerted to the drop until the last possible moment, by which time the impetus of the stampeding herd behind would force the animals at the front to leap to their deaths. Stone cairns were erected in a great funnel-like pattern that led to the jump; the most skilled hunters would stalk the herd for days or even weeks; a failed attempt to drive them could result in the herd leaving the area for many months; patience was therefore of the utmost importance. Dressed in the skins of wolves, hunters would get sufficiently close to the herd; often one would take the skin of a baby and imitate the cries of a lost infant to attract the herd to the correct position. When the moment was right the hunters would discard their camouflage and stampede the herd into the funnel; members of the tribe would now step out from behind the stone cairns and drive the bison along in the funnel, the herd instinct forcing them to run into the trap. None were permitted to escape; even in times of plenty every last bison in the herd was slaughtered as the Indians believed that a survivor would tell all other bison of the tactic and thus prevent any future hunts. The successful nature of this hunt can be demonstrated by the excavation at the foot of the cliff; here archaeologists have uncovered a layer of bison bones thirty feet deep! Surprisingly the "Head Smashed In" name is not due to the thousands of buffalo that tumbled over the cliff but the result of one particular Indian brave who managed to get himself crushed to death at the foot of the drop!

At Medicine Hat we passed by the world's largest tepee, a huge skeletal steel structure several storeys high which dominates the skyline of the flat grassland as you approach the town. With the sunset flaring a fiery dominant red and faded pink on the huge darkening sky we headed out into the prairie, surrounded on all sides by burnished gold and shadowed oranges that delight the eye and lift the spirit. The sense of freedom that one experiences in such massive landscapes, where the horizon is endless, met only by the huge sweeping dome of the sky, is hard to explain, but the complete lack of confining structures, concrete and iron is exhilarating.

We came eventually to Saskatoon where we stopped for three days to catch up on old friends. This town, set in the very heart of the great prairies, is a strange sprawling place with a skyscrapered centre and every urban facility, but which manages to maintain an air of small town charm sadly lacking in so many other cities. Constructed on the banks of the wide Saskatchewan river it is a pretty place of clipped lawns and old trees, where you may find a faded memorial bandstand dedicated to the massive sacrifice of Canadian troops at Vimy and a huge university campus which caters for the many hundreds of agriculture students sent in from the provinces to maintain the legacy of farming that sustained the growth of this truly gargantuan country. Close by the city is the historical site of Batoche where a heavy-handed colonial administration stamped down with arrogant contempt on a provisional government instigated by the indigenous Metis. The white-painted wooden church still bears the bullet holes of the Maxim machine guns that were deployed against the civilian population, and a walk through the magnificent collection of memorabilia that is on display is a lesson in British manufacturing and export policy that quickly brings home the truth of how close our nations were in those not too distant days.

We left Saskatoon and headed south for the border, past more tiny farming towns guarded by the ever-present sentinel grain elevators. In gas stations and local stores permeated by the deep aroma of coffee, denim-clad farmers bemoaned the price of seed and the weather. Broken-down cabins and barns, listing drunkenly, could be seen on the horizons and the historical markers of buffalo rubbing stones and long forgotten forts were interspersed with that most unique North American art form of giant statues, a massive thirty-foot tall coffee pot, a man constructed from giant rolled bales of straw, and in Moose Jaw, obviously, the world's largest moose!

The town of Moose Jaw is a fascinating place; it is a city of grand architecture, square solid buildings with beautifully crafted decorations that look as if they were transplanted here on freight cars from the far end of the connecting railroad line which terminated in Chicago. If the buildings were not imported from Chicago, the gangsters certainly were! This small town once held the dubious record for more killings than New York; in the roaring twenties it was the favoured haunt of Al Capone, a centre for bootlegging operations conveniently close to the American border but outside of the sphere of the prohibition laws. During the construction of the railways in Canada many thousands of Chinese coolies had been imported as cheap labour; when the railroad was completed the government attempted to deport these workers and many hundreds of them promptly disappeared underground. In Moose Jaw that is not a figurative term; the whole of the town is riddled with a honeycomb of underground passages, tunnels and chambers from which Chinese laundries and sweatshops were run with sadistic relish by unscrupulous characters. When the gangsters arrived this labyrinth was a ready-made asset for their nefarious activities and they quickly took possession of the unseen maze, installing stills, brothels and speakeasy bars, secret doors and camouflaged exits in false boilers and laundry machinery. The going rate in 1920 for hooch and a woman for the night was two Canadian dollars; this dubious snippet of social history was so deeply resented by the townspeople that when I first visited Moose Jaw some ten years ago there were still some businesses and shops that refused to accept the Canadian two dollar bill due to its immoral associations!

I am sad to say that the experience of visiting these tunnels has been changed for the worse since my first visit. The beautiful station which held its original benches and decoration is now a wine supermarket and the old style elegance of the restaurant that had a magnificent original tin ceiling has been destroyed forever. The emphasis is now firmly on the theme park experience with animated characters and actor guides who play for laughs. You still get some of the more salient facts but I was rather sad that the old chap who had taken me around on my first visit and imparted his enthusiasm for the unique history had decided to take the money and run.

We left Moose Jaw heading south into the dreary brown and brackish Big Muddy Valley, a place of curious eroded buttes where Sitting Bull, Crazy Horse and seven hundred Sioux had eventually given up the struggle and returned to the USA and the confinement of reservation life. We crossed the border at the tiny post of Big Beaver, where despite my repeated polite requests for a souvenir the Canadian customs official resolutely refused to stamp my passport. Thirty yards further south we came upon an abrupt reminder of the new post-September eleventh regime in the States. The American customs official greeted us with the usual passive indifference, but close at his shoulder was a huge stony faced marine in full combat dress complete with side arm.

Satisfied that we were not an imminent threat to national security, they allowed us to pass into Montana. The sunset flared in broad perfectly horizontal bands of yellow and orange like a television test card, and we watched pelicans drifting lazily on a mirrored lake of polished gunmetal whilst we beat off great clouds of stinging midges and flies. Moonless nights in the prairies are of a total blackness that defies description, the car headlights lance a narrow path of vision down which you stare with concentrated attention, hoping to spot the shining reflective eyes and avoid collision with one of the dozens of white tail deer or pronghorn antelope which leap with suicidal abandon into the path of your vehicle.

North and South Dakota are the heart of the Indian territories; these are the states that hold the remnants of the Indian nations, gathered together now in small and often run-down reservation lands. South Dakota boasts the geographical centre of the States, along with many of the most well-known tourist attractions of North America, but North Dakota harbours a truly magnificent national park that seems to be neglected by the great majority of tourists. The two sections of the Theodore Roosevelt National Park are situated in North Dakota badlands, huge areas of eroded sediment deposited there from the youngest days of the Rockies. Centuries of rain, flood and wind have created a fantastic landscape littered with thousands of conical ridges that resemble upturned egg boxes decorated with multiple layers of coloured rock, each band representing the deposited debris of mountains destroyed millennia before. Bison roam freely here and herds may be seen perched between the juniper bushes on the steep slump formations of stone and clay. Meadowlarks sing their loud piercing songs in the clear unpolluted air and on the lower grasslands you may see bison nursing calves whilst well-fed coyotes walk nonchalantly through the herd.

Every few miles you will encounter prairie dog towns of such immense size they should really be called cities. These engaging rodents, about the size of a rabbit, are a strange cross between squirrel and rat; they build their colonies on open flat ground where they excavate deep multi-chambered living quarters, each entrance marked clearly by a neat pile of excavated silver sand so that when your eye sweeps over the whole extent of the area it looks as if several thousand bags of sugar have been spilt on the dark, sun-scorched earth. They graze continuously, maintaining a nervous vigilance for the coyotes which prey upon them; at the approach of danger they jump up onto their back legs, straining their heads backwards as they emit piercing squeaks of alarm before darting rapidly into the safety of their burrow. Theodore Roosevelt said, "I never would have been president if it had not been for my experiences in North Dakota." He came there as a young man with the intention of enjoying big game hunting but the buffalo were already gone and he stayed to run various cattle ranches, eventually instigating some of the first ever conservation in America.

We left North Dakota and drove into the gravel back roads of Wyoming, long straight ribbons of unpacked stone where you pull a great cloud of boiling dust in your wake and your eye becomes fixated on the point in the far distance where the road pierces the distant horizon. Stretching away on both sides are great endless tracts of parched grasslands inhabited by huge grazing herds of pronghorn antelope.

In the late blue-black twilight of evening with glowering thunderheads brewing in the sky and gusts of icy windswept rain slapping into the car we approached our destination of the Devils Tower. For any one who remembers the Steven Spielberg film *Close Encounters of the Third Kind*, the atmospheric energy of an imminent thunderstorm over the massive flat-topped thrusting cone of the Devil's Tower is pure Hollywood imagery. This is a truly remarkable feature of nature, the core of an extinct volcano, surging up from the ground in hundreds of huge vertically straight columns of rock that form an almost perfect upturned yoghurt pot shape. The earth in the near vicinity of the tower is a deep rich red and orange and the many trees which grow at its base hide the great field of shattered and broken columns which have fallen away from the tower since it was left exposed to the elements by the erosion of the surrounding softer ground. The flat grey faces of the columns are a softly mottled blue, green and yellow caused by the growth of lichens, and the angular cornices are so perfectly shaped they appear to have been carved by the hands of master masons engaged in the construction of a medieval cathedral. As you pass around the huge base of the tower amongst trees where the bark has been stripped away by gnawing porcupines you realise that each of the faces that you are presented with has a different character. The Indians believe that this mountain was shaped by a great spirit bear who was chasing some brothers who had stolen his tail, the great scarred columns resulting from his tearing claws as he attempted to reclaim his appendage from the men who had hidden on the flat top of the tower.

We stopped briefly in Sundance, the town which provided the pseudonym for Harry Longabaugh, the legendary Sundance Kid; its only remarkable feature were the number of specialist shops selling huge arrays of skulls and pelts from every form of North American wildlife from grizzly bears to gophers. We wound our way southwards through areas of heavy pine and cedar forest and eventually resurfaced in South Dakota at the Jewel Cave National Monument. Just like the Carlsbad Caverns in New Mexico there is not the slightest visible hint of this massive subterranean complex on the surface, but the labyrinthine tangle of passages and chambers is second only to the truly gigantic Mammoth Cave in Kentucky. It boasts the usual array of nightmarish stalactite and stalagmite formations eerily dripping cold calcite-rich water from the ever-growing formations. But it has two very specific features that I had not seen before, it is called Jewel Cave for the almost complete covering of geode-type crystals that smother every available surface in a deep encrusting blanket of sparkling oddity. More impressive but less widespread are the long bacon formations that hang from the ceilings in vivid cream and red strips, perfectly replicated giant rashers of streaky bacon, twisted as if they had been pulled away from the other lengths in a chilled vacuum-packed plastic package. The cave also boasts the ability to breathe; the vast areas of space situated far below ground expel or inhale air dependent on the levels of pressure at the surface, a monotonous roar of moving air that drones in your ears and pushes the glass doors of the entrance firmly shut so that the ranger must exert his full strength to prise it open and grant access.

Our next stop was further south again, still in SD: the Mammoth Site close by the town of Hot Springs is a wondrous archaeological attraction of astonishing uniqueness. Somewhere around twenty-six thousand years ago, over a six or seven hundred year period, upwards of a hundred Woolly and Columbian Mammoths managed to entrap themselves in a spring-fed sinkhole; attracted there by the water they would slither down the steep sides of the hole and die from exhaustion whilst attempting to extricate themselves from the mire. In 1974 excavation for a new housing development uncovered the upper surface of the now fossilised hole complete with its hundred mammoth skeletons and various other prehistoric fauna such as giant short-faced bears, wolves and llama! The ongoing archaeological dig has so far reached down some sixty to eighty feet and the giant skeletons are left in their original positions supported by undisturbed pedestals of rock. The massive domed skulls, long curved tusks and giant molar teeth are clearly visible at dozens of locations in the pit; the skeletons are so perfectly preserved that the broken legs or fractured skulls that caused death can be clearly identified. It is as if you had stumbled onto a spy hole into the far distant past where you may view the last doomed struggles of these giant beasts as they fought in vain for their lives, the assembled predator wolves and bears sometimes tearing at their extended legs or faces as they reached up desperately from the steep slippery sides of the pit.

We stumbled upon the opening night of a three-day cowboy poetry festival in the town of Hot Springs; slow-talking men with rugged faces and large stetson hats read eloquent verses about life on the range or comical rhyming anecdotes relating to the cowboy phenomenon. Most impressive for us was the extremely old gentleman dressed in a cleanly pressed Roy Rogers-type cowboy outfit with high-heeled boots, patched trousers and chequered shirt complete with fanciful embroidery on the pockets and a steer's head bootlace tie. He perched himself on the stool in front of the microphone, and strumming on his polished guitar and nodding his head in time, he drawled out a series of original soft melodies that shining fictional comic book cowboys had supposedly sung to lull cattle during the night and prevent possible stampedes. It was a pure microcosm of nineteen-fifties America, a time of simple pleasures and stereotypical images that were complete untruths; it was made all the more astounding for me by the presence of an even older chap who I had assumed to be the singer's father but turned out to be his brother, an absolute double for the grizzly-looking Walter Huston in *The Treasure of the Sierra Madre*.

We passed through the Custer State Park several times during the next few days whilst we zigzagged back and forth around the closely situated attractions of South Dakota. This relatively small park is home to a very large herd of bison; they roam freely within the rolling, unfenced grasslands of the park and it is perhaps the only place in the world where you might actually see a genuine Buffalo Round-up. Each year the herd is gathered and corralled by genuine cowboys, inspected and inoculated and thinned through sales to an acceptable size for the land and forage available. You may view the bison here at an even closer range than in Yellowstone; huge lone bulls standing in the road will eye you with disinterest, declining to move before they have finished chewing their mouthful of cropped grass, their great humped shoulders clad in the dense matted fur that falls from their necks to mid-point on their backs like a draped cloak of coconut matting. We stopped to photograph a truly massive bull lying quietly at the side of the road and whilst I shot frame after frame of film he lazily curled his powerful head backwards, lifting his hind leg, and rolling out his huge, tacky, saliva-covered tongue to clean his belly, he immediately released a huge cloud of swarming flies and midges from beneath his legs that swarmed with angry buzzing at the intrusion. The agony that such tremendous amounts of biting insects must inflict on these animals is quite unimaginable; here in the wooded slopes of the black hills there is at least plenty of timber to rub against, which may provide some relief; roadsigns and crash barriers also provide convenient backscratchers but up in the prairies of Saskatchewan and Manitoba before roads were built and where trees were scarce, the buffalo would be hard-pressed to find something suitable to scratch themselves on. The few large boulders that had been deposited on the plains as the ice sheets retreated were worn perfectly smooth on their exposed surfaces by the thousands of buffalo which visited them to rasp off their old coats and salve their burning, irritated skins. So many animals would use these rocks that they have been left in deeply excavated hollows as if they were situated in their own protective moat.

Amongst the big horn sheep, mountain goats and elk, the other great wildlife attraction of the Custer State Park are the "Begging Burros"! These are donkeys, which live freely in the park and are totally habituated to the human visitors; they have quickly learned that grass is a poor second to the fast food alternatives found in vehicles and in the pockets of tourists. They are delightful characters who force their large dusty heads into the open windows of your car, imploring you to feed them with deeply sad eyes or cheeky nudges of the muzzle; they curl their tensile upper lips back over their nostrils to hold in your scent and in doing so they present such a huge toothy grin that one cannot help but offer up the goods!

To the north of Custer are the largest of all giant sculptures in North America: Mount Rushmore and the even bigger Crazy Horse Memorial. Rushmore is everything that one expects; the polished granite faces of Washington, Jefferson, Lincoln and Roosevelt expertly crafted into the mountainside by Gutzon Borglum are just as you have always seen them in every encyclopaedia or reference book. In the clear sunlight the faces are magnificently solid, flawless recreations projecting the character and humanity of the individual presidents out onto the thousands of assembled visitors. At night when the massive floodlights are brought into action the sculpture takes on a much more ephemeral quality; the complete surrounding blackness and the clearly defined shadows produce a ghostly apparition as if the faces were a projected image floating freely in space. I was greatly interested to witness the nightly ceremony of lowering the national flag, attended by a large crowd wrapped in duvets and car blankets, the national anthem sung with complete sincerity, not at all the half-hearted, apologetic effort that we Brits achieve. The ranger officiating over the ceremony suggested that any veterans of the forces who were present should come down onto the stage of the amphitheatre beneath the mountain so that they might assist in the lowering and folding of the flag. The assembled circle of middle-aged men clad in baseball hats and bomber jackets, chewing gum, looked completely incongruous in that majestic surrounding, but as they introduced themselves and their service records via the ranger's microphone the crowd applauded warmly and I was moved to reflect, that whilst we here in Britain manage a decent level of support and turnout for Remembrance, recognition of our ex-servicemen and women is sadly not an everyday occurrence such as you find in the States.

The Crazy Horse Memorial, some twenty miles away from Rushmore, is a work in progress. The gigantic sculpture of the legendary Indian warrior would swallow the heads at Rushmore several times over and is said to be the world's largest! It was the dream of a man called Korczak Ziolkowski, without a penny of government funding; he and his family have been working on the project for sixty years. At this time only the nine-storey-high face has been completed and I shall be long dead before Crazy Horse finally stretches out his arm above the head of his stallion and points to where his "dead are buried".

Ziolkowski himself is already dead, but his large family are still dedicated to completing his life's work; in the huge and fascinating Indian museum that is part of the memorial I was left in awe of this man's dedication to providing a lasting memorial to the native Indian; with broken-down second-hand machinery and rickety old ladders strung up the mountainside he had laboured alone for years until his sons and daughters had grown old enough to lend a hand. The faded and scratched film footage of him with the Indian chiefs who sanctioned the plan said it all; here the Indians, some of whom had actually fought Custer at the Little Bighorn, were all dressed in dark sombre suits, a silent reminder that they had succumbed to the savage pressure of our so-called civilisation, whilst Ziolkowski was adorned in traditional fringed buckskin clothing, Indian jewellery and pony tail!

Neil Pepper MBE, FRGS

Close by Rushmore is the town of Keystone, a mass of hotels and boarding houses for travellers visiting the many state attractions. A seasonally adapted town that hibernates in winter and surges with business in summer, it is home to the "Rolling Thunder" festival, the largest gathering of Harley Davidson motorcycles in the world. So many bikers descend upon this town in summer that often it is necessary to travel into the next two adjoining states to find any free accommodation! The dozens of shops along the main street are packed to overflowing with Harley merchandise and biker apparel, racks of tee-shirts proclaiming every imaginable allegiance, pressed metal signs with abusive slogans, shot glasses, sunglasses, knives, knuckledusters and Viking helmets emblazoned with the winged logo of the Milwaukee company.

A few minutes outside of town you may take your choice from any amount of theme parks where you may encounter anything from hand-reared billy goats to Komodo dragons! My particular favourite was Bear Country USA, a huge area of fenced land that contained over two hundred free-roaming black bears and multiple wolf packs. In a country where almost every second attraction is said to be the largest, longest or tallest in the world it is not surprising that this is said to be the most bears collected together in any one place; whether that is true I have no idea, but the animals are well-fed and seem content, they ramble around the huge enclosures, digging, swimming or scratching as the mood takes them, bears and wolves mingling as they wish although we did witness one unfortunate bear being attacked and chased by several very large wolves!

The real "aahh" factor of this place is the pens which hold the site-bred animals: there are infant bobcats, wolves and mountain lions but the undisputed show-stealers are the twenty tiny bear cubs held together in one large nursery pen; these mischievous bundles of energised fur maraud around their home in playful abandonment completely unaware of the delight they produce in the assembled onlookers; their frantic tumbling antics and impromptu naps are straight from the dreams of anyone who ever owned or loved a teddy bear, and after two hours Debbie eventually managed to persuade me that we should be on our way!

We headed off eastwards in search of the famous Wall Drug Store. This is an oddity of American enterprise which one has to admire. In 1931 a man called Ted Hustead purchased the only drug store in a tiny town named Wall; situated in the huge open expanse of the South Dakota prairies it was truly "the middle of nowhere", freezing in winter and unbearably hot in summer, a population of just over three hundred. The Husteads struggled along barely scratching a living for five years or so and then the wife had the idea of advertising free iced water for frazzled travellers grinding their way across the continent on the nearby Route 16. They fixed up a whole bunch of signs advertising their free iced water along the highway and never looked back! Today the Wall Drug as it is known covers several blocks; on an average summer's day they have twenty thousand visitors and serve five thousand glasses of iced water! The signs along the new Interstate Highway 90 stretch for a hundred miles in both directions; welcome points of focus in the flat dull landscape, they still tempt you with free iced water as well as many other attractions, "five-cent coffee", "free doughnuts for veterans", "see the T Rex". Hustead's original shop has developed into a huge sprawling maze of shops and dining rooms; it is an extravaganza of the curious, odd and unusual; there are animated life-size orchestras and automated characters who will play country and western songs or sell you snake oil for the price of a quarter. The restaurants are hung with fine oil paintings or collections of Indian artefacts; you may find a six-foot stuffed rabbit, a singing gorilla or dancing reindeer, and every space is filled with memorabilia or photos of people who have taken one of the free "Wall Drug" signs to the furthest reaches of the earth, including both poles!

A few miles directly South of Wall is the entrance to the Badlands National Park, a huge area of wilderness with some of the most unique scenery I have ever come across. Named "Badlands" by both the Dakota Indians and the French trappers who found the area "bad land" to cross, they hold similar cone and slump formations such as those found in North Dakota, but there the similarity ends. This is an area of enormous scale, a massive Martian red landscape serrated and ridged as if ploughed by the hand of God. The intricate wind and rain-eroded spires imitate the battlements and crenellations of massive fantasy Camelot-like castles. There are valleys where huge pedestals of scoured sandstone appear to have been carved into fanciful collections of statues, where your imagination and the passing clouds may seek out unlimited combinations of light and shade in the vibrant layered colours of purple iron oxide, white volcanic ash and orange clay. There are incredible fossil deposits in these ancient strata; perfect examples of sabre-tooth tiger, three-toed horses and crocodiles can be found in the now exposed former seabed and long-lost marshlands.

If you leave the main area of the park via the Sage Creek Road you pass through an area of native grassland frequented by lone bison, jack rabbits and prairie dogs and eventually you will arrive at the tiny settlement of "Scenic". If you have a taste for the unusual then Scenic is a destination you should seek out. It is a run-down, dilapidated near ghost town of few people but with two unique features. The first is an open-air gaol, or pokey, its thick rusted bars and huge lock sturdy and stentorian. This lock-up is situated conveniently next door to the only bar in town, the "Longhorn Saloon". The exterior is decorated with dozens of bleached steer skulls and the large battered sign on the roof proudly proclaims "Indians Welcome"; through the barred windows the neon Budweiser signs throw a vague light into the dark and dingy interior and your mind is filled with visions of sawdust-covered floors, spittoons and knife fights!

A short distance further south from Scenic brings you to the least visited area of the Badlands National Park, where you may slither and slide your way along barely passable mud tracks into Sheep Mountain Table. If you make it to the end of the road up the ever-increasing gradient and through the sludge and mire of deeply rutted chicanes you will be rewarded with views from a high vantage point out over several astonishing valleys that defy description. Thousands of years of erosion have left these canyons filled with uncountable spires crowded together in such close formation that the only way to describe them is as if they were the bristles of a well-worn and upturned broom head.

Leaving the Badlands behind us we continued south into the Pine Ridge Indian Reservation, a landscape of gently rolling hills blanketed in deep flowing seas of prairie grass that sway and shiver to every gentle breeze that sweeps it. Our destination was Wounded Knee. Here, at the very end of the genocidal campaign waged against the native Indians of North America, the white settlers managed to perpetrate a final barbaric act in the massacre of almost a whole tribe of starving, demoralised and sickening families.

Inspired by the visions of a new Messiah, many Indian tribes had adopted the Ghost Dance religion; it promised the removal of the white settlers, the return of the buffalo and the old ways of life and the resurrection of the dead. Those taking part in ghost dances would entrance themselves in days of non-stop dancing, eventually falling to the ground in an exhausted stupor where they would hallucinate about their long-lost friends and relatives. Shirts bearing magical symbols were produced for the dancers and those wearing them believed they would be protected from the bullets of the white man's guns. The national government and the army became increasingly nervous about what they saw as an imminent rebellion and stamped down ruthlessly on all ghost dances and tribes known to be practising the new religion.

A tribe of Minneconjous led by Chief Big Foot surrendered to the US Cavalry and were moved to a location on the Wounded Knee creek during Christmas of 1890; whilst attempting to disarm the warriors shots were fired and the cavalry brought the early Hotchkiss machine guns to bear on the assembled tribe. One hundred and fifty-three men, women and children are known to have died and estimates of the total dead who crawled away to die of their wounds or were left to die of exposure in open wagons during a fierce blizzard take the total up to around three hundred and fifty.

The massacre site at Wounded Knee sits in a large hollowed bowl surrounded by low hills; the story is set out in text on both sides of a large painted billboard and in the large script of the title, the word "Massacre" has been painted onto a board and screwed into place as a correction, so that I wondered what it had originally said beneath? Close by on the hillside is the mass grave and memorial enclosed in a wire fence with dozens of native symbols of fabric, animal bones and jewellery tied onto the links; young children in worn clothes wait at the gate of the cemetery to beg for donations for their basketball club and in the nearby village of run-down single-storey wooden homes, the yards littered with redundant cars and children's bikes, hand-made painted signs have been erected along the roadside imploring speeding motor-ists to "stop killing our children". The militant slogan "The WAR is not over" painted around the inside of a circular concrete dome that may once have been a community centre but was now being used by a family selling native jewellery made me wonder if there would ever be a way to appease these people for their immeasurable loss.

We turned north and threaded our way back through the full breadth of South Dakota to the legendary town of Deadwood. What a feast of imagination can be con-jured up on the back of this evocative name: Wild Bill Hickock, Calamity Jane, the famous stage route to Cheyenne! The small museum was packed to overflowing with wonderful memorabilia from all the famous residents; in the Number Ten Saloon Wild Bill is shot in the back whilst playing cards three times daily and in the huge Boot Hill Cemetery perched high on a cliff overlooking the full sweep of the town you may find the grave of Calamity Jane, a direct neighbour to the magnificent polished bronze memorial on Hickock`s final resting place. I had expected another Tombstone-style town, original structures, wooden boardwalks, dusty roads, the frontier held in per-petuity. I couldn't have been more wrong and was completely unprepared for the dozen or more slick casinos and shiny restaurants that lined the beautifully paved main street. It is as if a tiny themed piece of Las Vegas had been dropped here in the Black Hills. Showpiece of the town is the "sports bar" owned by the actor Kevin Cost-ner, who hailed from the nearby town of Spearfish. In this three-storey establishment you may eat, drink and, of course, gamble, surrounded by glass-cased costumes and props from all of his many films.

Despite my disappointment at the lack of originality we enjoyed a very late Sat-urday night watching a redneck band from Texas performing in the smoke-ridden, sawdust-scattered back room of the Number Ten Saloon. Whilst the energetic drum-mer thumped out a series of foot stomping polka style tunes on drums, harmonica and scrubbing board; the dance floor became a heaving tangle of violently colliding bodies and high-pitched rebel yells! We made the acquaintance of several people, a young bride to be, her tee-shirt printed with a checklist of salacious exploits which she had to complete before the end of her hen night, graciously allowed me to remove my shirt for her and subsequently sign my name in the appropriate box! A young couple spending an anniversary weekend away from the kids chatted with us; the husband, a builder by trade, questioned us closely on the use of bricks as a construction method and the "big fires" we had had in London. Debbie and I sat in bemused confusion, wondering if we had missed some significant disaster whilst we had been away, and it was only when our companion referred to the "rats" that I realised he was asking me about 1666 and the Great Fire! How does one politely tell someone that his or her grasp of English current affairs is roughly three hundred years out of date?

On a bright Sunday morning we headed out on the interstate highway, crossing westwards over the state border into Wyoming. I had been tempted by a note in a guidebook, which said the huge area of open plains between the Big Horn Mountains and the Black Hills was rarely visited by anyone! So at Gillette we left the security of the huge number ninety Interstate freeway and headed off into the russet-red and orange gravel of the Wyoming back routes in search of the hamlets of Spotted Horse and Otter. Some five hours later I was beginning to realise why it was that no one ventured here! We found Spotted Horse, a single bar, telephone kiosk and large statue of a rearing Appaloosa horse set in vast open grassland, but after this the maps became useless. The gravel tracks became more and more narrow, their orange ribbon snaking away to the horizon over endless ridges like a huge funicular railway. We never did find Otter! Eventually, low on fuel, I abandoned the maps and fell back on the compass, navigating slowly northwards in the hope of intersecting the main highway I knew existed somewhere out of sight.

With the fuel gauge reading empty, our reserve cans already used, I was greatly relieved to break out onto the highway within a couple of miles of Busby in the North Cheyenne Indian Reservation. We arrived at the only store in town to find the gas pumps redundant, rusting and empty! We turned back onto the highway heading for the gas station I knew existed some thirty miles distant at the Crow Agency. One hopes against hope that the gas will last until you feel the dreaded shudders which precede the final chugging death of the engine. We coasted to a stop on the roadside, the sultry silence of the warm afternoon enveloping us quickly; it is always a shock when you realise that the enclosing shell of the vehicle is not the safe warm cocoon that you thought it to be.

We had stopped within yards of a driveway that led up a small hill to a low single-storey wooden house with two battered old cars outside. I trudged up the dirt drive and stepped up onto the porch; there was no sound, no TV or radio playing, just the chirruping of unseen crickets. A young cat lay sprawled along the bottom of the screen door; I pushed her aside whilst she stretched lazily at my touch. My knock on the door was answered with a cry of 'come in' and I gingerly pushed open the door, trying not to step too far inside. We were in the very centre of an Indian reservation yet for some reason I was surprised to find Indians! Two round-faced women and a very sunburnt man with a craggy weathered face, all had the predictable long jet-black hair; they looked at me, I looked at them; they were seated at a large table eating a meal, the plates of food squeezed tightly amongst a large collection of finely crafted ceramic figures, intricate tableaux that depicted Indians in all manner of actions and dress and which covered almost the whole surface of the table. I explained my situation and they provided a can of gas without any great fuss, as if it was an everyday occurrence for their lunch to be interrupted by a stranded

Englishman. It was only when I returned the empty can to their living room that they curiously asked where I was from, warned me about the remoteness of the area and suggested that I would find it best to buy just a gallon or two of gas at the "expensive" Crow Agency filling station! Smiling broadly and marvelling at the incredible luck of this unexpected rescue I drove away with a warmed heart.

Having been rescued by Indians it was rather ironic that our next port of call was the Custer Memorial at the Little Bighorn battlefield. The stone obelisk, which marks the site of the famous last stand, sits perched high on a grassy hill where the dry prairie grass wafts quietly against the granite of the individual headstones. It is an area of quiet solitude where the bright blue sky reaches down to the earth unimpeded in every direction, where larks call and insects chatter, a place of beauty where the rolling plains are split by the meandering silt-laden Bighorn river and the arid brown and yellow grass is relieved by vivid green trees which thrive along the water's edge. When Custer led his troop of 7th Cavalry into this river valley, hoping to entrap the women and children and thereby entice the Indian warriors to surrender, he was confronted with a village of tepees which stretched five miles; the resultant massacre of his entire column as they attempted to retreat has become legendary. Study any painting or drawing of this event and it will always show the figure of Custer with his long blond hair billowing in the wind as he stands on the summit of a hill, gun in hand, his troopers dying at his feet as the Indians surge around the horses that the soldiers shot to provide a breastwork. The only sign of the horrific terror that descended on these men is the stone markers scattering out from the Last Stand Memorial, each stone representing the place where the fleeing soldiers met their deaths. One can hear no echoes here; the land is indifferent to the events and if you seek Custer you must look in the museum which houses a collection of his clothing and other belongings.

We passed from Montana back into Wyoming, heading south as night fell. In the early morning of the following day we climbed into the Bighorn Mountains, spectacular alpine scenery where every twist and turn of the hairpin roads opens new vistas of endless forest and meadow; on the high passes when you stop to squint out into the breathless far horizon friendly striped chipmunks run between your feet and cling to your trouser legs, soliciting a fix for their fast food addiction. On one of the very highest ridges close to Route 14 you may view an authentic "medicine wheel" perched on the mountainside; this ancient Indian symbol is constructed of stones positioned in the shape of a wagon wheel, the stone spokes radiating out to cairns on the circular perimeter. Even now we remain unaware of the true significance of this mystical structure; it may have been used in religious ceremonies long forgotten or may possibly have been a migratory navigation aid, the spokes aligning with various significant places of worship or potential hunting grounds. Whatever it was used for, its position high up on the very top of a remote mountainside appears to be the primary reason that it has survived. The steel cables of the fence which protect it are hung with charms, offerings and magic symbols, many containing fragments of animal skin and bones, bird skulls and feathers.

We descended from the Bighorn Mountains, and arriving at Cody we plunged into the famous Buffalo Bill Historical Center. This is a huge complex of fascinating museums dedicated to the larger-than-life character of William Cody: the five museums contain treasures ranging from Cody's many personal belongings to Calamity Jane's guns and the original Deadwood Stage; you may view wonderful Indian artefacts that include ghost shirts, buffalo skin bonnets or necklaces made from dozens of grizzly bear claws; the massive collection of firearms overflows from hundreds of glass cases into a basement annexe and the sculpture and art galleries house magnificent paintings and bronzes by Frederic Remington and C. M. Russell. If you have a taste for the Wild West this is without doubt "the" museum to visit! Cody may have been partly responsible for the wanton destruction of the great bison herds but there is no denying his awesome persona; one wonders who else could ever have concocted the idea of the live Wild West Show and then signed Chief Sitting Bull, conqueror of the legendary Custer, to appear twice daily?

If you leave Cody on Route 296 you pass through the Shoshone National Forest on "Chief Joseph Scenic Byway"; this high mountain road, lined with signs warning travellers they are in grizzly bear country, winds its way along the approximate route that Joseph took when he and the Nez Perce fought a desperate but ultimately successful eighteen-hundred-mile retreat from the ever-pursuing US Cavalry.

When you descend from the Colter Pass, eight thousand feet above sea level, you are entering the indescribable beauty of Yellowstone National Park!

No matter how often I visit Yellowstone I am always overawed by its spectacular beauty; each time I find some new thermal feature that I had overlooked during previous visits and the wildlife encounters are always an indescribable pleasure.

The great thermal caldera beneath the park erupts onto the surface at hundreds of locations in whispering steam vents, boiling mud pots, bubbling volcanoes and pressurised geysers; in some areas where the mineral-rich water has deposited its heavy contents, the richly coloured stone has formed into frozen cascade waterfalls feeding into algae-laden terraces where pungent sulphur steam rises in great billowing clouds. Old Faithful shoots its high plume of superheated water into the air with clockwork regularity and in the middle and upper geyser basins, bison sleep sprawled on their sides in piles of sulphur dust or roam amongst the boiling pools of crystal-clear water, risking horrendous death from scalding should they break through the fragile crust.

Some of the geysers have formed grotesque twisted statues of stone above their vents, each new eruption adding an infinitesimal new facet to the work in progress; there are deep funnel-shaped pools of water that contain rich beds of algae living in the varying degrees of heat as the water reaches the upper surface so that the beautiful coloration of the plume changes from clear turquoise blue to soft yellow to deep orange in such perfect fading shades that the eye can hardly believe the reality. At the Grand Prismatic Spring the beds of algae that surround the huge circular pool splinter out from the edges toward the centre of the pool in drifts of orange and red that resemble large licking flames sometimes seen painted on the bodywork of fast cars. The Yellowstone, from which the park takes its name, is split into a plunging canyon at one point; two high waterfalls recklessly hurl millions of tons of surging white water down through steep-sided and crumbling ravine walls that shine brightly lemon and gold in the dazzling water-sprayed sunlight.

The magnificent wildlife is everywhere: you may witness bison herds plunging into rivers where they swim with their massive heads held above the water, their huge eyes rolling fearfully in their exertions, followed by the joyous rolling, rubbing and nuzzling in dirt and dust when the far bank is reached. There are huge ponderous grizzly bears who plod thoughtfully up the steep sides of mountains digging for roots and grubs as their sensitive noses locate each new delicacy, great clouds of displaced earth and debris erupting into the air from their powerful giant claws. Brown bears gorge contentedly on large stands of berry-laden bushes, and from high vantage points you may view sweeping valleys filled with hundreds of elk feeding on the lower slopes, unaware of your presence, the magnificent whistling calls of the bulls shepherding their harems reaching clearly up to your delighted ears. And of course there are wolves! If you have time and if you have patience you may wait in the Lamar Valley, home to the Widows Peak Pack, the most accessible of the parks eleven reintroduced family units containing between them over one hundred and seventy animals; here you will hold your breath painfully and screw the binoculars tightly into your eyes whilst you revel in the glory of a genuinely wild wolf pack interacting in their native environment; for an animal lover there can be few more rewarding moments!

If you leave Yellowstone via the south entrance you pass directly into the adjacent National Park of Grand Teton; this remarkable linear mountain range has no foothills, and its snow-capped serrated peaks that are reflected in perfect mirror image in the huge lakes at their base resemble a giant upturned rip saw; there are deer and antelope, coyote and bighorns and in the low-lying areas adjacent to the snake river, at the aptly named Moose Junction, you may see the huge antlers and muscled necks of bull moose above the tops of the low purple-tinted brambles and green willows.

We bypassed the huge luxury ski resort of Jackson Hole and passed eastwards over the border into Idaho, threading our way slowly through winding gravel byways to eventually stay the night in Idaho Falls, an unremarkable industrialised flat city split by the Snake River, where signs outside every restaurant and fast food outlet

187

proudly proclaim "Idaho Potatoes available". The following day, free of the city limits, passing into green agricultural land we swept past huge farmhouses, with carefully manicured lawns, barred iron gates and fluttering stars and stripes; one home had a large brightly painted farm trailer positioned outside with an equally large professionally produced sign which read "Stack dead terrorists here". I began to remember all the tales I had heard about Idaho being the preferred state of survivalists, with a larger than normal percentage of gun-owning white Anglo-Saxon Protestants; we drove on quickly ...

We stopped briefly in Arco, a small town of nineteen-fifties' architecture which lays claim to having been the very first nuclear-powered town in the world! Futuristic visions of labour-saving kitchens, silent cars and efficiently heated homes were posted proudly on information boards detailing the atomic energy boom! As you leave Arco to the west the sky at the horizon becomes noticeably hazy and the air quality muggy and dense; huge amounts of pollution generated on the far distant west coast are said to collect here due to a peculiarity of geographical and meteorological conditions. I couldn't help wondering if it wasn't more likely to have been a by-product of the giant nuclear power plant squatting on the horizon like a brooding oblong black and red monster.

The Craters of the Moon National Monument sits below the great cloud of murky polluted air but does not detract from the awesome nature of these vast lava beds. The tremendous volcanic action which produced this incredible landscape is said to have ceased only two thousand years ago; one can hardly comprehend the shattering explosive energy that spewed out of the earth's crust here as it literally tore apart and bled molten lava. There are seven hundred and fifty thousand acres of lava-coated landscape within the confines of this national monument, a truly alien lunar landscape of twisted and tortured shapes which defy imagination; there are endless carpets of folded slithering lava, its enveloping forward progress frozen in time like a thousand curling waves breaking on a flat seashore; elsewhere you find huge cinder cones in the shape of sooty chimney pots or lampshades, some blasted open, the tumbled serrated debris scattered wildly around its circular base. There are deep caves where your torch barely provides adequate illumination; clear ice can be found in open crevices on the floor and the clammy cold air crawls on your face and exposed skin, and beneath your feet the brittle razor-edged lava creates a jangling, tinkling symphony of broken porcelain and bone china. There are magnificent lava tubes with high vaulted ceilings that arch seventy or eighty feet above your head, swirling and rotating in multiple petrified ribs of mottled blue, orange and red decoration where the insulated inner lava fell away from the cooled outer surface. The huge sloping cones of the larger craters are covered in complete blankets of soft black lava granules and ash, speckled with uncountable tiny white and yellow wild flower blooms; each mountain appears as if wrapped in a delicate lace-embroidered velvet cloak.

Turning north onto Route 75 we passed through neat towns with multiple antique shops and coffee houses where people went about their business with torpid nonchalance; in Sun Valley the postmistress declined to terminate her telephone call and continued to whisper reams of salacious town gossip whilst she stuck stamps onto my letters! We climbed into the foothills of the Saw Tooth Mountains and were soon enveloped in the now familiar pristine alpine beauty. We passed through Stanley and headed west into Salmon River Mountains in the beautiful pastel, shimmering, dust-heavy light of late afternoon. A briefly glimpsed road sign offered us the prospect of a short-cut and we plunged off into tiny gravel roads pressed in on both sides by the dense shadowy green of cedar and spruce trees. A large signboard in a clearing told us that we had entered an area for the experimental reintroduction of wolves; these packs, it said, were protected from hunting, but could be "withdrawn" at any time whilst they were regarded as an experiment! We squinted hard into the dense foliage as we passed by slowly on the soft gravel; we never did see any wolves but as the twilight settled and a steady light rain began to fall we entered an area of dark, menacing groves where we encountered several solitary hunters in full camouflage outfits. Sitting motionless in the undergrowth at the roadside, the rain dripping from the peaks of their baseball caps onto their plastic-covered shoulders, menacing high-powered rifles cradled protectively against their chests, their cheeks extended with what I imagined was chewing tobacco, they watched us with sullen half-closed eyes as we passed by. I in turn watched them carefully in the rear-view mirror.

Our short-cut turned out to be an unexpected detour through uninhabited, dark and foreboding river valleys that were not on any of our maps; when night closed in on us we counted the miles from the speedometer after we passed a sign which promised McCall in thirty-five miles, only to be crushed with disappointment when we arrived at the thirty-fifth mile and found a further sign also saying that McCall was still thirty-five miles distant! Fighting the heavy four-wheel-drive Jeep on twisting gravel roads that hang on the very edge of steep valley walls when you are fatigued, when the brakes are barely adequate to hold the vehicle on steep gradients even at the most minimal speed and the blackness of the impenetrable forest heaves down on you like a crushing burden, all you can think of is a place to stop. The destination becomes everything in your mind; fingers tight on the wheel, jaw clenched, you fight the heavy eyelids, the knotted and abused muscles in your neck and shoulders, and focus completely on the short tunnel of light that cuts the black threatening forest. The relief that you feel when you reach that destination is wonderful; it is not something I recommend for every day that you drive in the back routes of Idaho, but it certainly makes an unforgettable memory. As it turned out, we arrived in the town of McCall from a direction I could not have foreseen and our first point of human contact was a late night convenience store; whilst Debbie sought directions to the nearest motel I was amazed to see three beautifully mature red foxes, their coats shining thickly red and vibrant, come to sit before the front door of the shop! This turned out to be part of a nightly ritual which involved the shop assistant, a young, friendly and very helpful lady, feeding the assembled foxes with items of fast food that were to be discarded at the completion of the day's trading: we watched in fascination as she placed eggs on the ground and the foxes gently picked them up and departed!

We stayed the night in McCall, a pleasant little town on the shores of Payette Lake, a resort centre for upmarket wilderness experiences and outdoor activities complete with golf courses, water sports and expensive shops, all a little too slick and tailor-made for my own tastes, and we set out in bright sunshine the following morning, the memory of the previous night's dark journey fading fast. From McCall you may pass northwards on Route 95 and then thread your way eastwards into the Hell's Canyon National Recreation Area, a massive expanse of wilderness centred on the rushing Snake River which plunges through valley walls eight thousand feet deep.

To reach the rim you must drive ever upwards on winding switchback hairpin roads where each new rise offers the false promise of a view into the incredible torn crevice of red earth, peering into the dusty, warmed air the multiple ridges and peaks of the mountains create an optical illusion which makes them appear foreshortened and devoid of any perspective so that they present to the eye like flat painted images similar to those produced in China or Japan. Autumn had a firm grip on the trees and your eye was assaulted with riotous clumps of colour where the wind swept the dying leaves and displayed their magnificent burnished gold, dappled honey, crisp amber and shining silver like the rotating slides of a giant kaleidoscope.

At Cottonwood we visited the world's largest beagle, a huge wooden sculpture that reminded me of the Trojan Horse, set close to the highway where a husband and wife turn out chainsaw carvings of cats and dogs as decorations for garden and porch. A few miles further north, tempted by a sign, we detoured off the main highway into the picturesque small town of Winchester in search of wolves! The Wolf Center close by the town had two packs of captive-bred wolves that were obviously far too intelligent to venture out from their shady dens in the sultry heat of the afternoon, and we left having seen only the huge wooden Winchester rifle which hung above the gates of the town park! We ate lunch in a tiny nineteen-fifties-style diner tacked onto a gas station, where the fans hummed and the radio played quietly; the owner, a friendly chap, had recently taken up residence with his family after moving from Maine. He talked of his new stress-free lifestyle, where he had time to look at the night-time stars and enjoy the endless open space, and in the quiet sleepy afternoon when we and one other family were his only customers, I felt the stirring of envy at this quiet corner of what was his paradise. Further along the same road we blundered into the tiny town of Cul de Sac, the usual deserted dusty main street where once-prosperous agricultural banks and grain merchants were decaying with faded elegance, the only place in town that was open doubled as general store and junk or antique shop; we poked around in the dusty items looking for treasure but I was more interested in watching the Nez Perce Indian couple who were also sifting through the junk. The man was huge, his wife only marginally smaller; they were both in their mid-thirties and wore faded jeans and denim jackets, he with the mandatory large metal belt buckle; both wore items of handcrafted personal jewellery and rather romantically, they held hands as they walked; what fascinated me most was their almost childlike innocence and obvious enjoyment in the items which they studiously examined; their enthusiasm made me smile and the large carved soapstone walrus that I purchased from that dilapidated and dirty old shop is a constant reminder of that happy couple.

We had already covered a large area of the Nez Perce Reservation, and now in the late evening we arrived at Spalding; the visitor centre here is home to a remarkable collection of genuine artefacts: there are beautiful ceremonial costumes, beaded garments, dugout canoes and original weapons. The Nez Perce are a fascinating tribe, particularly peaceful; they fished and hunted the valleys of the Clearwater and Snake River, often digging for the edible bulbs of the Camas Lily on the nearby high plateaus. They were instrumental in aiding the legendary expedition of Lewis and Clark and in 1855, influenced by Christian missionaries, they agreed to the allocation of a large reservation that would encompass most of their traditional homeland. Within five short years, a result of the discovery of gold, the government reneged on the deal, reducing the reservation to one tenth of its original size; the resultant faction which chose not to accept the new treaty were eventually threatened with forcible incarceration inside the new reservation in 1877. The remarkable Chief Joseph led his tribe in an escape attempt, fighting a series of inspired skirmishes that left the army red-faced and smarting; eventually Joseph and his followers were defeated just forty miles short of the Canadian border and freedom. At Spalding it is possible to view the remains of the mission settlement that was foisted on the Nez Perce, the original Indian Agency and mission buildings are gone, but the trading post and church still stand and most damning of all, the railway, driven through the very heart of their ancient homeland, in the beautiful valleys where the tribe camped in summer, with total disregard for the devastating and colossal impact it delivered.

We passed back into Washington State, navigating our way slowly through winding back roads which were hugged tightly on both sides by rolling grassy banks, passing through the tiny towns of Dodge and Starbuck. In Washtunca a portly gentleman in green baize apron and shirt sleeves stood on the sidewalk in front of the dimly lit general store where rows of canned goods could be seen on sparsely stacked shelves; a faded stars and stripes fluttered in the sultry evening air above the meeting hall of the American Legion; our presence went unremarked and unnoticed in the timelessness of such backwaters. We rested for the night in the town of Othello; for a place with such a romantic name it has nothing to commend it: broad streets with multiple self-service car wash units or laundromats, a large jet suspended on a pedestal in the groomed memorial gardens. It sits in the centre of a huge fruit-growing area where every road is lined with orchards and huge piles of fruit boxes, and at ten in the evening the only place that seemed even remotely interested in serving food was a dive bar populated almost exclusively with Mexican fruit pickers. Deeply tanned, dressed in open necked, short sleeve linen shirts and lightweight straw field hats, they drank heavily and ignored us completely; only the collection of second-rate game trophies paid us any attention, their wonky skewed eyes peering glassily at us from beneath a broken antler or moth-eaten, dust-covered feathers.

At Vantage we passed back into the world of four-lane interstate highways and by a convoluted route we managed to pass through Mount Rainier National Park on the morning that we returned to Seattle; this was very definitely not worth the effort involved; the huge peak of Mount Rainier remained shrouded in deep fluffy banks of cloud and the water sodden rainforest was not as spectacular as that of Olympic. And so it was that we came back into the city of Seattle on a Saturday afternoon, when thousands of football fans were descending on the city stadium which sits in an amazing downtown location. There was not a single parking place in the city, and as we circled the stadium area, attempting to locate our very last port of call, an angry policeman blew his whistle at us in shrill blasts and stopped our car with an imperiously raised hand, and as I sat there wondering what we had done, a large bus swept around the corner and into the stadium, the huge bulky shapes of professional football players in crimson blazer jackets clearly visible in the windows. Eventually, with time running very short, our flight departure time looming, I paid twenty dollars in order to park on a section of wasteland close by our destination, the Klondike Gold Rush National Park in Pioneer Square. This tiny National Park, one of just a handful which are actually inside buildings, documents the incredible exodus of people to the Yukon in 1897. When the first ship loaded with two tons of Klondike gold docked in Seattle the race was on; thousands of gold seekers set out for the arduous trek to the goldfields, and whilst some did strike pay dirt, the real fortunes were made by the outfitters and supply shops that can still be seen around Pioneer Square.

America provides a remarkable collection of truly unique locations; the world famous theme parks on either coast and the huge glitz and brash neon magnet of Las Vegas remain glorious mass attractions populated by millions of tourists every year, but contained in the deep expansive heartland there are areas of staggering exoticism equal to any fictional desert islands, unexplored jungles or far-flung intergalactic alien civilisations; to reach them no rocket ship or space suit is required, just a driving licence and a credit card!

fig 26.   Bison dust bathing, Yellowstone Park, USA

fig 27. Bull bison, Wyoming, USA

fig 28. Bull elk, Estes Park, Colorado, USA

fig 29. Prairie dog, Theodore Roosevelt National Park, North Dakota

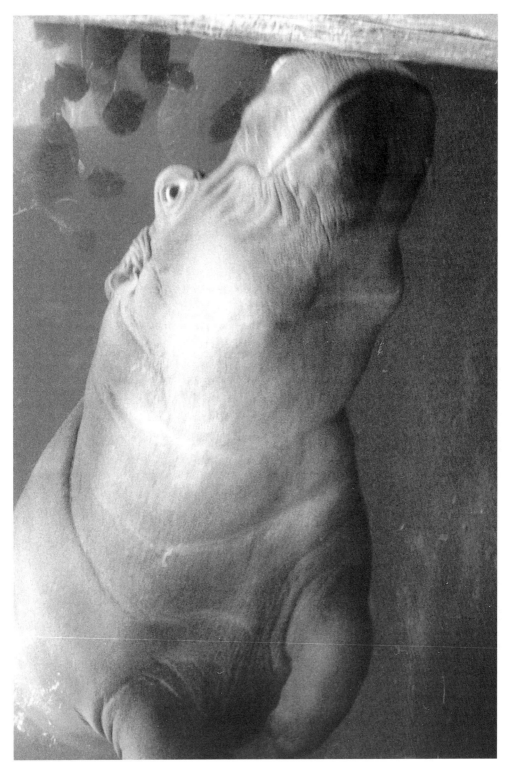

fig 30.   St Louis Zoo, Missouri, USA

14. *In Crowded Eden*

S hould you ever venture to the island of Madagascar do not expect to find yourself alone! There is a fair chance that you will manage some privacy when you retire to bed each night but certainly not if the legion of hotel night porters and bell-boys perceive that you are in need of female company …

The world famous biodiversity, the wonderful exotic name and remote location some three hundred miles off the east coast of Africa inveigle your mind with images of pristine wilderness devoid of human habitation and tourist infrastructure, a place where one can commune quietly with glorious, unique and often unimaginable species!

The truth, as I was to very quickly discover, is somewhat different; the location is indeed remote, the name is certainly exotic, the wildlife unique and awe-inspiring. But the idea that you may experience this strange place in some degree of privacy or solitude is completely false. Aside from the large indigenous population of Malagasy there are an astounding number of tourists; predominantly French, with large contingents of German and Dutch, they swarm over the island in escorted "eco tour" groups seeking out the beautiful endangered wildlife with such timed punctuality that one could quickly predict where you might encounter the various groups of middle-aged Brits with guidebooks and binoculars or the young French travellers with beaded hair and deep suntans when you next ventured into the jungles!

One has to admire the tenacity and dedication of such travellers, who despite their advanced age, discomfort and obvious lack of physical fitness would emerge from the mists of deep primal rainforest on precipitously steep trails choked with treacherous, decaying vegetation waiting to turn an ankle or break a leg, and pass me by with polite nods or an occasional "good morning" before they disappeared back into the deep camouflage of the jungle.

No matter how early I rose and how far I subsequently travelled into the forests or how high on the mountain you climbed, I was always astounded to find these groups of other tourists sweating and puffing on the steep hillsides where the terrain was more suited to members of the SAS rather than to elderly ladies who appeared to be stereotypical members of the WI.

Some were better than others, taking care not to impinge on your space or, more importantly, not to scare the animal or bird that you might be observing, and some, the Italians in particular, were a complete nightmare, shouting loudly and talking excitedly when they chanced upon any animal. On several occasions, much to my annoyance, moments of quiet close-range observation of a feeding lemur or a bathing bird just two or three feet away were often completely destroyed by such behaviour. Eventually I found that the only way to beat the crowd was to outwait it! Sometimes the luxury of travelling alone is not always obvious, but here the lack of schedule and the ability to adapt your plan paid multiple dividends. If I found myself in an area overrun with great hordes of tourists I would settle down to patiently wait for their departure and an hour or two later I would be able to enjoy the wildlife in complete solitude, my guide usually having fallen asleep in the intervening time.

One other aspect of travelling in Madagascar that caught me by surprise was the enormous time that it took to move between the various cities, parks and special reserves. The time expended on the dreadful, tortuous roads bears absolutely no relation to the distance which you might expect to cover; on some of the very worst stretches fifteen hours might see you progress just one hundred miles, and so my intended visits to the various national parks and private reserves were eternally under revision and I eventually managed to stop at five of the twenty available. Even so, I was not disappointed with the enthralling wildlife experience.

It is never good to arrive in a new and unknown destination after dark; it is even less advisable to arrive in the very early hours of the morning when one is tired and irritable from twelve hours cramped up in an Air France jumbo, but if you are going to travel to such places you just have to get on with it as best you can. The dimly lit arrivals' hall of Antananarivo airport seemed to be unusually well populated with large collections of nuns, each group wearing the obligatory wimple headdress with its subtle Masonic-like code of affiliation woven into the edging. The tone of my visit was set immediately by the chief of airport security who inspected my passport and quickly offered to expedite the immigration procedures for the usual gratuity, and the passport control officer who deftly extracted twenty dollars from me for some unfathomable amendment required to update my visa which had been issued just a fortnight earlier.

Despite the hour, I emerged into the usual throng of hopeful money-changers and illegal taxi drivers, all of whom in an act of complete sorcery seemed to simultaneously secure one hand or the other onto my bags or the baggage trolley. I eventually managed to shake off my escort by entering one of the official exchange bureaus that had remained open for the arrival of the flight, where I underwent the slow and careful process of converting my crisp new sterling into great bulging wads of torn, dog-eared, barely legible and foul-smelling francs. I left the airport building with just a few of the more resilient hawkers still in attendance and began the hopeless quest of locating an official taxi; eventually I had to abandon any pretence of being in control of the situation and with the help of two smartly uniformed gendarmes I was packed into a dilapidated and wobbly Citroën driven by "a friend" of the policemen who took charge of my high-speed induction on the Malagasy highway code for the next forty minutes.

First impressions are said to be important and these particular first impressions of a new country formed at this most disadvantageous time remain strong in my mind. We whizzed along the dimly lit roads, narrowly avoiding the unending procession of deeply excavated potholes, the unfixed passenger seat tilting alarmingly as we hurtled around each new obstacle in a dizzy slalom of repeated swerves. I peered intently through the worst of the cracks in the dirty windscreen and took in the surroundings that swept past. The deserted streets were dark and rather forbidding, the few lamp-posts casting barely discernible pools of illumination into the shadows gave glimpses of ramshackle houses capped with rough terracotta tiles, their windows shuttered with grubby heavyweight louvres and tiny narrow balconies enclosed by dust-soiled iron railings held grimy collections of tightly packed succulent plants in old paint cans and cooking oil tins. Between the houses steep alleyways snaked off into the shadows with dark intent, their smoothly worn cobbles like the embossed skins of giant slumbering crocodiles.

Antananarivo, or Tana as the locals refer to it, is a strange capital city; aside from the ruined Queen's Palace it has no great public buildings or important examples of architectural genius, there is no port and the river, the Ikopa, is sluggish, muddy and unremarkable. The city is divided by a deep valley into two sections, known as the upper and lower towns, and the houses ramble casually up and down the impossibly steep cobbled streets like a jumble of carelessly stacked infant's building blocks; solid white churches with soiled paint and stiff square steeples nestle between the shuttered fronts of red and orange homes where straggling unchecked branches of deeply purple bougainvillea drape the courtyard walls, and lines of damp washing are stretched between the railings of every balcony like strings of outsized ceremonial bunting. Despite the crushing poverty of the people the effect is one of charming fairytale curiosity, a delightful accumulated clutter of chaotic abandon where back lanes and narrow alleys beckon with confusing labyrinth-like promise and whole families draw water from ancient cast iron hand pumps, each adult and child filling containers of appropriately diminishing quantities relevant to the size and stature of those who must convey the load.

Away from the hillsides the congested roads are clogged with slowly moving traffic; hugely intimidating canvas-shrouded Mercedes trucks, buses overflowing with passengers and dented taxis are interspersed with outrageously laden bullock carts, bicycles crowded with multiple passengers and wary pedestrians, all of which are constantly shrouded in unending clouds of noxious foul smelling diesel fumes. Irregular acid green squares of flooded rice paddy populated by brightly coloured Muscovy ducks, herons and dippers reach into the city, and on the river tiny dugout canoes ferry passengers slowly back and forth, the dirty water barely inches from the upper edges of the timber gunwales.

The focus point of the city is the Avenue de l'Independence, a hugely wide boulevard which bisects the lower town, terminating at the little used railway station, its evocative French colonial façade cleanly painted despite its almost redundant status. Here during daylight hours you may stroll amongst the wealthy Malagasy who have money to spare to provide go-kart or pony rides for their children, and at the far end of the Avenue you may pick your way carefully through the mass of wares and produce strewn on the crowded dirty pavements by thousands of eager traders. Bowls of vivid powder-paint spices, huge verdant watermelons, piles of wilting carrots and small potatoes infested with eyes vie with all the gaudy cheap produce that China and Taiwan can market; here you may haggle over nasty plastic toys, shiny kitchen utensils, padlocks, keyrings and flashlights, mobile phone covers and cassettes, all of which will be immediately inflated in price suitable to the contents of a foreign pocket. You are as likely to see a woman dressed in smart western-style clothing complete with high heels, mobile phone, carrying her handbag upon her head, as you are to find one demonstrating the more usual circus-like skill of balancing humungous bundles of cauliflower or numerous packages and pots upon her cranium.

During the hours of darkness the streets take on a less pleasant aspect, the smell of urine is all-pervasive and in the doorways of shops and businesses such as Interflora and Air France, or at the sides of the high class hotels with their restaurants and night clubs, you will pass homeless bundles of destitute humanity wrapped against the cold night air in soiled blankets and deteriorating rags. The pavements are haunted by young prostitutes and beggars clutching grimy snot-encrusted children who are thrust repeatedly into your face with hopeful appeals for assistance and on most corners small quiet groups of adults squat against walls using squares of torn cardboard to fan tiny fires beneath metal dishes of roasting nuts or popcorn. It is difficult to gauge who are the genuine needy amongst the many professional beggars; having parted with a donation, your escort of pleading imploring hopefuls would depart immediately with huge happy grins and even the most apparently desperate mothers would dissolve into an hilarity of giggling laughter when I inflated a balloon for their dirty offspring.

Despite the fact that many of the animals are housed in Victorian-style cages, a visit to the Zoological Gardens in Tana is definitely worth the effort; a huge sprawling area of unkempt trees and shrubs enclosed by dilapidated fences, it is watched over from the ridge by the destroyed Queen's Palace where the giant window apertures, devoid now of both frames and glass and backlit by the open sky, gaze down like sightless damaged eyes. The Zoo is perhaps the best place to watch Malagasy people; it was thronged with crowds of happy smiling families and boisterous groups of scouts and teenage students and the queue for entry tickets snaked out of the main entrance and up the steep hill where the patient crowd appeared to be in mortal danger from speeding traffic, which hurtled past, almost pinning them against the high brick perimeter wall.

They do not have a particularly huge collection of animals and oddly enough, in a land of astonishingly exotic wildlife, the African ostrich appeared to be the biggest crowd pleaser, but they do have lots of lemurs and at six pm, with the night darkness in full bloom, I presented myself back at the entrance gate with my specially purchased ticket and a hastily bought Chinese torch so that I might view the most unique and unusual of all lemurs, the "Aye-aye".

The island of Madagascar has no woodpeckers and in line with Darwin's theory of adaptation the Aye-aye has developed to fill the niche. It is an animal that almost defies description for it is not like any other single animal or bird that you may have ever seen; it is about the size of a badger with the same brittle grey and black hair beneath which you may glimpse the pink moist skin; it has a magnificent brush-like tail as long as its entire body and equal to that of a fully grown fox. Its face is a study of ugliness, with huge paper thin ears that would be suited to a gigantic pipistrelle bat and large round yellow eyes like those of a frightened bushbaby, a pink wet snout devoid of hair such as you might see on a mole rat and a turned back upper lip that exposes huge rabbit teeth. Most astonishing of all are the hands which look like the crooked claws of someone suffering from swan's neck arthritis, or perhaps large bony black tarantula spiders crouching before they pounce onto unsuspecting prey; the centre toe of each front paw is an elongated, skeletally thin wand of bone which the Aye-aye uses to sound the trunks and branches of trees for the hollow tunnels of grubs and larvae. Its massive super-sensitive ears are able to detect grubs moving beneath bark and the clawed fingers are kept contracted in the spider-like configuration so that the long bony probe may be inserted harpoon-like into holes which it gnaws once the prey is located. It is so adept in the use of its long claw that it can drink coconut milk by flicking the liquid into its open mouth!

Watching these remarkable animals in the dim light of a torch is a truly hypnotic experience; it is such an oddity that is just impossible to take your eyes from its astonishing visage. It is extremely agile, moving quickly in the branches of its enclosure with a free-flowing athletic grace far beyond that which one may expect from its almost deformed appearance; its agility in the canopy is outstripped only by its clumsy progress on the floor, where it moves in a slow crouching waddle, its claws ticking loudly as it ambles around in small circles, depositing perfectly formed rings of urine on the ground that were swept carelessly by its sodden dripping tail.

Perhaps the most memorable part of the Aye-aye is the remarkable noises which it produces; it is continually sniffing and snorting like a person attempting to relieve a congested sinus, or the puffing, sighing noise which a disappointed dog will make when presented with a treat that it feels is unequal to its recent performance! The Aye-aye is gravely endangered and may even now be on the verge of extinction; it has suffered gravely from loss of habitat and has been hunted for food by some Malagasy tribes and is even persecuted for its supposed evil powers in some rural communities which believe its tapping presence to be the herald of death. To see an Aye-aye close to any settlement in daylight is regarded as incredibly bad luck and the poor animal is usually dispatched at once in a frenzy of dread panic. Some villages have even been burnt to the ground in attempts to appease the evil spirits of a visiting Aye-aye!

Fifty miles east of Tana you may find the equally impressive, though certainly less odd, Indri. This is the largest of all the lemurs, standing over a metre tall; it is a perfect study in teddy bear cuteness. Its soft piebald markings sweep elegantly from its stumpy, almost non-existent tail up past its permanently startled expression to its huge Mickey Mouse ears. They have an enormously endearing way of peering down at you from the crook of a branch or whilst clinging to a tree trunk, their wide-stretched yellow eyes framed perfectly in the soft coal-black fur of their round mask. They produce huge, seemingly effortless, silent leaps of thirty metres or more, executing flawless mid-air turns and arriving at their chosen tree with a confident hugging grasp and calm indifference to the swaying branches and tumbling leaves. The Indri live in Perinet or Andasibe Special Reserve and the nearby Mantadia National Park where they are protected by the law and also by the more ancient Fady or Taboo belief. Perinet is a tiny island remnant of mid-altitude rainforest centred on a high ridge where you may find small family groups of four or five Indri snoozing soundly, cuddled together in tangled furry balls in the higher reaches of the canopy some eighty feet above your head.

The superb primal forest of Mantadia is a magnificent tangle of ancient full-grown hardwood trees and dense undergrowth, there is little if any flat ground and exploring here is enormously strenuous work but the rewards are immense. In the early morning light the thick undulating canopy is partly shrouded in banks of curling rain-laden mist, every branch and leaf sheds tiny jewel-like droplets of clean fresh water and the air is alive with the drone of countless frogs and insects. Massive moss-covered eucalyptus trees surge upwards from amongst dank piles of rotten leaves and mouldering, discarded vegetation, their monstrous trunks dividing into great buttress roots that resemble giant claymore battle axes piled together by soldiers on an ancient battlefield. Huge fronds of virescent raffia palm curve in quivering predatory arches above your head and prodigious spiders hang in the midst of tangled mesh-like webs, immobile in their patient vigil amongst the deadly gossamer.

Parasitic strangler figs swoop down from their host tree with springy twisted stems that impede your slow progress, and needle-sharp thorns of varying size and ferocity snag in clothing and abrade your skin with every careless step. Tiny copper coloured bamboo lemurs scurry through the swaying canopy high above, a flurry of silently falling leaves twisting slowly to the forest floor the only evidence of their lithe, darting progress. When the sun has risen high enough to penetrate the high-level foliage the lower forest is lit in tender pools of dappled, shivering sunlight and small streams of churning water bridged by decaying trunks of fallen trees throw off shimmering, luminescent sparkles that dance reflectively on the polished bevelled edges and emerald underside of countless immobile leaves. The humidity in this rainforest is intense and the sweat pours from your body, attracting leeches which plummet from branches onto your exposed skin with unerring accuracy, a tiny slithering itch the only indication of their silent arrival. The horrible spine-shivering revulsion that this miniscule slug-like creature produces, gyrating upon your body with its silky arched back, is quite astonishing and you sweep them off your arm or face in a snap reaction of shuddering disgust.

Aside from the astonishing beauty of the rainforest the other principal reason for early morning expeditions is to hear the indri sing! These beautiful animals range over large territories far too big to be effectively marked with scent and so each morning they communicate with family members and rival groups by calling their positions loudly. Other lemurs grunt, chuckle and swear but the indri performs on a magnificent operatic scale, its magical aria a mix of whale song and police siren which rises slowly and builds to an abrupt crescendo rippling out over the forest; it is answered from half a dozen remote locations so that the haunting melody washes over you in repeated rhythmic cycles from all sides. Indri song is clearly audible for two miles and should you be lucky enough to be in close proximity to one that is singing, the volume is astonishing, the mouth forms into a deep tunnel-like maw, the bright red of the inner cheeks clearly visible, its head held aloft, the throat stretched and eyes shining fixedly on some point in the middle distance; the exquisite ululating song wails out, assaulting your ears in repetitive bursts rising and falling like an air-raid warning.

The abiding colour of Madagascar is orange! The land baked in harsh sunlight ranges through a variance of ochre, amber, russet and bronze, but the common theme is orange.

The solid oblong shaped houses with untidy thatched roofs and shuttered windows are constructed with orange bricks manufactured from the clay of the drained paddy fields, and rendered in rough orange screed; the only relief is the wide blackened fans of soot and scorching that sweep upwards from the lintels of doorways and windows where, in the absence of chimney stacks, the cooking fires disgorge their smoke and fumes.

As you travel through the constant hills and valleys the enormous levels of defor-estation become quickly evident, the roads are lined with hacked burgundy coloured stumps of decapitated hardwood trees, the shattered and torn remnants of the trunks surrounded by piles of chipped and splintered debris and, without fail, every one of the few remaining trees standing alongside or close to the roads is mutilated with axe cuts or missing wedges of timber denoting their brief stay of execution.

Timber appears to be one of the few resources available to the rural communi-ties and you pass by groups of women on steep, winding gradients bowed under huge bundles of plundered limbs tied with lengths of old rag and balanced precariously upon their heads. While the women walk, the men, it seems, have the monopoly on wheeled transport; logs along with every other imaginable commodity are transported on ingenious trolleys, which resemble children's box carts. These elongated go-karts conform to the usual design but have cleverly designed brakes and mechanical steer-ing often attached to a full-size car steering wheel; it is not at all uncommon to pass such trolleys equipped only with small casters from an old armchair hurtling down-hill loaded with both lumber and multiple passengers whilst the captain stands erect on the stern of his vessel hauling murderously on the wheel as he attempts to avoid oncoming traffic!

In many locations newly built, brightly painted steel bridges span rivers directly adjacent to the twisted, torn and half submerged skeletons of the original structures, destroyed with explosives by one or another of the factions fighting for the disputed presidency in 2001. The river banks in close proximity to most villages are often draped in brightly coloured patchwork quilts of freshly washed garments, the cloudy, turbid waters crowded with a host of half-naked children and labouring women scrubbing diligently at the laundry, whilst bent double beneath protective wide-brimmed hats. Malagasy people appear to have an enormous predilection for hats and the array of astonishing and sometimes incongruous styles never failed to amaze me; they ranged through carefully stitched leather trilbies, multicoloured balaclavas, homburgs and occasionally even broad fedoras on the men, to turbans, pillboxes and elegant sum-mer bonnets decorated with collections of twisted flowers and bright primary col-oured ribbons on the women. There were regions of obvious tribal uniformity where the men could be seen wrapped against the early morning chills in clean yellow or pink floral blankets and neat porkpie headgear, but equally it was not unusual to find a teenage male sporting sandals, sweatshirt and jogging pants topped with a purple or black creation more suited to the bride's mother at a society wedding than an ado-lescent boy!

Away from the cities, magnificent longhorned oxen known as zebu are still the primary source of motive power; in the rice fields men with trousers rolled up above the knee stumble and struggle behind decrepit ploughshares, their clothes stained and sodden with splashes of sickly yellow mud. In the narrow smaller paddies these huge rotund beasts, imprisoned in wide, smoothly worn antique wooden yokes, seem barely able to execute the constricted U-turn required at the completion of each of the invisible short furrows. On the roads you pass ancient wooden bullock carts uniformly decorated in fading cornflower blue, hauled by pairs of massive zebu, their great humps swaying slowly in time with the oscillation of their heads as they strain passively against the load, a biblical image of such timeless quality it appears to have sprung directly from the pages of dusty old Sunday school books.

Elsewhere carts transporting stacks of hay are often loaded so high and have such voluminous, untidy skirts of dried grass tumbling over the sides and sweeping the floor that from behind the huge harvested piles appear to be floating along under their own volition as if possessed by some magical power of levitation. Occasionally you may pass an open air blacksmith's shop where sweating men wield hammers in gentle ringing symphonies as they carefully ease iron tyre rings onto the enormous dished wooden wheels of restored vehicles.

At various locations along National Route Seven tremendous smoking structures shaped like military pillboxes or gun emplacements stand sentinel amongst the flat treeless landscape. These are giant brick kilns constructed from alternate layers of newly fabricated unbaked bricks and beds of dried straw; they are stacked into massive free-standing khaki-coloured cubes, intricately riddled with narrow ventilation shafts to allow the fire to breathe; the whole exterior is plastered over with wet clay, sealing in the heat and generating temperatures of sufficient strength to ensure the bricks are adequately fired. White clouds of smoke and ash trail away from the upper vents or cracks in the mud-packed façade like encrypted Indian smoke signals and when the fire is extinguished and the mass adequately cooled, the structure is dismantled brick by brick by cheerful young women ably transporting stacks of the clinking buff-coloured stocks balanced upon woven circlets of straw atop their heads.

The road to Ranomafana is truly one of the worst I have ever travelled on; during the several hours of interminable muscle-clenched, mind-numbing lurching where we slipped violently in and out of deep turgid pools of liquid mud; the only other traffic was either mighty heavyweight trucks broken down and sunk to the axles in the mire or mud-spattered four-wheel-drive Land Cruisers packed with happy smiling nuns! We passed tiny villages where soiled and grimy houses lined the rainwashed dirt road and children crowded around little thatched kiosks to purchase dubious sweets that were dispensed through a tiny hatch beneath the single heavily barred and filthy window. Indignant squawking chickens and startled plump ducks scattered noisily from the path of our Jeep and I have a particularly vivid memory of one young boy of seven or eight smiling broadly and waving enthusiastically as he stomped around amongst the scattered debris in front of his home on a finely made pair of wooden stilts!

The National Park at Ranomafana was only designated in 1991 following the discovery of a new species of golden bamboo lemur. Since then the steep forested slopes that press in on the surging Namorona river have been found to contain some of the most important wildlife in the whole of Madagascar; there are twelve kinds of lemur, over a hundred types of birds, and new species are still being discovered on a regular basis. This mid-altitude montane forest is extremely dense and humid, the trails are depressingly steep and slippery and it rains almost every day. However the biodiversity is incredible and every tree, bush or fern seems to house its own collection of leaf-tailed geckos, warty chameleons or spine-shivering insects dressed with armour-plated carapace shells. Thrush-like ground rollers, vivid blue vangas and charcoal black drongos pipe their trilling songs throughout the tops of the canopy.

In the valley floors, as you pick your way cautiously along the contours of gently flowing streams or tread carefully on moss-laden stepping-stones amid the gurgling current, you will catch brief glimpses of sleekly fat, red forest rats scuttling through the pungent mulch of decaying leaves, discarded bark and tangled vines. You may view soft, velvet-coated bamboo lemurs feeding with quiet preoccupation on the poisonous stems of rampant bamboo plants. This unique food source, which contains arsenic, is fatal to any other species, and the hollow, shredded poles, split along the vertical grain pulled into drooping crowns of curled fibre where the segment knuckle resists the tear, is definite indication of the lemurs' range.

Many wear the small red or blue dog collars allocated to them by members of the huge community of research students who work in the forest, and along the trails the trees are often draped with multiple lengths of coloured nylon ribbon marked in fibre tip pen with personalised hieroglyphics recording the time and date of visiting species. Large red bellied lemurs, their white face markings resembling bandit masks, dislodge concrete hard figs from bulky green clusters amongst the high branches of trees where they are feeding as if your inquisitive upturned face were an irresistible target for unripened projectile fruit and painful impacts upon your head are sometimes unavoidable.

Although lemurs traverse their jungle homes with huge graceful leaps they are surprisingly easy to follow; even in the thickest undergrowth the parks are riven with innumerable trails, and unless they become alarmed you may maintain contact with relative ease once you have located a troop, slowly wrestling your way up and down the steep inclines where you can position yourself on almost the same horizontal level as the animals travelling across the treetops! A vast proportion of the species in Madagascar is nocturnal and seeking them out at night in the depths of primal forest is no easy task; somewhat oddly, should you be lucky enough to find them tucked securely beneath a platform of foliage, birds can be viewed at leisure during darkness but the mammals are a very different prospect. You must search the tangled undergrowth and the towering banks of shadow with torches, looking for the reflective flash of shining eyes, and often you are rewarded with the briefest glimpse of a flashing body and tail as the animal darts for cover. In Ranomafana however you are guaranteed sightings of two of the more unique nocturnal residents. In a small clearing close to a high lookout point rangers have habituated pygmy mouse lemurs and striped civet cats to the presence of humans by providing titbits of food. Segments of banana are smeared onto the branches of the enclosing bushes from where this tiny wide-eyed lemur, no bigger than a hamster, may be watched as it carefully licks the sweet residue from the twigs. It has an orange-yellow coat of soft downy fur and an exceptionally long, prehensile tail that it uses to great effect along with its opposable thumbs; its enormous globe-like eyes fill most of the space in its tiny moon face and fur-covered ears twitch with constant radar sensitivity.

The civets, known as fanlaoka, are similarly enticed from concealment amongst the thick cloaking undergrowth with small offerings of zebu fat; they are beautifully sleek felines with magnificent striped or spotted markings that wash over their graceful shape like the painted lines of the early thoroughbred racing cars so popular in the twenties. They are slightly smaller than the average fox with a similar bushy brush-like tail and the same sharp predatory eyes. They live in pairs in the eastern rainforests hunting mice, rats, birds' eggs, earthworms and carrion and building fat reserves in their tails in order to survive the lean winter months. The three that came to the edge of the clearing to receive their tribute of greasy meat were exquisitely beautiful, sitting beneath the low branches of bushes at the very edge of the clearing with their tails wrapped around their feet like an expensive fur stole. They waited patiently for the tiny segments of fat, darting quickly into the bush to devour their prize before returning for further offerings; occasionally there would be some small disagreement amongst the assembled hierarchy or a clamorous face-off with raised hackles, drawn teeth and loud spitting reminiscent of domestic tomcats fighting for territorial command. Rather strangely, Madagascar does not have a great number of carnivores, but the largest and most fearsome is also a member of the civet family; the fosa is a slender puma like creature with a large stubby head; it has noticeably short legs and an exceptionally long tail that accounts for half of its two-metre body length; a solitary creature, it feeds primarily on lemurs, hunting them amongst the high canopy of the jungles where it demonstrates expert climbing ability, employing its huge tail as a balance pole. Unfortunately the fosa is rarely seen by anyone and so the park administrators sanction the feeding of the civets in Ranomafana in order that visitors may view at least one of carnivore species.

We travelled westwards back into the centre of the island and out onto the flat volcanic plain which contains the urban sprawl of Antsirabe; the earth in this location must be extremely nutrient-rich for the streets are lined with numerous vegetable stalls piled high with huge succulent carrots and large healthy potatoes; the many women transporting great bundles of produce upon their heads appeared as if they were auditioning for some elaborate South American cabaret, the alternating layers of orange tubers and delicate green foliage reminiscent of those astonishingly lofty headdresses worn by Carmen Miranda.

I stayed the night in an old persons' home, a huge building that must once have been either a hospital or a school, its impressive columns and long wings of grand architectural splendour now home to dozens of Malagasy pensioners. The town appeared to be completely overrun with pousse-pousses; these rickshaws have not changed in their design for centuries and whilst the brightly decorated shade is now more likely to be made from plywood than linen and the tiny cowbells worn on the wrist to solicit business have now given way to mechanical bicycle bells, the original concept remains unchanged, a man runs between the shafts and on the steeper gradients he may be assisted by another individual pushing, hence the name of "push push". They were apparently introduced to Madagascar by British missionaries eager to replace the traditional palanquin chair and its association with slavery, a subject that echoes vaguely in the posters displayed in many restaurants which warn of the consequences to those who indulge in sexual tourism.

On the outskirts of Antsirabe you pass dozens of vegetable plots where men and women irrigate the ranks of plants with shiny galvanised watering cans, the sun reflecting brightly in the showered water spraying from the rose as it is swept back and forth in wide leisurely arcs. As you head south the cultivation peters out and you enter cattle country, a repetitive, expansive landscape of rolling hills and wide distant horizons where great herds of zebu graze on brittle scorched yellow grass. The roads wend circuitously with numerous hairpin curves on the steeper hills and often you will encounter a small boy lazing on the side of the road displaying a hand drawn sign of a capital letter H, the upper portions of the letter elongated outwards from the normal vertical position into a representation of stretched horns. These young sentinels are the vanguard for massive divisions of cattle journeying through the mountains as they are driven between grazing pastures, great heaving seas of zebu jostling in a dusty close-packed confusion of giant horns and swaying humps, the herders casually controlling direction and pace with shouts, whistles and leafy fresh-cut switches applied to the rump. Occasionally on the edges of these wide prairies far from any village you pass by small groups of women and children squatting passively amidst untidy piles of firewood, cast iron pots and various dilapidated canisters of water; positioned in these remote locations, such enterprising women offer fast food refreshment services for the many passing cowboys!

The Malagasy people are extremely friendly, but initially wary of Vazha or "white strangers". Like the little boy who stood as far away as he could, a worried dark frown on his face as he stretched his arms full length to accept a small toy from me, they are cautious at first meetings. However, just a few brief words of Malagasy greeting and their nervous trepidation would dissolve immediately into broad smiles of curious amusement, their surprise and appreciation both gratifying and enchanting to observe. It never failed to amaze me that the collections of moulded plastic farm animals that I gave to various small children would be taken by mothers or fathers and distributed with careful impartiality to everyone in the assembled group, adults included! To give a present to just one member of a group or family was obviously a considerable faux pas and adults, often more insistent than the children, received balloons, pens, badges and keyrings with equal delight to that displayed by their offspring! They appear to have charmingly innocent minds and when during the course of our conversations in the car I mentioned that I had been in America, my driver asked me with grave seriousness whether the native Indians were friendly or whether one might still expect to be shot and scalped! Dami lived in a house with no running water or electricity, lighting was achieved by candles, and television was a much-coveted luxury. Much of his understanding of the world appeared to have been gleaned from his weekly visits with his family to video parlours in Tana where films can be viewed communally for a fraction of the price of a cinema ticket. His great favourite was *King Kong* and he was most interested to know whether such forty-foot giant gorillas actually existed?

The markets of most towns are fascinating jumbles of stunningly bright colours and raucous jangling noise; tribes of hopeful dogs lie in patient, watchful groups before opulent butcher stalls, the strings of dubious plump grey sausages and large slabs of roughly hewn beef mantled in thick coats of sickly yellow fat are barely shaded from the fierce sun and swarming flies. Women traders with beautiful plaits of shining inky black hair sit beside dozens of shallow bowls loaded with vibrant multicoloured conical piles of pepper, nutmeg and saffron. You may purchase freshly baked, deliciously crusty baguettes, rusty cans of ancient sardines or cheap oil lamps ingeniously manufactured from old tins of Nestlé's condensed milk or Campbell's soup. Other tables are covered in the paraphernalia of traditional herbal remedies ranging from bundles of carefully labelled tiny wooden logs to the shells from giant land snails and large desiccated starfish. On the roads leading in and out of town you pass by anxious farmers driving small groups of grubby, quarrelsome piglets or striding breathlessly behind enormous solitary hogs, their snouts held aloft and ears flapping recklessly as they perambulate in wobbling, portly eminence at the end of a frayed and knotted length of rope. Groups of men stand about in small knots deep in conversation, with fat black and white Muscovy ducks clenched tightly beneath an arm, surveying the passing traffic with sternly bemused curiosity. Not all such game birds are treated so lovingly, and some, those of perhaps a lower fiscal value, are grasped only by their legs, the unfortunate creature swinging head down against the lower legs of its owner with outflung wings and craning neck as it attempts to maintain some small vestige of equilibrium. Shabby old pick-up trucks listing perilously on ancient and abused suspension chatter along the roads amongst astringent belching clouds of thick black diesel fumes; in the canvas-covered rear compartments the tightly packed mass of passengers, singing and clapping loudly, wave enthusiastically as you overtake, a happy communal choir of gleeful smiling faces amidst the choking exhaust vapours.

A former colony of France, the island has many Gallic reminders of times gone by; there is the decaying and faded elegance of the crumbling rural railway stations where the high windows, chipped mouldings and cornices, elaborate rusted metal railings and solid cast iron post boxes fill your mind with images of rotund, frock-coated stationmasters with coloured flags and enormous fob watches carefully supervising the puffing departure of narrow gauge steam trains. On the roads the security checkpoints are manned by Gendarmes in smart blue uniforms with polished boots and starched kepis; somewhat astonishingly for policemen in a developing country, these fellows are remarkably well- behaved and never once attempted to extract the usual fraudulent backhander! The signs and impacts of the most recent and ongoing cultural colonisation are slightly more subtle but there nonetheless if you care to look: dozens of beautifully handcrafted scale wooden models of articulated trucks and diggers displayed on various stalls along a remote country road were all painted in the glossy red and white enamel livery of Coca-Cola!

If you travel far enough south from Tana you will eventually come to the National Park of Isalo, a phenomenal area of eroded sandstone, deep canyons, tribal burial caves and wide sweeping savannah. The huge, vertically sheer cliffs of the Isalo massif surge upwards for hundreds of feet from the flat surrounding plain like the giant walls of a medieval fortress. The buff-coloured crumbling stone is riven with precipitously deep slot canyons that cleave the rock in narrow V-shaped fractures plummeting from the very top of the flat, table-like plateau to the jumbled piles of fallen rock at the feet of the perpendicular walls. In the bottoms of these canyons there are tiny isolated remnants of secretive, Elysian jungles; gently flowing streams of exquisitely clear water wind enticingly between shining banks of soft golden sand where yellow wagtails strut amongst the babbling shallows and darting kingfishers skim the water's surface, their magnificent plumage blurring into high-speed streaks of vivid rusty orange and metallic sapphire blue. Hypnotic waterfalls tumble lazily over giant polished boulders in shimmering, ethereal sheets that patter into deep limpid pools, reflecting the dense tropical vegetation that surrounds them. Black and white Verreaux's sifaka swarm in the spindly upper branches of the tall trees; sheltered from the wind by the enclosing ramparts these cute, long-armed lemurs make inconceivably huge leaps, their tiny infants clinging tightly to their backs or beneath the woolly stomachs as they soar between the supple and elastic limbs of the upper canopy. Tubby brown lemurs preen their long fluffy tails with serious preoccupied attention, occasionally wrapping the flowing appendage about their necks and heads like a sensuous knitted scarf as they sit wedged in the crook of some suitable branch. Ring tails feed on great bunches of ripened figs, tearing the husk from the succulent fruits with a combined effort of nimble fingers, dexterous feet and carefully applied teeth. Occasionally they descend to the forest floor, their striped tails held rigidly straight as they patrol their territory and chase away other species of lemur with an arrogant four-legged swagger that takes no account of the watchful hawks perched on tiny ledges in the jagged rock face high above the forests. These beautiful canyons hold forgotten memories of the paradise that we have squandered; they are places of such gentle tranquillity and natural balance that, even as you stand amid the unparalleled beauty, your heart aches painfully with a sense of irretrievable loss.

Out on the flat plains of scorched yellow grasslands a beautifully sleek kestrel surveyed his hunting ground from atop a dry twisted branch of the single lifeless tree, and in the thriving thorn bushes amongst the delicate new buds and painful finger-length spines, an immobile, jade-coloured chameleon posed with silent watchfulness, his long tail tightly curled into a target-like cipher resembling the iced swirls of a Chelsea bun or a fossil ammonite. Close by a tiny hamlet of thatched mud huts I was shown an even larger chameleon; this one had a grey-brown body and serrated frills along its mouth and across its thick reptilian head, but it was outmatched in its curious appearance by the three young girls who had corralled it with sticks in a dense stand of parched long grass. Each had protected their faces from the fierce sun with primitive mudpacks and despite their western-style clothes the caked white clay produced an image of fearful ceremonial masks with grinning mouths and wide staring eyes.

Isalo is a fascinating park full of remarkable features; it is at its absolute best in the few minutes before sunset each evening when the enormous fiery sun scours the wide horizon with fields of delicate orange, pink and red and the fanciful sculptured spires and battlements of the weather-beaten rocks are painted with ever-changing shades of soft pastel-tinted light and deep, wallowing shadows.

When all was said and done perhaps I should not have been surprised at the huge numbers of tourists travelling abroad in this remarkable island. Madagascar is a small land mass renowned for the tremendous, isolated development of its wildlife, stranded there millions of years previously when the island separated from the continent of Africa. It contains approximately eighty percent of all living species in the world, amongst which are many that are completely unique and often desperately endangered. The island constantly surprises you with its incredibly varied array of landscapes: you may travel in the dried savannah grasslands of Kenya or the red dust deserts of outback Australia, you can pass from the Dolomite Mountains of Italy to Dakota prairies or the eroded monuments of Arizona and Utah and the jungles of Latin America. Despite the immense fines and long prison sentences which are meted out to poverty-stricken locals who cut the trees, its forests are under threat and it is known throughout the world as the hottest of all eco hot-spots; perhaps the great scale of tourist activity here represents an awareness of the irreparable fragility and a faint hope for a chance at conserving the remaining fragments of what must once have truly been the Garden of Eden.

fig 31. Striped civet, Madagascar

fig 32.   Indri lemur, singing teddy bears, Madagascar

Afterword

People will often tell you "the world is a small place" and in all fairness, with the massive development of instant communication and super-fast travel services, you could actually find it so.

For me however the more I travel the bigger the world becomes. Each new trip generates more possible destinations and potential adventures to be sought out and explored. More people to be encountered and animal species to be observed.

On top of that there are those truly bewitching places like the icy reaches of the high Arctic or the Falklands Islands which beckon me back with relentless gentle tugging on some invisible strings attached to my heart.

It occurred to me recently that as I grow older there is now relatively insufficient time available for me to go back even once more to all the most enchanting places that haunt my vivid memories.

This wonderful planet that we inhabit constantly astonishes me with its excess of magnificent biodiversity, often far beyond any human imagination; the truth of weird and wondrous nature is greater than any conjured science fiction.

In the very sincere wish that we as a species can check and hopefully repair the massive damage we have perpetrated here on earth I hope that this collection of writings may encourage you to lend even a small hand in that pressing task.